I0006919

Performance and Evaluation of Lisp Systems

MIT Press Series in Computer Systems

Herb Schwetman, editor

Metamodeling: A Study of Approximations in Queueing Models, by Subhash Chandra Agrawal, 1985

Logic Testing and Design for Testability, by Hideo Fujiwara, 1985

Performance and Evaluation of Lisp Systems, by Richard P. Gabriel, 1985

The LOCUS Distributed System Architecture, by Gerald J. Popek, 1985

Performance and Evaluation of Lisp Systems

Richard P. Gabriel

The MIT Press
Cambridge, Massachusetts
London, England

PUBLISHER'S NOTE

This format is intended to reduce the cost of publishing certain works in book form and to shorten the gap between editorial preparation and final publication. Detailed editing and composition have been avoided by photographing the text of this book from the author's prepared copy.

Third printing, 1986
©1985 by The Massachusetts Institute of Technology

All rights reserved. No part of this book may be reproduced in any form by any electronic or mechanical means (including photocopying, recording, or information storage and retrieval) without permission in writing from the publisher.

Printed and bound in the United States
of America by Halliday Lithograph Company

Library of Congress Cataloging-in-Publication Data

Gabriel, Richard P.
  Performance and evaluation of Lisp systems.

  (MIT Press series in computer systems)
  Bibliography: p.
  Includes index.
  1. LISP (Computer program language) 2. Computer
architecture. I. Title. II. Series.
  QA76.73.L23G32 1985   005.13'3   85-15161
  ISBN 0-262-07093-6

MIT Press

0262070936

ISBN 0-262-57193-5 (Paperback)

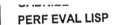

PERF EVAL LISP

Contents

Series Foreword vii

Preface ix

Acknowledgments xiii

Chapter 1 Introduction 1

1.1 Levels of Lisp System Architecture 2

1.2 Lisp Operation Level 18

1.3 Major Lisp Facilities 20

1.4 The Art of Benchmarking 23

Chapter 2 The Implementations 31

2.1 MacLisp 31

2.2 MIT CADR 34

2.3 Symbolics 36

2.4 LMI Lambda 42

2.5 S-1 Lisp 46

2.6 Franz Lisp 51

2.7 NIL 54

2.8 Spice Lisp 58

2.9 Vax Common Lisp 63

2.10 Portable Standard Lisp 66

2.11 Xerox D-Machine 73

2.12 Data General Common Lisp 76

Chapter 3 The Benchmarks 81

3.1 Tak 81

3.2 Stak 93

3.3 Ctak 99

3.4 Takl 105

3.5 Takr 110

3.6 Boyer 116

3.7 Browse 136

3.8 Destructive 146

3.9 Traverse 153

3.10 Derivative 170

3.11 Data-Driven Derivative 175

3.12 Another Data-Driven Derivative 181

vi

3.13 Division by 2 186

3.14 FFT 193

3.15 Puzzle 203

3.16 Triangle 217

3.17 File Print 227

3.18 File Read 232

3.19 Terminal Print 236

3.20 Polynomial Manipulation 240

3.21 Conclusions 275

References **277**

Index **281**

Series Foreword

This series is devoted to all aspects of computer systems. This means that subjects ranging from circuit components and microprocessors to architecture to supercomputers and systems programming will be appropriate. Analysis of systems will be important as well. System theories are developing, theories that permit deeper understandings of complex interrelationships and their effects on performance, reliability, and usefulness.

We expect to offer books that not only develop new material but also describe projects and systems. In addition to understanding concepts, we need to benefit from the decision making that goes into actual development projects; selection from various alternatives can be crucial to success. We are soliciting contributions in which several aspects of systems are classified and compared. A better understanding of both the similarities and the differences found in systems is needed.

It is an exciting time in the area of computer systems. New technologies mean that architectures that were at one time interesting but not feasible are now feasible. Better software engineering means that we can consider several software alternatives, instead of "more of the same old thing," in terms of operating systems and system software. Faster and cheaper communications mean that intercomponent distances are less important. We hope that this series contributes to the excitement in the area of computer systems by chronicling past achievements and publicizing new concepts. The format allows publication of lengthy presentations that are of interest to a select readership.

Herb Schwetman

Preface

The distance is commonly very great between actual performances and speculative possibility, It is natural to suppose that as much as has been done today may be done tomorrow: but on the morrow some difficulty emerges, or some external impediment obstructs. Indolence, interruption, business, and pleasure, all take their turns of retardation; and every long work is lengthened by a thousand causes that can, and ten thousand that cannot, be recounted. Perhaps no extensive and multifarious performance was ever effected within the term originally fixed in the undertaker's mind. He that runs against Time has an antagonist not subject to casualties.　　Samuel Johnson (Gibbon's *Miscellaneous Works*)

When I ran across this quote, I was at first jubilant to have found something profound about performance written by Samuel Johnson which I could use as a centerpiece for the preface to this book. But as I read I saw that he was talking much too specifically about human performance to be an appropriate general statement about performance—a statement that could be applied to the performance of a computer program. It took me a few days to see that the point Johnson made addressed the very center of what should be learned about the performance of Lisp systems by anyone who cares to study the material I've presented in this book.

That point is that people work very hard to attain every microsecond of speed that a computer demonstrates, and there are two major problems facing an implementor when he embarks on producing a Lisp system: the first problem is the myriad of decisions to be made, the interactions of various parts of the Lisp system when they are brought together, the unfortunate choice in one aspect of the system turning around and influencing, badly, the performance of another; the second problem is that writing a Lisp system is a monumental undertaking, and this undertaking is executed within the context of living a life as well. And, although an implementor might start out with large goals and spectacular intentions, the time it takes to do the thorough job required to produce an excellent Lisp system will bring many obstacles and intrusions, impediments and obstructions, and in the end, Time will have won out, in that every microsecond the implementor grabs from the hands of Time are bought with hours or days or weeks or months of effort expended by the implementor.

When I began the adventure on which I am reporting in this book, I had the belief that I would simply gather benchmark programs, distribute them to a handful of implementors, and get back the results; my major job would be to distribute the results to all interested parties. When I first sent out the initial benchmarks, there was an uproar because the benchmarks weren't fair, they weren't representative of real Lisp programs, people didn't care about performance now so why bring up this minor concern as a major one, and what was I trying to do, embarrass one group of implementors for the benefit of others?

Throughout the adventure, which lasted four years, I was praised for performing a public service, I was praised for helping find performance and correctness bugs, I was praised for taking the lead in a necessary area—gathering accurate and objective performance information—where others would fear to tread or would be too burdened to tread; and I was accused of favoritism, accused of industrial espionage, even a computer account was closed while I was using it because a system administrator was told that I was possibly gathering proprietary information.

Some people requested that this book not contain any charts, but that the benchmark results be included in running text, the idea being that it would take a significant effort on the part of a reader to make a chart of his own.

But despite the extremes of reaction to my activities, the most common reaction was for the Lisp implementor to look at the results he got running my benchmarks compared with the results from other Lisp implementations, and to turn, quietly and patiently, to his terminal to improve the results. Over the course of the four-year study I've watched the performance of some Lisp systems improve by factors of up to four on some benchmarks, and by factors of two and three overall. These results took the full four years to achieve in some cases, and I think it was the existence of a widely available, common set of benchmarks along with the results of those benchmarks for a number of Lisp implementations that have contributed to these improvements.

It is a gift to be born beautiful or rich or intelligent, to be given, by birth, the possibilities of excellent education, to be endowed with gifts that allow one to make important and stunning contributions. And I respect those individuals who use their talents when those talents have been cultivated 'in the usual manner.' But I admire, much more, people who are born ugly or poor or of average intelligence, who have minimal opportunities for first-class education, who work their ways through bad schools and bad breaks to make contributions. Perhaps the contributions are less important or less frequent than from those who are blessed, but the contributions are the result of a strong will and advantageous application of available talent and skills.

And so it is with the performance of Lisp systems: I respect the performance of Lisp systems based on special hardware designed by wizards, but I admire the performance of Lisp systems on stock hardware and written by the common implementor, especially when I've watched the performance of those latter systems creep up over the years, by small increments, and accomplished during periods of busy activity in other areas.

Acknowledgments

This book is really the confluence of works and results provided to me by many people: I did not run every benchmark reported here, I did not write every benchmark, and I did not create every section of this book. However, I gathered the raw material together and unified it into a book. The sections describing the various implementations was written based on information provided to me by the implementors of those systems. In these acknowledgments I hope to credit as accurately as I can remember those people who did most of the work reported here.

L. Peter Deutsch got the project started by turning a simple suggestion by me for a methodology into a statement of volunteering. Early comments, criticisms, benchmarks, and benchmark results were provided by Charles Hedrick, Mabry Tyson, Paul Martin, Gerrold Ginsparg, Jon L. White, Richard Fateman, and Larry Masinter. Larry Masinter and I wrote a paper, entitled 'Performance of Lisp Systems,' which was presented at the 1982 ACM Symposium on Lisp and Functional Programming, and which is largely reproduced, with revision, in Chapter 1. Bob Boyer, Harry Barrow, and Richard Fateman contributed three of the more important benchmarks contained herein: BOYER, FFT, and FRPOLY. Forest Baskett wrote, for another context, PUZZLE. Larry Masinter contributed TAKL and TAKR. John McCarthy's bad memory was responsible for TAK.

The material for the sections on the Symbolics Lisp machines and the CADR was put together by Paul Wieneke, working from Symbolics and MIT documents, and the material on the instruction fetch unit was provided by Bruce Edwards; the material for the LMI section was contributed by Morris (Mache) Creeger of Lisp Machines Inc.; the S-1 Lisp section is an adaptation of a paper presented at the 1982 ACM Symposium on Lisp and Functional Programming written by Guy L. Steele Jr., Rod Brooks, and myself; the material for the Franz section was contributed by John Foderaro and Richard Fateman; the material for the NIL section was contributed by Glenn Burke; the material for Spice section was contributed by Skef Wholey; the material for the Vax Common Lisp section was contributed by Walter van Roggen; the material for the PSL section was contributed by Robert Kessler, Martin Griss, and Jim McDonald; the material for the Xerox section was contributed by Jon L White and Larry Masinter; and the material for the Data General section was contributed by Dan Oldman.

The following people ran benchmarks and provided a great deal of support and information about the benchmark results:

Raymond Bates, Alan Bawden, Eric Benson, Bob Boyer, Rod Brooks, Gary Brown, Howard Cannon, George Carrette, Scott Fahlman, Mike Farmwald, William Galway, Jim Gay, Erik Gilbert, Joe Ginder, Bernie Greenberg, Richard Greenblatt, Carl W. Hoffman, Earl Killian, Paul Martin, Dave Moon, Vaughan Pratt, Tom Rindfleisch, Eric Schoen, Beau Sheil, Guy L. Steele, Jr., Bill vanMelle, and Dan Weinreb.

Virginia Kean did a major editing job on this book.

— R. P. G.

Palo Alto, California
May 1985

Performance and Evaluation of Lisp Systems

Chapter 1

Introduction

This is the final report of the Stanford Lisp Performance Study, which was conducted by the author during the period from February 1981 through October 1984. This report is divided into three major parts: the first is the theoretical background, which is an exposition of the factors that go into evaluating the performance of a Lisp system; the second part is a description of the Lisp implementations that appear in the benchmark study; and the last part is a description of the benchmark suite that was used during the bulk of the study and the results themselves.

This chapter describes the issues involved in evaluating the performance of Lisp systems and is largely a reprint of the paper "Performance of Lisp Systems" by Richard P. Gabriel and Larry Masinter. The various levels at which quantitative statements can be made about the performance of a Lisp system are explored, and examples from existing implementations are given wherever possible. The thesis is that benchmarking is most effective when performed in conjunction with an analysis of the underlying Lisp implementation and computer architecture. Some simple benchmarks which have been used to measure Lisp systems examined, as well as some of the complexities of evaluating the resulting timings, are examined.

Performance is not the only—or even the most important—measure of a Lisp implementation. Trade-offs are often made that balance performance against flexibility, ease of debugging, and address space.

'Performance' evaluation of a Lisp implementation can be expressed as a sequence of statements about the implementation on a number of distinct, but related, levels. Implementation details on each level can have an effect on the evaluation of a given Lisp implementation.

Benchmarking and analysis of implementations will be viewed as complementary aspects in the comparison of Lisps: benchmarking without analysis is as useless as analysis without benchmarking.

The technical issues and trade-offs that determine the efficiency and usability of a Lisp implementation will be explained in detail; though there will appear to be a plethora of facts, only those aspects of a Lisp implementation that are the most important for evaluation will be discussed. Throughout, the impact of these issues and trade-offs on benchmarks and benchmarking methodologies will be explored.

The Lisp implementations that will be used for most examples are: INTERLISP-10 [Teitelman 1978], INTERLISP-D [Burton 1981], INTERLISP-Vax [Masinter 1981a] [Bates 1982], Vax NIL [White 1979], S-1 Lisp [Brooks 1982b], FRANZ Lisp [Foderaro 1982], and PDP-10 MacLisp [Moon 1974],

1.1 Levels of Lisp System Architecture

The performance of a Lisp system can be viewed from the lowest level of the hardware implementation to the highest level of user program functionality. Understanding and predicting Lisp system performance depends upon understanding the mechanisms at each of these levels. The following levels are important for characterizing Lisp systems: basic hardware, Lisp 'instructions,' simple Lisp functions, and major Lisp facilities.

There is a range of methodologies for determining the speed of an implementation. The most basic methodology is to examine the machine instructions that are used to implement constructs in the language, to look up in the hardware manual the timings for these instructions, and then to add up the times needed. Another methodology is to propose a sequence of relatively small benchmarks and to time each one under the conditions that are important to the investigator (under typical load average, with expected working-set sizes, etc). Finally, real (naturally occurring) code can be used for the benchmarks.

Unfortunately, each of these representative methodologies has problems. The simple instruction-counting methodology does not adequately take into account the effects of cache memories, system services (such as disk service), and other interactions within the machine and operating system. The middle, small-benchmark methodology is susceptible to 'edge' effects: that is, the small size of the benchmark may cause it to straddle a boundary of some sort and this leads to unrepresentative results. For instance, a small benchmark may be partly on one page and partly on another, which may cause many page faults. Finally, the real-code methodology, while accurately measuring a particular implementation,[1] is not necessarily accurate when comparing implementations. For example, programmers, knowing the performance profile of their machine and implementation, will typically bias their style of programming on that piece of code. Hence, had an expert on another system attempted to program the same algorithms, a different program might have resulted.

1.1.1 *Hardware Level*

At the lowest level, things like the machine clock speed and memory bandwidth affect the speed of a Lisp implementation. One might expect a CPU with a basic clock rate of 50 nanoseconds to run a Lisp system faster than the same architecture with a clock rate of 500 nanoseconds. This, however, is not necessarily true, since a slow or small memory can cause delays in instruction and operand fetch.

Several hardware facilities complicate the understanding of basic system performance, especially on microcoded machines: the memory system, the instruction buffering and decoding, and the size of data paths. The most important of these facilities will be described in the rest of this section.

Cache memory is an important and difficult-to-quantify determiner of performance. It is designed to improve the speed of programs that demonstrate a lot of locality[2] by supplying a small high-speed memory that is used in conjunction with a larger, but slower (and less expensive) main memory. An alternative to a cache is a stack buffer, which keeps some number of the top elements of the stack in a circular queue of relatively high-speed memory. The Symbolics 3600 has such a PDL buffer.

Getting a quantitative estimate of the performance improvement yielded by a cache memory can best be done by measurement and benchmarking. Lisp has less locality than many other programming languages, so that a small benchmark may fail to accurately measure the total performance by failing to demonstrate 'normal' locality. Hence, one would expect the small-benchmark methodology to

---

[1] Namely, the implementation on which the program was developed.

[2] *Locality* is the extent to which the locus of memory references—both instruction fetches and data references—span a 'small' number of memory cells 'most' of the time.

tend to result in optimistic measurements, since small programs have atypically higher locality than large Lisp programs.

An instruction *pipeline* is used to overlap instruction decode, operand decode, operand fetch, and execution. On some machines the pipeline can become blocked when a register is written into and then referenced by the next instruction. Similarly, if a cache does not have parallel write-through, then such things as stack instructions can be significantly slower than register instructions.

Memory bandwidth is important—without a relatively high bandwidth for a given CPU speed, there will not be an effective utilization of that CPU. As an extreme case, consider a 50-nanosecond machine with 3-μsec memory and no cache. Though the machine may execute instructions rapidly once fetched, fetching the instructions and the operands will operate at memory speed at best. There are two factors involved in memory speeds: the time it takes to fetch instructions and decode them and the time it takes to access data once a path to the data is known to the hardware. Instruction pre-fetch units and pipelining can improve the first of these quite a bit, while the latter can generally only be aided by a large cache or a separate instruction and data cache.

Internal bus size can have a dramatic effect. For example, if a machine has 16-bit internal data paths but is processing 32-bit data to support the Lisp, more microinstructions may be required to accomplish the same data movement than on a machine that has the same clock rate but wider paths. Narrow bus architecture can be compensated for by a highly parallel microinstruction interpreter because a significant number of the total machine cycles go into things, such as condition testing and instruction dispatch, that are not data-path limited.

Many other subtle aspects of the architecture can make a measurable difference on Lisp performance. For example, if error correction is done on a 64-bit quantity so that storing a 32-bit quantity takes significantly longer than storing a 64-bit quantity, arranging things throughout the system to align data appropriately on these 64-bit quantities will take advantage of the higher memory bandwidth possible when the quad-word alignment is guaranteed. However, the effect of this alignment is small compared to the above factors.

1.1.2 *Lisp 'Instruction' Level*

Above the hardware level, the Lisp 'instruction' level includes such things as local variable assignment and reference, free/special[3] variable assignment, binding, and unbinding; function call and return; data structure creation, modification, and reference; and arithmetic operations.

At the 'instruction level' Lisp is more complex than a language such as PASCAL because many of the Lisp 'instructions' have several implementation strategies in addition to several implementation tactics for each strategy. In contrast, PASCAL compilers generally implement the constructs of the language the same way—that is, they share the same implementation strategy. For example, there are two distinct strategies for implementing free/special variables in Lisp—*deep binding* and *shallow binding*. These strategies implement the same functionality, but each optimizes certain operations at the expense of others. Deep-binding Lisps may cache pointers to stack-allocated value cells. This is a tactic for accomplishing speed in free/special variable lookups.

The timings associated with these operations can be determined either by analysis of the implementation or by designing simple test programs (benchmarks) that contain that operation exclusively and that time the execution in one of several ways. The operations will be discussed before the benchmarking techniques.

1.1.2.1 *Variable/Constant Reference*

The first major category of Lisp 'instruction' consists of variable reference, variable assignment, and constant manipulation. References to variables and constants appear in several contexts, including passing a variable as an argument, referencing a constant, and referencing lexical and global variables.

Typically, bound variables are treated as lexical variables by the compiler. The compiler is free to assign a lexical variable to any location (or more prop-

---

[3] In the literature there are several terms used to describe the types of variables and how they are bound in the various implementations. *Global* variables have a value cell that can be set and examined at any lexical level but cannot be lambda-bound. A *special* variable can sometimes mean a global variable, and sometimes it can mean a *free, fluid,* or *dynamic* variable; these synonymous terms refer to a variable that is not lexically apparent, but that can be lambda-bound. In this report the terms *lexical* or *local* will be used for nonglobal, nonfluid variables, *global* for global variables, and *free/special* for global and fluid variables.

erly, to assign any location the name of the lexical variable at various times). Typical locations for temporaries, both user-defined and compiler-defined, are the registers, the stack, and memory. Since Lisp code has a high proportion of function calls to other operations, one expects register protection considerations to mean that temporaries are generally stored on the stack or in memory. In addition, since many Lisp programs are recursive, their code must be re-entrant and, hence, must be read-only. This argues against general memory assignment of temporaries. Consequently, most lexical variables are assigned to the stack in many Lisp implementations. Variables that are in registers can be accessed faster than those in memory, although cache memories reduce the differential.[4]

Compilation of references to constants can be complicated by the fact that, depending on the garbage collection strategy, the constants can move. Thus, either the garbage collector must be prepared to relocate constant pointers from inside code streams or the references must be made indirect through a reference-table. Sometimes, the constants are 'immediate' (i.e., the bits can be computed at compile time). On some systems, constants are in a read-only area, and pointers to them are computed at load time. Immediate data are normally faster to reference than other kinds, since the operand-fetch-and-decode unit performs most of the work.

1.1.2.2 *Free/Special Variable Lookup and Binding*

There are two primary methods for storing the values of free/special variables: *shallow binding* and *deep binding*. Deep binding is conceptually similar to ALIST binding; ⟨variable name, value⟩ pairs are kept on a stack, and looking up the value of a variable consists of finding the most recently bound ⟨variable name, value⟩ pair. Binding a free/special variable is simply placing on the stack a new pair that will be found before any previous pairs with the same variable name in a sequential search backwards along the variable lookup path (typically this is along the control stack).

A shallow-binding system has a cell called the *value cell* for each variable. The current value of the variable with the corresponding name is always found

---

[4] And, in fact, on some machines the cache may be faster than the registers, making some memory references faster than register references. A good example is the KL-10, where, unlike KA-10, it is slower to execute instructions out of registers and to fetch registers as memory operands than it is to perform those operations from the cache.

there. When a variable is bound, a ⟨variable name, old value⟩ pair is placed on a
stack so that when control is returned beyond the binding point, the old value is
restored to the value cell. Hence, lookup time is constant in this scheme.

The performance profiles for free/special lookup and binding are very different depending on whether you have deep or shallow binding. In shallow-binding
implementations, times for function call and internal binding of free/special variables are inflated because of the additional work of swapping bindings. On some
deep-binding systems, referencing a dynamically bound variable (which includes
all variable references from the interpreter) can require a search along the access
path to find the value. Other systems cache pointers to the value cells of freely
referenced free/special variables on top of the stack; caching can take place upon
variable reference/assignment or upon entry to a new lexical contour,[5] and at each
of these points the search can be one variable at a time or all/some variables in
parallel. Shallow-binding systems look up and store into value cells, the pointers
to which are computed at load time. Deep-binding systems bind and unbind faster
than shallow-binding systems, but shallow-binding systems look up and store values faster.[6] Context-switching can be performed much faster in a deep-binding
implementation than in a shallow-binding one. Deep binding therefore may be
the better strategy for a multi-processing Lisp.[7]

A complication to these free/special problems occurs if a function can be
returned as a value. In this case the binding context or environment must be
retained as part of a *closure* and re-established when the closure is invoked. Logically, this involves a tree rather than a stack model of the current execution
environment, since portions of the stack must be retained to preserve the binding
environment.

In a deep-binding system, changing the current execution environment (in-

---

[5] A *lexical contour* is the real or imaginary boundary that occurs at a LAMBDA, a PROG,
a function definition, or at any other environment construct. This terminology is not universal.

[6] Shallow-binding systems look up and store in constant time. Deep-binding systems must
search for the ⟨variable name, value⟩ pairs, and in cached, deep-binding systems this search time
may be amortized over several references and assignments.

[7] A shallow-binding system can take an arbitrary time to context switch, and for the
same reason, a deep-binding system can take an arbitrary amount of time to search for the
⟨variable name, value⟩ pairs.[Baker 1978b]

voking a closure) can be accomplished by altering the search path in the tree. In cached systems one must also invalidate relevant caches.

In a shallow-binding system, the current value cells must be updated, essentially by a tree traversal that simulates the unbinding and rebinding of variables.

Some shallow-binding Lisps (LISP370, for instance) have a hybrid scheme in which the value cell is treated more like a cache than like an absolute repository of the value and does cache updates and write-throughs in the normal manner for caches.

Some Lisps (the Common Lisp family, for example) are partially *lexical* in that free variables are by default free/special, but the visibility of a bound variable is limited to the lexical context of the binding unless the binding specifies it as free/special. Lisp compilers assign locations to these variables according to the best possible coding techniques available in the local context rather than demand a canonical or default implementation in all cases.[8]

As hinted, variable access and storage times can vary greatly from implementation to implementation and also from case to case within an implementation. Timing just variable references can be difficult because a compiler can make decisions that may not reflect intuition, such as optimizing out unreferenced variables.

1.1.2.3 *Function Call/Return*

The performance of function call and return is more important in Lisp than in most other high-level languages due to Lisp's emphasis on functional style. In many Lisp implementations, call/return accounts for about 25% of total execution time. Call/return involves one of two major operations: 1) building a stack frame, moving addresses of computed arguments into that frame, placing a return address in it, and transferring control; and 2) moving arguments to registers, placing the return address on the stack, and transferring control. In addition, function calling may require the callee to move arguments to various places in order to reflect temporary name bindings (referred to as *stashing* below), to default arguments not supplied, and to allocate temporary storage. Furthermore, saving and restoring registers over the function call can be done either by the caller or the callee, or

---

[8] Canonical implementations allow separately compiled or interpreted functions to access free/special variables.

by some cache type of operation that saves/restores on demand [Lampson 1982] [Steele 1979]. As noted in the previous section, function calling can require caching deep-binding free/special variables on the stack.

Function call and return time are grouped together because every function call is normally paired with a function return. It is possible for a function to exit via other means, for example, via the nonlocal exits such as RETFROM in INTERLISP and THROW in MacLisp. As it searches for the matching CATCH, THROW does free/special unbinds along the way (referred to as *unwinding*).

The following two paragraphs constitute an example of the kind of analysis that is possible from an examination of the implementation.

In PDP-10 (KL-10B or DEC-2060) MacLisp, a function call is either a PUSHJ/POPJ (3 μsec) for the saving and restoring of the return address and transfer of control, a MOVE from memory to register (with possible indexing off the stack—.4–.8 μsec) for each argument up to 5, or a PUSH and maybe a MOVEM (MOVE to Memory—.6 μsec) for each argument when the total number of arguments is more than 5. Function entry is usually a sequence of PUSH's to the stack from registers. Return is a MOVE to register plus the POPJ already mentioned. Upon function entry, numeric code 'unboxes' numbers (converts from pointer format to machine format) via a MOVE Indirect (.5 μsec) to obtain the machine format number.

Function call without arguments in INTERLISP-10 on a DEC 2060 has a range of about 3 μsec for an internal call in a block (PUSHJ, POPJ) to around 30 μsec for the shortest non-block-compiled call (builds a frame in about 60 instructions) to around 100 μsec (function call to a swapped function).

Some Lisps (Common Lisp [Steele 1982], Lisp Machine Lisp [Weinreb 1981]) have multiple values. The implementation of multiple values can have great impact on the performance of a Lisp. For example, if multiple values are pervasive, then there is a constant overhead for marking or recognizing the common, single-value case, and some tail-recursive cases may require that an arbitrary amount of storage be allocated to store values that will be passed on—for example, (prog1 (multiple-values) ...). If some multiple values are passed in registers (S-1 [Correll 1979]), there may be an impact on how the register allocator can operate, and this may cause memory bottlenecks. If they are all on the stack

(Lisp machine, SEUS [Weyhrauch 1981]), a count of the number of values that must be examined must be made at various times. Sometimes an implementation may put multiple values in heap-allocated storage. This could severely degrade performance.

Timing function calls has several pitfalls that should be noted as analyses such as the ones given above can be misleading. First, the number of arguments passed may make more than a linear difference. For example, the last of several arguments could naturally be computed into the correct register or stack location, causing zero time beyond the computation for evaluating the argument. Second, if several functions are compiled together or with cross declarations, special cases can be much faster, eliminating the move to a canonical place by the caller followed by a stashing operation by the callee. In this case also, complete knowledge of register use by each routine can eliminate unnecessary register saving and restoring. Third, numeric function calls can be made faster given suitable representations of numbers. In MacLisp, as noted, stashing and unboxing can be incorporated into a single instruction, MOVE Indirect. Note that these performance improvements are often at the expense either of type safety or of flexibility (separate compilation; defaulting unsupplied arguments, for instance).

An expression such as

```
((lambda (x ...) ...) ...)
```

is also an example of a function call, even though control is not transferred. If x is a free/special variable, then in a shallow-binding Lisp there will be a binding operation upon entry to the lambda and an unbinding upon exit, even in compiled code; in a deep-binding Lisp, caching of free/special variables freely referenced in the body of the lambda may take place at entry. In some Lisps the values of lexical variables may be freely substituted for, so that the code

```
((lambda (x)
  (plus (foo) x)) 3)
```

may be exactly equivalent to

```
(plus (foo) 3)
```

Some machine architectures (e.g., Vax) have special features for making function call easier, although these features may be difficult to use in a given Lisp implementation. For example, on the Vax the CALLS instruction assumes a right to left evaluation order, which is the opposite of Lisp's evaluation order.

Calls from compiled and interpreted functions must be analyzed separately. Calls from interpreted code involve locating the functional object (in some Lisp implementations this requires a search of the property list of the atom whose name is the name of the function.) Calls from compiled functions involve either the same lookup followed by a transfer of control to the code or a simple, machine-specific subroutine call; usually a Lisp will attempt to transform the former into the latter once the function has been looked up. This transformation is called *fast links*, *link smashing*, or *UUO-link smashing* on various systems. Some Lisps (Vax NIL and S-1 Lisp) implement calls to interpreted code via a heap-allocated piece of machine code that simply calls the interpreter on the appropriate function application. Hence, calls to both compiled and interpreted code from compiled code look the same. When benchmarking function calls, it is imperative to note which of these is being tested.

The requirement for this function lookup is a result of the Lisp philosophy that functions may be defined on the fly by the user, that functions can be compiled separately, that compiled and interpreted calls can be intermixed, and that when an error or interrupt occurs, the stack can be decoded within the context of the error. While link-smashing allows separate compilation and free mixing of compiled and interpreted code, it does not allow for frame retention and often does not leave enough information on the stack for debugging tools to decode the call history.

Franz Lisp is a good example of an implementation with several types of function-calling mechanisms. It has *slow function call*, which interprets the pointer to the function for each call.[9] This setting allows one to redefine functions at any time. Franz also has *normal function call*, which smashes the address of the function and a direct machine-level call to that code into instances of calls to that function. This usually disallows free redefinitions and hence reduces the debugability[10] of the resulting code. Finally Franz has *local function call*, which uses a simple load-register-and-jump-to-subroutine sequence in place of a full stack-frame-building call. Functions compiled this way cannot be called from outside the file where they are defined. This is similar to INTERLISP-10 *block compilation*. A final type of function call is a variant of APPLY called FUNCALL, which takes

---

[9] Corresponding to the variable NOUUO being T in MacLisp.

[10] As contrasted with *Debuggabilly*, the music of hayseed hackers.

a function with some arguments and applies the function to those arguments. In Franz, if normal function call is time 1.0 on a function-call-heavy benchmark (TAK', described below) running on a Vax 11/780, slow function call is 3.95, and local function call is .523. FUNCALL for this same benchmark (involving an extra argument to each function) is time 2.05.[11]

In addition, if the formal parameters to a function are free/special, then the binding described earlier must be performed, and this adds additional overhead to the function call.

Direct timing, then, requires that the experimenter report the computation needed for argument evaluation, the method of compilation, the number of arguments, and the number of values. The timing must be done over a range of all of these parameters, with each being duly noted.

1.1.2.4 *Data Structure Manipulation*

There are three important data structure manipulations: accessing data, storing into data, and creating new data. For list cells, these are CAR/CDR, RPLACA/RPLACD, and CONS.

In addition to CONS cells, several implementations provide other basic data structures that are useful for building more complex objects. Vectors and vector-like objects[12] help build sequences and record structures; arrays build vectors (in implementations without vectors), matrices, and multidimensional records; and strings are a useful specialization of vectors of characters.

Further, many Lisps incorporate abstract data structuring facilities such as the INTERLISP DATATYPE facility, the MacLisp EXTEND, DEFSTRUCT, and DEFVST facilities, and the Lisp Machine DEFSTRUCT and FLAVOR facilities. Several of these, especially the FLAVOR facility, also support Object Oriented Programming, much in the style of SMALLTALK.

The following is an example analysis of CONS cell manipulations.

---

[11] The reason that FUNCALL is faster than the slow-function-call case is that the slow-function-call case pushes additional information on the stack so that it is possible to examine the stack upon error.

[12] For instance, *hunks* are short, fixed-length vectors in MacLisp.

In INTERLISP-10 on a DEC 2060, times for the simple operations are as follows:
CAR compiles into a HRRZ, which is on the order of .5 μsec. RPLACA is either
.5 μsec (for FRPLACA) or 40–50 μsec (function call + type test). CONS is about
10 μsec (an average of 20 PDP-10 instructions). MacLisp timings are the same
for CAR and RPLACA but faster for CONS, which takes 5 instructions in the
non-garbage collection initiating case.

Creating data structures like arrays consists of creating a header and allocating contiguous (usually) storage cells for the elements; changing an element is
often modifying a cell; and accessing an element is finding a cell. Finding a cell
from indices requires arithmetic for multidimensional arrays.

In MacLisp, for example, array access is on the order of 5 PDP-10 instructions for each dimension when compiled in-line. For fixed-point and floating-point
arrays in which the numeric data are stored in machine representation, access may
also involve a number-CONS. Similarly, storing into an array of a specific numeric
type may require an unbox.

In some implementations, changing array elements involves range checking on
the indices, coercing offsets into array type. Pointer array entries in MacLisp are
stored two per word, so there is coercion to this indexing scheme, which performs
a rotate, a test for parity, and a conditional jump to a half-word move to memory.
This adds a constant 5 instructions to the $5n$, where n is the number of dimensions
that are needed to locate the entry. Hence, storing into an n-dimensional pointer
array is on the order of $5(n + 1)$ PDP-10 instructions.

Timing CAR/CDR and vector access is most simply done by observing the
implementation. Array access is similar, but getting the timings involves understanding how the multidimension arithmetic is done if one is to generalize from a
small number of benchmarks.

A basic feature of Lisp systems is that they do automatic storage management, which means that allocating or creating a new object can cause a garbage
collection—a reclamation of unreferenced objects. Hence, object creation has a
potential cost in garbage collection time, which can be amortized over all object
creations. Some implementations do incremental garbage collection with each operation (such as CAR/CDR/RPLACA/RPLACD) on the data type performing a
few steps of the process. Others delay garbage collection until there are no more

free objects or until a threshold is reached. Garbage collection will be discussed in detail in a subsequent section.

It is sometimes possible to economize storage requirements or shrink the working-set size by changing the implementation strategy for data structures. The primary compound data structure is the CONS cell, which is simply a pair of pointers to other objects. Typically these CONS cells are used to represent lists, and for that case, it has been observed that the CDR part of the CONS cell often happens to be allocated sequentially after the CONS. As a compaction scheme and as a strategy for increasing the locality (and hence, reducing the working-set), a method called *CDR-coding* was developed that allows a CONS cell to efficiently state that the CDR is the next cell in memory. However, doing a RPLACD on such an object can mean putting a forwarding pointer in the old CONS cell and finding another cell to which the forwarding pointer will point and which will contain the old CAR and the new CDR. All this could bring the cost of this relatively simple operation way beyond what is expected. In a reference-count garbage collection scheme, this operation added to the reference count updating can add quite a few more operations in some cases. Therefore, on a machine with CDR-coding it is possible to construct a program that performs many RPLACDs and that by doing so will show the machine to be much worse than expected (where that expectation is based on other benchmarks).

The point is that there is a trade-off between compacting data structures and the time required for performing certain operations on them.

1.1.2.5 *Type Computations*

Lisp supports a runtime typing system. This means that at runtime it is possible to determine the type of an object and take various actions depending on that type. The typing information accounts for a significant amount of the complexity of an implementation; type decoding can be a frequent operation.

There is a spectrum of methods for encoding the type of a Lisp object and the following are the two extremes: the typing information can be encoded in the pointer or it can be encoded in the object. If the type information is encoded in the pointer, then either the pointer is large enough to hold a machine address plus some tag bits (tagged architecture) or the address itself encodes the type. As an example, in the latter case, the memory can be partitioned into segments, and for each segment there is an entry in a master type table (indexed by segment number) describing the data type of the objects in the segment. In MacLisp this is called the *BIBOP* scheme (Big Bag Of Pages) [Steele 1977a].

In most Lisps, types are encoded in the pointer. However, if there are not enough bits to describe the subtype of an object in the pointer, the main type is encoded in the pointer, and the subtype is encoded in the object. For instance, in S-1 Lisp a fixed-point vector has the vector type in the tag portion of the pointer and the fixed-point subtype tag in the vector header. In SMALLTALK-80 and MDL, the type is in the object not the pointer.

In tagged architectures (such as the Lisp Machine [Weinreb 1981]), the tags of arguments are automatically used to dispatch to the right routines by the microcode in generic arithmetic. In INTERLISP-D operations such as CAR compute the type for error-checking purposes. In MacLisp, interpreted functions check types more often than compiled code where safety is sacrificed for speed. The speed of MacLisp numeric compiled code is due to the ability to avoid computing runtime types as much as possible.

Microcoded machines typically can arrange for the tag field to be easily or automatically extracted upon memory fetch. Stock hardware can either have byte instructions suitable for tag extraction or can arrange for other field extraction, relying on shift and/or mask instructions in the worst case. Runtime management of types is one of the main attractions of microcoded Lisp machines.

The following paragraph is an example analysis of some common type checks.

In MacLisp, type checking is about 7 instructions totalling about 7 μsec, while in S-1 Lisp it is 2 shift instructions totalling about .1 μsec. In MacLisp, NIL is the pointer 0, so the NULL test is the machine-equality-to-0 test. In S-1 Lisp and Vax NIL, there is a NULL type, which must be computed and compared for. S-1 Lisp keeps a copy of NIL in a vector pointed to by a dedicated register, so a NULL test is a compare against this entry (an indirection through the register).

Since type checking is so pervasive in the language, it is difficult to benchmark the 'type checking facility' effectively.

16

1.1.2.6 *Arithmetic*

Arithmetic is complicated because Lisp passes pointers to machine format numbers rather than passing machine format numbers directly. Converting to and from pointer representation is called *boxing* and *unboxing*, respectively. Boxing is also called *number-CONSing*.

The speed of Lisp on arithmetic depends on the boxing/unboxing strategy and on the ability of the compiler to minimize the number of box/unbox operations. To a lesser extent the register allocation performed by the compiler can influence the speed of arithmetic.

Some Lisps attempt to improve the speed of arithmetic by clever encoding techniques. In S-1 Lisp, for instance, the tag field is defined so that all positive and negative single-precision fixed-point numbers consisting of 31 bits of data are both immediate data and machine format integers with their tags in place.[13] Thus, unboxing of these numbers is not needed (though type checking is), but after an arithmetic operation on fixed-point numbers, a range check is performed to validate the type. See [Brooks 1982b] for more details on the numeric data types in S-1 Lisp.

MacLisp is noted for its handling of arithmetic on the PDP-10, mainly because of PDL-numbers and a fast small-number scheme [Fateman 1973] [Steele 1977b]. These ideas have been carried over into S-1 Lisp [Brooks 1982a].

A PDL-number is a number in machine representation on a stack. This reduces the conversion to pointer format in some Lisps, since creating the pointer to the stack-allocated number is simpler than allocating a cell in heap space. The compiler is able to generate code to stack-allocate (and deallocate) a number and to create a pointer to it rather than to heap-allocate it; hence, arithmetic in which all boxing is PDL-number boxing does not pay a steep number-CONS penalty. In MacLisp there are fixed-point and floating-point stacks; numbers allocated on these stacks are only safe through function calls and are deallocated when the function that created them is exited.

The small-number scheme is simply the pre-CONSing of some range of small integers, so that boxing a number in that range is nothing more than adding

---

[13] The Vax Portable Standard Lisp implementation uses a similar scheme for immediate fixed-point numbers.

the number to the base address of the table. In MacLisp there is actually a table containing these small numbers, while in INTERLISP-10 the table is in an inaccessible area, and the indices, not the contents, are used. The MacLisp small-number scheme gains speed at the expense of space.

The range of numbers that a Lisp supports can determine speed. On some machines there are several number-format sizes (single, double, and tetraword, for instance), and the times to operate on each format may vary. When evaluating the numeric characteristics of a Lisp, it is important to study the architecture manual to see how arithmetic is done and to know whether the architecture is fully utilized by the Lisp.

A constant theme in the possible trade-offs in Lisp implementation design is that the inherent flexibility of runtime type checking is often balanced against the speed advantages of compile-time decisions regarding types. This is especially emphasized in the distinction between microcoded implementations in which the runtime type checking can be performed nearly in parallel by the hardware and stock-hardware implementations in which code must be emitted to perform the type checks. Stock-hardware implementations of Lisp often have type-specific arithmetic operations (+ is the FIXNUM version of PLUS in MacLisp), while machines with tagged architectures matched to Lisp processing may not support special type-specific arithmetic operators aside from providing entry points to the generic arithmetic operations corresponding to their names.

With arithmetic it is to the benefit of stock hardware to unbox all relevant numbers and perform as many computations in the machine representation as possible. Performing unboxing and issuing type specific instructions in the underlying machine language is often referred to as *open-compiling* or *open-coding*, while emitting calls to the runtime system routines to perform the type dispatches on the arguments is referred to as *closed-compiling* or *closed-coding*.

A further complicating factor in evaluating the performance of Lisp on arithmetic is that some Lisps support arbitrary precision fixed-point (BIGNUM) and arbitrary precision floating-point (BIGFLOAT) numbers.

Benchmarking is an excellent means of evaluating Lisp performance on arithmetic. Since each audience (or user community) can easily find benchmarks to suit its own needs, only a few caveats will be mentioned.

18

Different rounding modes in the floating-point hardware can cause the 'same' Lisp code running on two different implementations to have different execution behavior, and a numeric algorithm that converges on one may diverge on the other.

Comparing stock hardware with microcoded hardware may be difficult, since a large variability between declared or type-specific arithmetic is possible in non-generic systems. To get the best performance out of a stock-hardware Lisp, one must compile with declarations that are as detailed as possible. For example, in MacLisp the code

```
(defun test (n)
       (do ((i 1 (1+ i)))
           ((= i n) ())
           <form>))
```

compiles into 9 loop management instructions when no declarations aside from the implicit fixed-point in the operations 1+ and = are given, and into 5 loop management instructions when i and n are declared fixed-point. The 40% difference is due to the increased use of PDL-numbers.

1.2 Lisp Operation Level

Simple Lisp 'operations,' i.e., simple, common subroutines such as MAPCAR, ASSOC, APPEND, and REVERSE, are located above the instruction level. Each is used by many user-coded programs.

If a benchmark uses one of these operations and if one implementation has coded it much more efficiently than another, then the timings can be influenced more by this coding difference than by other implementation differences. Similarly, using some of these functions to generally compare implementations may be misleading; for instance, microcoded machines may put some of these facilities in firmware.

For example, consider the function DRECONC, which takes two lists, destructively reverses the first, and NCONCs it with the second. This can be written (without error checking) as

```
(defun dreconc (current previous)
  (prog (next)
   b
    (cond ((null current) (return previous)))
    (setq next (cdr current))
    (rplacd current previous)
    (setq previous current current next)
    (go b))))))
```

With this implementation the inner loop compiles into 16 instructions in MacLisp.
Notice that NEXT is the next CURRENT, and CURRENT is the next PREVIOUS. If
we let PREVIOUS be the next NEXT, then we can eliminate the SETQ and unroll
the loop. Once the loop is unrolled, we can reason the same way again to get

```
(defun dreconc (current previous)
  (prog (next)
   b
    (cond ((null current) (return previous)))
    (setq next (cdr current))
    (rplacd current previous)
    (cond ((null next) (return current)))
    (setq previous (cdr next))
    (rplacd next current)
    (cond ((null previous) (return next)))
    (setq current (cdr previous))
    (rplacd previous next)
    (go b)))
```

With this definition the (unrolled) loop compiles into 29 instructions in MacLisp,
which is 9.7 instructions per iteration, or roughly $\frac{2}{3}$ the number of original instructions. It pays an 80% code size cost.

Such things as MAPCAR can be open-coded, and it is important to understand
when the compiler in question codes operations open versus closed. INTERLISP
uses the LISTP type check for the termination condition for MAPping operations.
This is unlike the MacLisp/Common Lisp MAPping operations, which use the
faster NULL test for termination. On the other hand, if CDR does not type-check,
then this NULL test can lead to nontermination of a MAP on a nonlist.

1.3 Major Lisp Facilities

There are several major facilities in Lisp systems that are orthogonal to the subroutine level but are important to the overall runtime efficiency of an implementation. These include the garbage collector, the interpreter, the file system, and the compiler.

1.3.1 *Interpreter*

Interpreter speed depends primarily on the speed of type dispatching, variable lookup and binding, macro expansion, and call-frame construction. Lexically bound Lisps spend time keeping the proper contours visible or hidden, so that a price is paid at either environment creation time or lookup/assignment time. Some interpreters support elaborate error correction facilities, such as declaration checking in S-1 Lisp, that can slow down some operations.

Interpreters usually are carefully handcoded, and this handcoding can make a difference of a factor of two. Having interpreter primitives in microcode may help, but in stock hardware this handcoding can result in difficult-to-understand encodings of data. The time to dispatch to internal routines (e.g., to determine that a particular form is a COND and to dispatch to the COND handler) is of critical importance in the speed of an interpreter.

Shallow binding versus deep binding matters more in interpreted code than in compiled code, since a deep-binding system looks up each of the variables when it is used unless there is a lambda-contour-entry penalty. For example, when a lambda is encountered in S-1 Lisp, a scan of the lambda-form is performed, and the free/special variables are cached (S-1 Lisp is deep-binding).

The interpreter is mainly used for debugging; when compiled and interpreted code are mixed, the ratio of compiled to interpreted code execution speeds is the important performance measure. Of course, the relative speed of interpreted to compiled code is not constant over all programs, since a program that performs 90% of its computation in compiled code will not suffer much from the interpreter dispatching to that code. Similarly, on some deep-binding Lisps, the interpreter can be made to spend an arbitrary amount of time searching the stack for variable references, when the compiler can find these at compile-time (e.g., globals).

Also, one's intuitions on the relative speeds of interpreted operations may be wrong. For example, consider the case of testing a fixed-point number for 0.

There are three basic techniques:

```
(zerop n)
(equal n 0)
(= n 0)
```

Where declarations of numeric type are used in compiled code, one expects that ZEROP and = would be about the same and EQUAL would be slowest; this is true in MacLisp. However, in the MacLisp interpreter, ZEROP is fastest, then EQUAL, and finally =. This is odd because = is supposedly the fixed-point-specific function that implicitly declares its arguments. The discrepancy is about 20% from ZEROP to =.

The analysis is that ZEROP takes only one argument, and so the time spent managing arguments is substantially smaller. Once the argument is obtained, a type dispatch and a machine-equality-to-0 are performed.

EQUAL first tests for EQ, which is machine-equality-of-address, after managing arguments. In the case of equal small integers in a small-number system, the EQ test succeeds. Testing for EQUAL of two numbers beyond the small-integer range (or comparing two unequal small integers in a small-number system) is then handled by type dispatch on the first argument; next, machine equality of the values is pointed to by the pointers.

= manages two arguments and then dispatches individually on the arguments, so that if one supplies a wrong type argument, they can both be described to the user.

1.3.2 *File Management*

The time spent interacting with the programming environment itself has become an increasingly important part of the 'feel' of a Lisp, and its importance should not be underestimated. There are three times when file read time comes into play: when loading program text, when loading compiled code (this code may be in a different format), and when reading user data structures. The time for most of these is in the READ, PRINT (PRETTYPRINT), and filing system, in basic file access (e.g., disk or network management), and in the operating system interface.

Loading files involves locating atoms on the atom table (often referred to as the *oblist* or *obarray*); in most Lisps, this is a hash table. Something can be learned by studying the size of the table, the distribution of the buckets, etc. One can time atom hash table operations to effect, but getting a good range of variable names (to test the distribution of the hashing function) might be hard, and getting the table loaded up effectively can be difficult.

On personal machines with a relatively small amount of local file storage, access to files may require operation over a local network. Typically these are contention networks in the 1–10 megabit per second speed range (examples are 3-megabit Ethernet, 10-megabit Ethernet, Chaosnet). The response time on a contention network can be slow when it is heavily loaded, and this can degrade the perceived pep of the implementation. Additionally, the file server can be a source of slowdown.

1.3.3 *Compiler*

Lisp compiler technology has grown rapidly in the last 15 years. Early recursive-descent compilers generated simple and often ridiculous code on backing out of an execution-order treewalk of the program. Some modern Lisp compilers resemble the best optimizing compilers for algorithmic languages [Brooks 1982a], [Masinter 1981b].

Interpreting a language like Lisp involves examining an expression and determining the proper runtime code to execute. Simple compilers essentially eliminate the dispatching routine and generate calls to the correct routines, with some bookkeeping for values in between.

Fancier compilers do a lot of open-coding, generating the body of a routine in-line with the code that calls it. A simple example is CAR, which consists of the instruction HRRZ on the PDP-10. The runtime routine for this will do the HRRZ and then POPJ on the PDP-10. The call to CAR (in MacLisp style) will look like

```
move a,<arg>
pushj p,<car>
move <dest>,a
```

And CAR would be

```
hrrz a,(a)
popj p,
```

if no type checking were done on its arguments. Open-coding of this would be simply

```
hrrz <dest>,@<arg>
```

Other types of open-coding involve generating the code for a control structure in-line. For example, MAPC will map down a list and apply a function to each element. Rather than simply calling such a function, a compiler might generate the control structure code directly, often doing this by transforming the input code into equivalent, in-line Lisp code and then compiling that.

Further optimizations involve delaying the boxing or number-CONSing of numbers in a numeric computation. Some compilers also rearrange the order of evaluation, do constant-folding, loop-unwinding, common-subexpression elimination, register optimization, cross optimizations (between functions), peephole optimization, and many of the other classical compiler techniques.

When evaluating a compiler, it is important to know what the compiler in question can do. Often looking at some sample code produced by the compiler for an interesting piece of code is a worthwhile evaluation technique for an expert. Knowing what is open-coded, what constructs are optimized, and how to declare facts to the compiler in order to help it produce code are the most important things for a user to know.

A separate issue is "How fast is the compiler?" In some cases the compiler is slow even if the code it generates is fast; for instance, it can spend a lot of time doing optimization.

1.4 The Art of Benchmarking

Benchmarking is a black art at best. Stating the results of a particular benchmark on two Lisp systems usually causes people to believe that a blanket statement ranking the systems in question is being made. The proper role of benchmarking is to measure various dimensions of Lisp system performance and to order those systems along each of these dimensions. At that point, informed users will be able to choose a system that meets their requirements or will be able to tune their programming style to the performance profile.

24

1.4.1 *Know What is Being Measured*

The first problem associated with benchmarking is knowing what is being tested.

Consider the following example of the TAK′ function:

```
(defun tak' (x y z)
  (cond ((not (< y x)) z)
        (t (tak' (tak' (1- x) y z)
                 (tak' (1- y) z x)
                 (tak' (1- z) x y))))))
```

If used as a benchmark, what does this function measure? Careful examination shows that function call, simple arithmetic (small-integer arithmetic, in fact), and a simple test are all that this function performs; no storage allocation is done. In fact, when applied to the arguments 18, 12 and 6, this function performs 63609 function calls, has a maximum recursion depth of 18, and has an average recursion depth of 15.4.

On a PDP-10 (in MacLisp) this means that this benchmark tests the stack instructions, data moving, and some arithmetic, as we see from the code the compiler produces:

```
tak':                          movei a,(fxp)
push p,[0,,fix1]               push fxp,tt
push fxp,(a)                   pushj p,tak'+1
push fxp,(b)                   move d,-3(fxp)
push fxp,(c)                   subi d,1
move tt,-1(fxp)                movei c,-4(fxp)
camge tt,-2(fxp)               movei b,-5(fxp)
jrst g2                        push fxp,d
move tt,(fxp)                  movei a,(fxp)
jrst g1                        push fxp,tt
g2:                            pushj p,tak'+1
move tt,-2(fxp)                push fxp,tt
subi tt,1                      movei c,(fxp)
push fxp,tt                    movei b,-1(fxp)
movei a,(fxp)                  movei a,-3(fxp)
pushj p,tak'+1                 pushj p,tak'+1
move d,-2(fxp)                 sub fxp,[6,,6]
subi d,1                       g1:
movei c,-3(fxp)                sub fxp,[3,,3]
movei b,-1(fxp)                popj p,
push fxp,d
```

One expects the following sorts of results. A fast stack machine might do much better than its average instruction speed would indicate. In fact, running this benchmark written in C on both the Vax 11/780 and a Motorola 4 megahertz MC68000 (using 16-bit arithmetic in the latter case), one finds that the MC68000 time is 71% of the Vax 11/780 time. Assuming that the Lisps on these machines maintain this ratio, one would expect the MC68000 to be a good Lisp processor. However, in a tagged implementation the MC68000 fares poorly, since field extraction is not as readily performed on the MC68000 as on the Vax. An examination of all instructions and of the results of a number of benchmarks that have been run leads to the conclusion that the MC68000 performs at about 40% of a Vax 11/780 when running Lisp.

As mentioned earlier, the locality profile of this benchmark is not typical of 'normal' Lisp programs, and the effect of the cache memory may dominate the performance. Let us consider the situation in MacLisp on the Stanford Artificial Intelligence Laboratory KL-10A (SAIL), which has a 2k-word 200-nanosecond cache memory and a main memory consisting of a 2-megaword 1.5-μsec memory and a 256-kiloword .9-μsec memory. On SAIL, the cache memory allows a very large, but slow, physical memory to behave reasonably well.

This benchmark was run with no load and the result was as follows:

```
cpu time = 0.595
elapsed time = 0.75
wholine time = 0.75
gc time = 0.0
load average before = 0.020
load average after  = 0.026
```

where CPU time is the EBOX time (no memory reference time included), elapsed time is real time, wholine time is EBOX + MBOX (memory reference) times, GC time is garbage collector time, and the load averages are given before and after the timing run; all times are in seconds, and the load average is the exponentially weighted average of the number of jobs in all runnable queues. With no load, wholine and elapsed times are the same.

There are two ways to measure the effect of the extreme locality of TAK': one is to run the benchmark with the cache memory shut off; another is to produce a sequence (called TAK$'_i$) of identical functions that call functions TAK$'_j$, TAK$'_k$, TAK$'_l$, and TAK$'_m$ with uniform distribution on j, k, l, and m.

With 100 such functions and no load the result on SAIL was

```
cpu time = 0.602
elapsed time = 1.02
wholine time = 1.02
gc time = 0.0
load average before = 0.27
load average after  = 0.28
```

which shows a 36% degradation. The question is how well do these 100 functions destroy the effect of the cache. The answer is that they do not destroy the effect very much. This makes sense because the total number of instructions for 100 copies of the function is about 3800, and the cache holds about 2000 words. Both benchmarks were run with the cache off at SAIL. Here is the result for the single function TAK':

```
cpu time = 0.6
elapsed time = 6.95
wholine time = 6.9
gc time = 0.0
load average before = 0.036
load average after  = 0.084
```

which shows a factor of 9.2 degradation. The 100 function version ran in the same time, within a few percent.

Hence, in order to destroy the effect of a cache, one must increase the size of the code to a size that is significantly beyond that of the cache. Also, the distribution of the locus of control must be roughly uniform or random.

This example also illustrates the point about memory bandwidth, which was discussed earlier. The CPU has remained constant in its speed with the cache on or off (.595 versus .6), but the memory speed of 1.5 μsec has caused a slowdown of more than a factor of 9 in the overall execution speed of Lisp.[14]

Some Lisp compilers perform *tail recursion* removal. A tail-recursive function is one whose value is sometimes returned by a function application (as opposed to an open-codable operation). Hence in the function TAK', the second arm of the COND states that the value of the function is the value of another call on TAK', but with different arguments. If a compiler does not handle this case, then another

---

[14] With the cache off, the 4-way interleaving of memory benefits are abandoned, further degrading the factor of 7.5 speed advantage the cache has over main memory on SAIL.

call frame will be set up, control will transfer to the other function (TAK', again, in this case), and control will return only to exit the first function immediately. Hence, there will be additional stack frame management overhead for no useful reason, and the compiled function will be correspondingly inefficient. A smarter compiler will re-use the current stack frame, and when the called function returns, it will return directly to the function that called the one that is currently invoked.

The INTERLISP-D compiler does tail recursion removal; the MacLisp compiler handles some simple cases of tail recursion, but it does no such removal in TAK'.

Previously it was mentioned that MacLisp has both small-number-CONSing and PDL numbers. It is true that

$$\text{TAK}'(x+n, y+n, z+n) = \text{TAK}'(x, y, z) + n$$

and therefore it might be expected that if MacLisp used the small-number-CONS in TAK' and if one chose n as the largest small-integer in MacLisp, the effects of small-number-CONSing could be observed. However, the PDP-10 code for TAK' shown above demonstrates that it is using PDL numbers. Also, by timing various values for n, one can see that there is no significant variation and that the coding technique therefore cannot be number-size dependent (up to BIGNUMs).

Thus analysis and benchmarking can be valid alternative methods for inferring the structure of Lisp implementations

1.4.2 *Measure the Right Thing*

Often a single operation is too fast to time directly, and therefore must be performed many times; the total time is then used to compute the speed of the operation. Although simple loops to accomplish this appear straightforward, the benchmark may be mainly testing the loop construct. Consider the MacLisp program

```
(defun test (n)
  (declare (special x)(fixnum i n x))
  (do ((i n (1- i)))
      ((= i 0))
    (setq x i)))
```

which assigns a number to the special variable x, n times. What does this program do? First, it number-CONSes for each assignment. Second, of the 6 instructions the MacLisp compiler generates for the inner loop, 4 manage the loop counter, its testing, its modification, and the flow of control; 1 is a fast, internal subroutine call to the number-CONSer; and 1 is used for the assignment (moving to memory). So 57% of the code is the loop management.

```
      push fxp,(a)
g2:   move tt,(fxp)
      jumpe tt,g4
      jsp t,fxcons
      movem a,(special x)
      sos fxp
      jrst g2
g4:   movei a,'()
      sub fxp,[1,,1]
      popj p,
```

To measure operations that require looping, measure the loop alone (i.e., measure the null operation) and subtract that from the results.

As mentioned in the previous section, even here one must be aware of what is being timed, since the number-CONSing is the time sink in the statement (setq x i).

In INTERLISP-D and in S-1 Lisp it makes a big difference whether you are doing a global/free or lexical variable assignment. If x were a local variable, the compiler would optimize the SETQ away (assignment to a dead variable).

1.4.3 *Know How the Facets Combine*

Sometimes a program that performs two basic Lisp operations will combine them nonlinearly. For instance, a compiler might optimize two operations in such a way that their operational characteristics are interleaved or unified; some garbage collection strategies can interfere with the effectiveness of the cache.

One way to measure those characteristics relevant to a particular audience is to benchmark large programs that are of interest to that audience and that are large enough so that the combinational aspects of the problem domain are reasonably unified. For example, part of an algebra simplification or symbolic integration system might be an appropriate benchmark for a group of users implementing and using a MACSYMA-like system.

The problems with using a large system for benchmarking are that the same Lisp code may or may not run on the various Lisp systems or the obvious translation might not be the best implementation of the benchmark for a different Lisp system. For instance, a Lisp without multidimensional arrays might choose to implement them as arrays whose elements are other arrays, or it might use lists of lists if the only operations on the multidimensional array involve scanning through the elements in a predetermined order. A reasoning program that uses floating-point numbers $0 \leq x \leq 1$ on one system might use fixed-point arithmetic with numbers $0 \leq x \leq 1000$ on another.

Another problem is that it is often difficult to control for certain facets in a large benchmark. The history of the address space that is being used for the timing—how many CONSes have been done and how full the atom hash table is, for example—can make a difference.

1.4.4 *Personal Versus Time-shared Systems*

The most important and difficult question associated with timing a benchmark is exactly how to time it. This is a problem, particularly when one is comparing a personal machine to a time-shared machine. Obviously, the final court of appeal is the amount of time that a person has to wait for a computation to finish. On time-shared machines one wants to know what the best possible time is and how that time varies. CPU time (including memory references) is a good measure for the former, while the latter is measured in elapsed time. For example, one could obtain an approximate mapping from CPU time to elapsed time under various loads and then do all of the timings under CPU time measurement. This mapping is at best approximate, since elapsed time depends not only on the load (number of other active users) but also on what all users are and were doing.

Time-sharing systems often do background processing that doesn't get charged to any one user. TENEX, for example, writes dirty pages to the disk as part of a system process rather than as part of the user process. On SAIL some system interrupts may be charged to a user process. When using runtime reported by the time-sharing system, one is sometimes not measuring these necessary background tasks.

Personal machines, it would seem, are easier to time because elapsed time and CPU time (with memory references) are the same. However, sometimes a personal machine will perform background tasks that can be disabled, such as monitoring the keyboard and the network. On the Xerox 1100 running INTERLISP, turning off the display can increase Lisp execution speed by more than 30%. When using elapsed time, one is measuring these stolen cycles as well as those going to execute Lisp.

A sequence of timings was done on SAIL with a variety of load averages. Each timing measures EBOX time, EBOX + MBOX (memory reference) time, elapsed time, garbage collection time, and the load averages before and after the benchmark. For load averages $.2 \leq L \leq 10$, the elapsed time, E, behaved as

$$E = \begin{cases} C(1 + K(L-1)), & L > 1; \\ C, & L \leq 1. \end{cases}$$

That is, the load had a linear effect for the range tested. The effect of load averages on elapsed time on other machines has not been tested.

The quality of interaction is an important consideration. In many cases the personal machine provides a much better environment. But in others, the need for high absolute performance means that a time-shared system is preferable.

1.4.5 *Measure the Hardware Under All Conditions*

In some architectures, jumps across page boundaries are slower than jumps within page boundaries, and the performance of a benchmark can thus depend on the alignment of inner loops within page boundaries. Further, working-set size can can make a large performance difference, and the physical memory size can be a more dominating factor than CPU speed on benchmarks with large working-sets. Measuring CPU time (without memory references) in conjunction with a knowledge of the approximate mapping from memory size to CPU + memory time would be an ideal methodology but is difficult to do.

An often informative test is to take some reasonably small benchmarks and to code them as efficiently as possible in an appropriate language in order to obtain the best possible performance of the hardware on those benchmarks. This was done on SAIL with the TAK' function, which was mentioned earlier. In MacLisp the time was .68 seconds of CPU + memory time; in assembly language (heavily optimized) it was .255 seconds, or about a factor of 2.5 better.[15]

---

[15] This factor is not necessarily expected to hold up uniformly over all benchmarks.

Chapter 2

The Implementations

The following sections contain descriptions of the implementations studied. Most of the descriptions were submitted by the implementors of the Lisp systems. In general, the aspects noted in the previous chapter as important to performance will be described for each implementation.

2.1 MacLisp

MacLisp was one of the first Lisps written on the PDP-10. Its primary author was JonL White, although many people contributed to it over the years. It was derived from the PDP-6 Lisp, which was written during the middle 1960's. MacLisp on the PDP-10 was introduced in 1972, and in 1984 it was in use on many DEC-20 installations.

MacLisp enjoys a large runtime system, which includes an interpreter written in assembly language. The listing of this runtime system is over 600 pages long. Nearly a decade passed before it was understood that a Lisp could be implemented in Lisp itself; no such implementations appeared until the mid 1970's.

2.1.1 *Types*

The PDP-10 has 36-bit words and a variety of half-word instructions. An address is 18 bits, and so a CONS cell fits nicely into one 36-bit word. To be able to look at a pointer (an address) and determine the type of the object to which the pointer points, the information must be encoded in the address. The method used is BIBOP. Memory is segmented into pages, each about 1k words long. Each page contains objects of one type only. To determine the type of a pointer, one must determine the type of the page to which it points. In general, this can be done by using a special table (as in MacLisp) or by looking at a header word at the beginning of the page in question.

Array headers are allocated in this way, and the array elements are placed elsewhere. Hunks are a short, vector-like data structure in MacLisp and are allocated using a buddy-block system.

2.1.2 *Function Call*

MacLisp function calling is quite simple; it uses a stack to hold PCs (program counters). Arguments are passed in five sequential registers (A, B, C, AR1, AR2A). If there are more than five arguments, they are passed on the stack, and the number of arguments passed is placed at the top of the stack.

When compiled code contains a call to a function, a user UUO (**Un Used Opcode**) is placed at the point of call. A UUO looks exactly like a machine instruction in format, but the opcode is not understandable to the CPU. When the CPU encounters such a UUO, it traps to a handler for it. This is how monitor calls are done on the PDP-10. UUOs not handled by the operating system can be handled by user code.

When loading compiled Lisp code, the loader does not fix up function references. Instead, it places a UUO with an operand, which is the address of the symbol that is the name of the function being called. When the UUO is encountered, the CPU traps to a user routine that finds out the address of the code to which the function corresponds.

This idea is refined by making a table of such UUO calls, with one entry for every call to a particular routine. Instead of the UUO appearing in the instruction stream, an XCT instruction is placed there. The XCT instruction executes the instruction located at the effective address of its operand as if it were located at the current PC.

When the UUO determines the correct address, it replaces the UUO call with

```
PUSHJ P,<function address>
```

This is the simple function-calling mechanism in MacLisp, and whenever the first call to a particular function is made, all subsequent calls to that function use this simple mechanism rather than the UUO mechanism.

The UUO mechanism, however, allows a great deal of debugging functionality. The UUO can invoke tracing or other debugging routines at function-call points. Hence, to extend the utility of this basic facility, the table of UUO calls is in two parts, one a copy of the other. All calls go through one half of the table. When the user wishes to invoke some debugging routines, he can cause the untouched copy of the table to be copied on top of the optimized table. Hence, we say that the so-called *UUOLINKS* table can be 'unsnapped.' Several other Lisp implementations—Franz Lisp, for example—use this scheme or one like it.

2.1.3 *Fast Arithmetic*

One of the most well-known aspects of MacLisp is its fast arithmetic. This is accomplished in two ways—both are variants of the 'do not number-CONS' philosophy.

What makes arithmetic slow in most Lisps is the need to make numbers into Lisp objects, which means there must be a pointer to them whose type can be deduced. In MacLisp, this means moving them into a page full of the required type of number and returning a pointer to that location. One key to fast arithmetic is doing this operation only when it is absolutely necessary. Because most fixnums, in practice, are in the range −1000 to 1000, these numbers are permanently preallocated, and number-CONSing one of them is nothing more than simply adding the base index of this preallocated table to the original number.

The second way to achieve fast arithmetic is to create two stacks, a FLPDL and a FXPDL. FLPDL contains only floating-point numbers, and FXPDL only fixed-point numbers. Arithmetic expressions can use these stacks as temporary storage, and hence the largest source of unnecessary number-CONSing is eliminated. S-1 Lisp uses this idea.

2.1.4 *Remarks*

MacLisp was the first high-performance Lisp implementation. For many years it was the standard against which all Lisp implementations were measured, not only in terms of performance but also in functionality. The people who were the primary implementors of NIL, Spice Lisp, ZetaLisp, S-1 Lisp, and Franz Lisp, and who were the primary architects of the CADR, the Lambda, and the Symbolics 3600 were brought up on MacLisp. Since the primary designers of Common Lisp were drawn from this group the intellectual debt to MacLisp is considerable.

In the tables, the name SAIL is used to refer to the Stanford Artificial Intelligence Laboratory's KL-10B, which runs the WAITS time-sharing system. The machine has 3.3 megawords of physical memory and does not page. The MacLisp dialect is identical to the MIT BIBOP version. The KL-10B CPU is identical to the DEC-2060 CPU.

2.2 MIT CADR

Symbolics Inc. and LISP Machine Inc. (LMI), both Lisp machine companies based in Cambridge, Massachusetts, were spin-offs of the MIT Artificial Intelligence Laboratory Lisp machine project. LMI was the first company to sell a commercial version of the MIT CADR, and Symbolics soon followed with a similar machine. Since then, these two companies have gone in different directions.

The following description is reasonably accurate for all three of the MIT CADR, the LMI CADR, and the Symbolics LM-2.

2.2.1 *CADR and LM-2*

The CADR is the MIT Lisp machine; it is quite similar to the Symbolics LM-2. Both machines run a dialect of Lisp called ZetaLisp, which is a direct outgrowth of the MIT Lisp Machine Lisp (in fact, the two dialects share a manual).

The CADR is 32-bit microprocessor with up to 16k of 48-bit words of writable control store and a 180-nanosecond microcycle time. The memory configuration ranges from 255k words, minimum, to 4 megawords. It was designed to emulate complex order codes, especially ones involving stacks and pointer manipulation. While not tied exclusively to Lisp, the CADR is well suited to it and contains hardware to support a virtual Lisp Machine. For example, there is hardware to aid in the processing of the 16-bit instruction stream generated by the Lisp compiler. In addition, the CADR has flexible type-dispatching, function calling, and byte manipulation capabilities; it also supports internal stack storage.

The CADR derives much of its power from extensive microcoding. This is assisted by a 14-bit microprogram counter that, acting as a traditional processor, permits up to 16k words of dynamically writable microprogram memory. There is also a 32-location microcode function return stack.

The CADR has linear, paged virtual memory comprising 65,536 pages of 256 32-bit words. A two-level memory map translates each virtual address of 24 bits into a 22-bit physical address.

There is a 1 kilobyte pointer-addressable RAM, which behaves like a cache for the top of the stack. Although the 3600 has more hardware for stack manipulation, the CADR has more microcode support, including a capability for microcompiled functions that use the hardware CALL instruction.

2.2.1.1 *Function Call*

The CADR uses an inverted calling sequence for function calls. The CALL instruction opens a stack frame (the maximum size is 128 words Then when the caller pushes arguments on the stack, they are placed where the callee expects them. This avoids the overhead of copying the arguments. The last argument value is moved to the destination D-LAST, which executes the function call.

2.2.1.2 *Types*

The combination of tagged data objects and a 32-bit word makes for non-standard number formats on the CADR. Fixnums are a 24-bit immediate datum. Word addresses are also 24-bits. Flonums (floating point numbers) are implemented as pairs of words; while larger than the single format on most systems, they are slower to access. The significand is 32 bits and the exponent is 11 bits.

2.3 Symbolics

2.3.1 *3600*

The 3600 is the current product offering of Symbolics. It is an intellectual descendent of the CADR and the LM-2 but has more hardware support for Lisp.

The Symbolics 3600 is built around a microcoded 36-bit processor (28/32 bits data, 4/8 bits tag) with a 180 to 250-nanosecond cycle time. The minimum memory configuration is 256k words and the maximum is 7.5 megawords. The architecture of the 3600 is based primarily on the requirements of Lisp. While it currently has less microcode support than the CADR, it benefits from a more appropriate hardware design and a more efficient instruction set.

The 3600 has a demand-paged virtual memory that is word addressable. Random access of a word takes 3 machine cycles (600 ns), while sequential access takes one cycle. The virtual memory address space is 256 megawords, approximately 5 megawords of which is occupied by system software. The 28-bit virtual address is passed through a hierarchy of map tables to obtain the appropriate address.

From a programming standpoint, one can think of main memory as a large cache. Virtual memory is not allocated by process, but rather is split up by AREA feature in ZetaLisp and then further carved up into Lisp objects. The user can create AREAs to contain related data and thus increase locality effects.

The default paging algorithm is based on a least-recently-used (LRU) replacement technique, but the user can optionally affect the storage scheme and paging algorithm by setting characteristics of a particular AREA. Common modifications include changing the number of pages swapped at a time, locking pages into memory, and specifying sequential rather than random access.

One of the unique features of the 3600 is hardware-supported type checking. Runtime typing happens during instruction execution rather than prior to it as in the CADR design. This is accomplished by examining the tag field appended to each Lisp object. Thus, macroinstructions such as '+' are generic and compiler declarations for number types are no-ops. For example, the ADD instruction checks the type of each operand while the addition is in progress, then the ADD completes if the arguments are fixnums; otherwise it traps to microcode for floats or to Lisp code for BIGNUMs.

2.3.1.1 *Types*

There are two basic formats for the 36-bit data word in the 3600. One format consists of an immediate number made up of a 2-bit tag, 2-bits for CDR-coding, and 32 bits of data. The other is a tagged pointer consisting of a 2-bit CDR code, a 6-bit data type tag, and 28 bits of address for the pointer itself. In main memory, these formats are augmented by 7 bits for error correction code (ECC) plus one spare bit for a total of 44 bits, which is the width of the 3600's data path.

Both the CADR and the 3600 make extensive use of a list compaction technique termed 'CDR-coding.' In both machines, data word formats dedicate 2 bits for the three values used for this method. One value, 'Cdr-normal,' indicates that the list element is the CAR of a CONS pair (i.e., the next word is a pointer to the CDR). This is the traditional pair representation for CAR and CDR. The other two values allow storage of lists as vectors in memory, and this cuts the storage required for lists in half. 'CDR-next' indicates that the next list element is the next word in memory. 'CDR-NIL' marks the last object in the list/vector.

Whether a list manipulating function produces a CDR-coded list or not depends on the nature of the function. For example, LIST produces a CDR-coded list, but CONS can't. As one might imagine, hybrid lists are common. The construct (CONS 1 (LIST 2 3 4)) would produce a list whose second, third, and fourth elements are logically a vector.

It may be useful here to give the sequence of operations that the 3600 completes to get the CDR of a list. First, CDR checks to see if it has a valid argument: NIL, a list, or a locative (a low-level pointer to a Lisp object cell on the CADR and the 3600). Then it branches on the argument type. If the argument is NIL, then it returns NIL. If the argument is a locative, it returns the contents of the cell to which it points. To take the CDR of a list, the microcode dispatches on the value in the CDR code field. If that value is CDR-next, it increments the current pointer and returns the new pointer. If the CDR code field is CDR-NIL, it returns NIL. Otherwise, in the CDR-normal case, it increments the word pointer and returns the contents of the cell being pointed to.

CDR of NIL takes 2 cycles, CDR of a locative takes 4 cycles, CDR of a CDR-next list takes 5 cycles, CDR of a a CDR-NIL list takes 6 cycles, and CDR of a CDR-normal list takes 6 cycles.

Most of the 3600's architecture is built around stacks, although it is not purely a stack machine. Most, though not all, of the 3600's instructions use the stack to get operands and stash results. There are no general purpose registers at the macroinstruction level. Stacks facilitate passing arguments to functions and flavor methods, returning single and multiple values, and making local data references. Given the importance of flexible function calling in modern Lisp dialects, this is a crucial design feature.

Associated with each process is a separate environment called a 'stack group.' Stack groups in ZetaLisp may be created and manipulated by the user. Stack groups have three components: the control stack, the binding stack, and the data stack.

The 3600's processor hardware handles most stack management tasks. There are two 1k word stack buffers, which behave like cache memory. These contain the top of the Lisp control stack, which is maintained by the virtual paging system. As mentioned above, most memory references in Lisp are passed through the stack. This speeds up access times considerably in CPU-bound programs. Several stack frames at the top of the stack are held in the stack buffer, which has faster access and more bandwidth than main memory.

Pointers to the stack buffers are also managed by the hardware. By eliminating the need for microcode to handle stack manipulations, stack instructions like PUSH and POP work in one machine cycle. There is also a special top-of-stack register.

One component of a stack group is the control stack, which consists of a series of concatenated frames that correspond to function calls ordered last in, first out. A frame is made up of a fixed header, slots for arguments and local variables, and a temporary stack area that holds the computed arguments and the result(s) returned from the called function.

As mentioned above, stack groups have two other components, namely, the binding stack and the data stack.

The binding stack is used to manage the binding of special variables. Each binding is represented by a pair of words. One is a locative to the value cell of the variable; the other contains the previous value. The CDR-codes of these words supply information about the binding, including whether or not it is a closure binding. The stack group that is associated with each binding stack keeps track of pointers to the base of the stack, the highest legal word, and the stack overflow limit.

Binding occurs by reading the value cell pointed to by the first word of the pair (following any invisible pointers), storing it in the second word, putting the new value in the original value cell, and finally incrementing the stack pointer.

To unbind, the word pair is read out of the binding stack, the old value is restored, and the binding stack pointer is decremented. Constructs such as THROW unbind as they unwind each appropriate stack.

The data stack is not implemented at the time of this writing. The data stack will contain objects of dynamic extent such as temporary arrays and lists to reduce garbage collection overhead.

2.3.1.2 *Function Call*

During a function call, the arguments are computed and then pushed onto the temporary stack. The function call instruction specifies the function to be called, the number of arguments, and what to do with the results (ignore them, push them on the temporary stack, return them as the caller's result, or accept multiple values on the stack). The caller sees if there is room in the stack buffer for a new frame, checks for the right number of arguments and the legality of the function being called. If all is well, the caller builds a frame and copies the new arguments to it. The frame itself may be up to 220 words long. &REST arguments are handled by passing the callee a pointer to a CDR-coded list of the arguments from earlier in the stack (created either by the current caller or by some previous caller). This avoids the necessity of variable length data in the main part of the frame. The caller then transfers control to the called function, which ultimately issues a return instruction. The return instruction insures that the caller's frame is in the stack buffer, removes the called function's frame, and replaces the caller's copy of the arguments with multiple returned values if any; otherwise it places the single returned value in the appropriate place.

The compiler for the 3600 does not produce as highly optimized code as it might. In part, this is because the 3600's hardware was designed to alleviate some of the problems that are usually addressed by an optimizing compiler. With the use of stack buffers, sophisticated register allocation is unnecessary.

Like the CADR, the compiler for the 3600 allows the user to specify source level optimizers. These are stored on the property list of the respective functions. Optimizers are used to specify functionally equivalent, but more efficient forms; for example, (= object 0) may become (ZEROP object).

The user can also control in-line coding by using the DEFSUBST special form and, of course, macros.

2.3.1.3 *Data Formats*

The 3600's data formats are significantly different from those of the CADR. On the 3600, pointers are 28 bits and fixnums are 32 bits. Floating-point numbers comprise 8 bits of exponent and 23 bits of significand. This corresponds to IEEE single precision specifications. Also, on the 3600 floating-point numbers are an immediate datum, while on the CADR they are larger but implemented as word pairs. This change is reflected in the improved times for the FFT benchmark and the floating-point tests in FRPOLY. This format also speeds up garbage collection of floating-point objects.

2.3.1.4 *Instruction Pre-Fetch*

The 3600 supports an optional instruction pre-fetch unit (the IFU), which fills the instruction cache asynchronously. This pre-fetcher is sufficiently fast (two instructions every machine cycle), so that it usually gets the instruction there before the processor needs it, even in straight-line code. Thus there are no wait states for straight-line code.

If there are branches, the pre-fetcher will not follow them. Thus, if the instruction streams remerge, there is a good chance that the pre-fetcher will have already fetched the next instruction. Backward branches are almost always in the cache. If the processor branches and the pre-fetcher has not fetched the instruction in time, one of two situations has occurred.

In the first situation the pre-fetcher does not know the virtual address translation for the page that was branched to (in other words, the branch was across a page boundary). Consequently, the pre-fetcher and instruction pipeline shut down until the execution state has emptied the pipe. Then, the execution state is redirected to do the page translation for the new page. There are 4 dead cycles until the first instruction comes back and is executed.

In the second situation the instruction branched to was on the same page and had not yet been loaded by the pre-fetcher. In this case, the pre-fetcher is shut down and restarted at the new address. It takes 5 cycles to get the instruction ready for the execution stage. However, this can be overlapped with the execution of the two instructions already in the instruction pipeline (in the case of an unconditional branch).

In a conditional branch, the CPU and pre-fetcher cannot proceed until the result of the branch is known, so there is at most a single instruction in the pipeline (the IFU fetches both the target and the fall-through of a conditional branch). If the instructions in the pipeline take more than 4 cycles, then there are no wait states; otherwise wait states are inserted. Another complication is that the pre-fetcher stays out of the way of the main processor memory requests, so that if the processor is requesting memory, then the pre-fetcher can fall behind. This almost never happens in actual code.

2.3.2 *Details on the Results*

The timing results presented are for the Common Lisp versions. Page time includes both time spent satisfying page faults and time spent creating new pages. Page time is highly dependent on the configuration of the system and the tuning of the garbage collector for the particular application. The numbers given here are the minimum expected time on the 3600—the configuration that was timed had 6 megabytes of physical memory, and the garbage collector was carefully tuned.

CPU time is real time less page time. The scheduler was disabled while the benchmarks were run to eliminate the effects of other processes. These CPU time figures are repeatable across different system configurations. These results were obtained on a Symbolics 3600 system running System 271.19 and microcode 319.

2.4 LMI Lambda

LISP Machine, Inc. (LMI) supports two versions of the Lisp Machine architecture originally developed at MIT. LMI's first machine, the CADR, was the first commercial incarnation of the MIT CADR. LMI's current product, the Lambda, is a lower-cost and higher-performance descendant of the CADR. The CADR and the Lambda both execute the Common Lisp dialect in addition to their traditional ZetaLisp software.

The CADR was discussed earlier.

2.4.1 *The Lambda Architecture*

The Lambda is a 32-bit microprogrammed processor with up to 64K 64-bit words of virtual control store and a 200 nanosecond microcycle time. Although the Lambda design is flexible enough to be adapted to other purposes, it is primarily a tagged architecture tailored for executing Lisp. It features 32 megawords of demand-paged virtual address space, a large number of internal registers, a byte-manipulation capability, a 4096-word instruction and data cache, a 2048-word stack cache, logic for tag comparison and boxing/unboxing tagged quantities, and pipelined logic for fetching and decoding the 16-bit order codes produced by the Lisp Machine compiler.

A unique feature of the Lambda is its pageable control store and microcompiler, which compiles Lisp into microcode. Under favorable conditions, the microcompiler can produce microcode for the Lambda processor, yielding improved performance in many cases. For example, the TAK benchmark microcompiled on a Lambda executes in 0.192 seconds, which is faster than all other reported results except for those of the Cray-1 and the IBM 3081.

The Lambda processor resides on the NuBus, a fast 32-bit synchronous bus developed at the MIT Laboratory for Computer Science and produced by Texas Instruments. The NuBus features a 10 Mhz clock, a low-latency arbitration scheme, and a bandwidth of 37.5 megabytes/second in one of several block-transfer modes. In addition, the NuBus supports multiple-processor operation with fair arbitration, which allows LMI to supply on a single bus low-cost configurations of multiple Lambda processors that share physical resources such as disks and network interfaces. With LMI's NuBus coupler, several NuBus card cages can be directly addressed.

2.4.2 *Performance Issues*

The Lambda derives much of its performance from its stack cache, a bank of fast memory acting as a specialized top-of-stack cache. The contents of this cache are managed by the microcode to contain the contents of the top of the control stack for the current stack group. The frame of the currently executing function is always resident in the stack cache, and references to elements of the frame (arguments, local variables, temporary values, or frame header words) are made by indexing off a frame pointer held in a special register. The stack level is checked on function entry and exit and adjusted as necessary by moving words to or from the stack image in main memory.

2.4.3 *Function Calling*

The Lambda uses an inverted function-calling sequence that eliminates the need to copy pieces of stack around during normal execution. A function call starts with a 'CALL' instruction, which builds a frame header, and then the arguments are pushed. The last argument is pushed to a special destination, which causes the function to be invoked. This can immediately push any local variables and temporaries and begin execution. The result of the function is pushed to another destination, which causes the frame to be popped and the value to be transmitted.

Many Common Lisp functions are implemented in microcode on the LMI Lambda. Conventional machines implement logically primitive operations such as ASSQ, ASSOC, MEMQ, MEMBER, property list manipulation, or BIGNUM arithmetic in macrocode or Lisp. In the Lambda, these functions are implemented in microcode.

The data/instruction cache in the Lambda speeds up typical Lisp execution by about 30%. Most of the benefit comes from faster macroinstruction fetching (the stack cache eliminates most data references to memory). The cache is a physical-address write-through design and achieves an LMI-estimated 85% hit rate. Using a two-level mapping scheme, virtual address translation proceeds in parallel with cache hit detection. There are a number of improvements to be made in the operation of the cache, including the use of block-mode NuBus memory cycles for cache updating in regions with high locality of reference; the benchmark figures do not reflect these enhancements.

The Lisp Machine uses CDR-coding to represent list structure efficiently.

Two bits in the tag field of every object indicate where the CDR of that object (if any exists) is to be found. If the CDR-code has the value CDR-normal, then the CDR of the object is found by following the pointer in the next higher location. If the CDR-code has the value CDR-next, then the CDR object is the next higher location. If the CDR-code is CDR-NIL, then the CDR of the object is NIL. CDR-coding is completely transparent to the user and reduces the space needed to store list structure by nearly 50%. This scheme is essentially the same as that used on the 3600.

2.4.4 *The Microcompiler*

The optimizing microcompiler eliminates all the overhead of macroinstruction processing and speeds up control flow and most forms of data manipulation. Compile-time declarations (using Common Lisp syntax) allow further optimization of function calling and open-coding of fixnum arithmetic.

As has been often noted, function-calling speed is quite central to the performance of most Lisp programs. When generating a call from one microcoded function to another, the microcompiler can generate a particularly fast form of function call termed a 'micro-micro' call. In the micro-micro function call, the call and return are only one microinstruction each and are pipelined using the delayed-branch mechanism of the Lambda micromachine. The overhead of calling and returning from a function is only 200 nanoseconds. Argument transmission is also efficient under microcompilation.

To produce optimal code the microcompiler requires special declarations in much the same manner as do Lisps running on conventional architectures. Microcode-to-microcode (micro-micro) calls can only be produced using appropriate declarations. First, the microcompiler needs assurance that the target function will indeed be microcoded and will reside in the control store when it is called. Second, the micro-micro call pushes return addresses on a special stack, 256-words deep, in the Lambda micromachine. Deeply recursing functions must arrange to check this stack for overflow occasionally—this process is controlled by declarations. It is interesting to note, however, that all of these benchmarks were run without overflow checks and without microstack overflow.

There are several language constructs that cannot appear in microcompiled functions. Currently these include &REST arguments, CATCH/THROW control

structures, and the return or receipt of multiple values. The other limitation is
that only 64k microinstructions can be loaded at one time, though more may
be resident in main memory and explicitly loaded before use. However, 64k is a
significant amount of microcode: the Lambda system microcode comprises about
14k instructions, and a program the size of the BOYER benchmark typically
requires less than 500 instructions.

2.4.5 *The Benchmarks*

The benchmark figures reported are for a Lambda running a preliminary
version of LMI's release 2.0 software (System version 99.67). The Lambda had
760k words of physical memory, and no other processors were running on the
NuBus at the time. Scheduling overhead, typically about 3%, is included in the
figures.

2.5 S-1 Lisp

S-1 Lisp runs on the S-1 Mark IIA computer, which is a supercomputer-class complex instruction set computer. S-1 Lisp is almost entirely written in Lisp.

2.5.1 *Architecture*

The S-1 architecture [Correll 1979] has some unusual features (as well as some ordinary ones):

— Words are 36 bits, quarter-word addressable (bytes are 9 bits, not 8).

— Virtual addresses are 31 bits plus a five-bit tag. Nine of the 32 possible tags have special meaning to the architecture (to implement MULTICS-like ring protection, among other things); the others may be used freely as user data-type tags.

— Most arithmetic instructions for binary operations are '2-1/2 address.' The three operands to ADD may be in three distinct places provided that one of them is one of the two special registers named RTA and RTB. If the destination and one source are identical, then both addresses may be general memory locations (as in the PDP-11). As an example, these patterns are permissible for the 'subtract' instruction (M1 and M2 are arbitrary memory or register addresses):

```
SUB M1,M2               ;M1 := M1 - M2
SUB RTA,M1,M2           ;RTA := M1 - M2
SUB RTB,M1,M2           ;RTB := M1 · M2
SUB M1,RTA,M2           ;M1 := RTA · M2
SUBV M1,M2              ;M1 := M2 - M1
SUBV M1,RTA,M2          ;M1 := M2 - RTA
```

— A variant of IEEE proposed standard floating-point is provided, including special 'overflow,' 'underflow,' and 'undefined' values.

There are sixteen rounding modes for floating-point operations and for integer division. (Thus FLOOR, CEIL, TRUNC, ROUND, MOD, and REMAINDER are all primitive instructions).

There are single instructions for complex arithmetic: SIN, COS, EXP, LOG, SQRT, ATAN, and so on.

— There are vector-processing instructions that perform component-wise arithmetic, vector dot product, matrix transposition, convolution, Fast Fourier Transform, and string processing.

2.5.2 *Hardware*

The Mark IIA has an 11-stage pipeline, a 16k-word data cache and an 8k-word instruction cache. The Mark IIA has 32 megawords of physical memory.

2.5.3 *Data Types*

In S-1 Lisp the type of a data object is encoded primarily in the pointer to that data object and secondarily in the storage associated with the object, if any. It is important that all pointers to a data object have a type field consistent with that object.

The format of a pointer in S-1 Lisp is a single-word with a type in bits <0:4> and an address or immediate datum in bits <5:35>. This is consistent with the S-1 Mark IIA pointer format.

The data types are defined as follows:
Type Use within S-1 Lisp

   0 Positive fixnum
   1 Unused
   2 Unbound marker
   3 Self-relative
   4 Program Counter
   5 Program Counter

  6 Program Counter

  7 Program Counter

  8 GC Pointer (used only by the garbage collector)

  9 reserved

10 Named vector (user data structure)

11 Named array (user data structure)

12 Halfword (immediate) floating-point number

13 Singleword floating-point number

14 Doubleword floating-point number

15 Tetraword floating-point number

16 Halfword complex floating-point number

17 Singleword complex floating-point number

18 Doubleword complex floating-point number

19 Tetraword complex floating-point number

20 Extended number

21 Code pointer

22 Procedure or stack group

23 Array

24 General vector

25 Specialized vector

26 String (vector of string-characters)

27 Character

28 Symbol

29 Pair (cons cell)

30 Empty list

31 Negative fixnum

Subtypes of vectors and arrays are encoded in the header word of the object. The subtype of a vector depends on the types of its components. These subtypes are pointer, bit, and numeric data types. The numeric data types are the quarterword integer, the halfword integer, the singleword integer, the doubleword integer, the signed byte integer, the unsigned byte integer, the halfword floating-point, the singleword floating-point, the doubleword floating-point, the tetraword floating-point, the halfword complex floating-point, the singleword complex floating-point, the doubleword complex floating-point, the tetraword complex floating-point, the halfword complex integer, and the singleword complex integer.

The subtypes of arrays are the same as those of vectors.

Numbers are represented internally in a variety of ways in order to conserve space and time for common situations. In particular, integers in the range $[-2_{31},$ $2_{31} - 1]$ as well as halfword floating-point numbers are represented in an 'immediate' format so that one need not allocate heap storage when such numbers are generated. Numbers are also represented in fixed-precision multiple-word formats and in indefinite-precision formats. The details are given below.

Numbers may be divided into scalars and complex numbers. Complex numbers are represented as pairs of scalars in one format or another. Scalars may be divided into integers, ratios, and floating-point numbers. These three classes are further subdivided by internal storage types. All classes of numbers have provision for a representation with indefinitely large precision.

Data type 0 is used for positive integers, and data type 31 for negative integers. This implies that an immediate integer is in fact in true two's-complement form and can be utilized directly by arithmetic instructions. (The results of such instructions must, however, be range-checked; they cannot in general be assumed to have this format.)

Floating-point numbers come in five representations: halfword, singleword, doubleword, tetraword, and indefinite precision. The first is an immediate data type; the half-word floating-point value is stored in the low eighteen bits of the pointer. In the singleword, doubleword, and tetraword representations, the pointer simply points to a singleword, doubleword, or tetraword containing the hardware data format. Indefinite-precision floating-point numbers are represented in extended-number format.

Similarly, complex numbers come in five formats. Those whose components are halfword floating-point numbers are represented as singlewords, those whose components are singleword floating-point numbers are represented as doublewords, those whose components are doubleword floating-point numbers are represented as four consecutive words, and those whose components are tetraword floating-point numbers are represented as eight consecutive words. In each case the representation consists of the real part followed by the imaginary part in standard floating-point format; the pointer points to the first of the words. A general complex number is a kind of extended number.

2.5.4 *Systemic Quantities Vector*

To speed up various operations, a vector of commonly referred to constants and procedures is pointed to by a register dedicated to the purpose. This vector contains the quantities T, (), the locks mentioned above, constants defining the sizes of some objects, the addresses of the CONSers, and addresses of routines that allocate, de-allocate, and search special lookup blocks on the stack. Calling these routines is inexpensive compared to the cost of a normal procedure call.

2.5.5 *Function Calls*

All arguments are passed on the stack. Temporary storage for each function is also on the stack. Six stack slots are allocated for the basic function call: a slot for one returned value (multiple values are handled separately), a spare PC slot, the return PC, an old temporaries pointer slot, an old closure pointer slot, and an old frame pointer slot. The arguments, pointer temporaries, and nonpointer temporaries are above these slots.

Self-recursive calls go to a distinguished label at the front of the compiled code. This saves an indirect memory reference through the function cell. The pipeline hardware can *value-predict* the new PC; this allows the pipeline to proceed more smoothly than it does in the indirect memory-reference case. However, tracing such calls is not possible.

2.5.6 *Remarks*

The S-1 supports PDL-allocated numbers in much the same fashion as MacLisp.

2.6 Franz Lisp

Franz Lisp was written at the University of California at Berkeley by Richard Fateman and his students. It was originally intended to be a Lisp that was suitable for running a version of MACSYMA on a Vax. It evolved into one of the most commonly available Lisp dialects on Unix machines.

2.6.1 *Data Types*

Typing is done with a BIBOP scheme using 512-byte pages. Pointers of the same type are allocated on a single page, and for each page there is a table entry that indicates the type for pointers on that page. There may be many pages for each type.

2.6.2 *Function Call*

Franz supports both a *normal* function call and a *local* function call. On the Vax, normal function calls use the Vax CALLS instruction for compatiblity with other languages. With local function compilation, a function invocation can be implemented by a JSB on the Vax directly to an entry point if enough information is known at compile time. This totally inhibits debugging, generally hides the name of the local function from functions not compiled 'at the same time,' and is very fast. In Franz one does (declare (localf tak)), for example, to declare a function as local.

In the tables that appear later in this report, *LclfYes* means that the functions in the benchmark were declared local, and *LclfNo* means they were not so declared.

When a reference to a function is made in a normal function call, that reference is made through a table of transfer vector pairs, where each pair is of the form <*name location*>. *Name* is the name of the function and *location* is the address of the code to which to jump.

For a function, FOO, this pair is initially <FOO QLINKER>. QLINKER is a general calling routine that refers to the atom's (FOO's) function definition cell. There is a flag, TRANSLINK, that can be set to influence the use of this transfer table. TRANSLINK can be set to either T or ().

If the function definition is binary code (where the appropriate address is BCD-FOO) and if TRANSLINK = T, then the pair in the table is updated to be <FOO BCD-FOO>.

The next time FOO is invoked, the branch to QLINKER is avoided, and the invocation goes much faster.

If FOO is not compiled or if TRANSLINK = (), then the transfer table remains unchanged, and the overhead of going through QLINKER is present each time FOO is called.

Setting TRANSLINK to T leaves somewhat less information on the stack, so if there is an error, the backtrace function has to work harder to find out the sequence of function-calls leading to the current state. Also, if FOO's definition cell is changed, a relinking has to be done. Implementationally, a reference to an entry in the table is resolved at load-time, so that no searching of the TRANSLINKs vector table need be done at runtime.

In the tables, *TrlOn* means that TRANSLINK = T, and *TrlOff* means that TRANSLINK = ().

2.6.3 *Data Representations*

All numbers are boxed. The compiler will open code fixnum operations in compact arithmetic expressions, but generally numbers are reboxed right after they are created. BIGNUMs are represented as lists of fixnums with a special 'BIGNUM-type' object at the head.

CONS cells are 8 bytes; the CDR is first because CDRs are more common than CARs, and this permits a CDR operation (without type checking) to be done with an indirect addressing mode.

An array is a very general data structure in Franz. A user-definable function is called to interpret the indices on each array reference. A vector data type exists for fast unidimensional array-like operations.

2.6.4 *Remarks*

In the benchmark runs, the Vax 11/750 and Vax 11/780 had 2–4 megabytes of physical memory. The MC68000 machines were 10 megahertz SUN II machines.

Franz programs try to be good time-sharing neighbors. Programs start inside a small Lisp, and when space gets short, that Lisp grows as needed. It is very easy to reduce the garbage collection time by preallocating space so that fewer garbage collections occur. Thus comparisons that include the garbage collection times may not be as meaningful if the fastest possible runtimes are desired.

2.7 NIL

NIL (New Implementation of Lisp) was done at MIT for the Vax family of computers. Originally designed as the first modern Lisp dialect on stock hardware after the development of Lisp-machine Lisp at MIT, it went on to become one of the main influences on the design of Common Lisp.

2.7.1 *Data Types*

In NIL, a pointer is 32 bits long. Five bits are type bits, and 27 are for address (in nonimmediate objects) or immediate data. The type bits are divided between the low two and high three bits in the 32-bit longword. This permits the 'address bits' to be in the correct position to be longword addresses—the VAX is byte-addressed, and NIL allocates storage in longword units. In effect, fewer than 3 bits of addressability are lost, rather than 5. This also permits address arithmetic to be used for operating on the data of a CONSed object. For instance, the type code of a CONS cell happens to be just 1, and the CAR and CDR are in two consecutive longwords. So to get the CAR of register r6 into register r7,

```
movl -1(r6),r7
```

and likewise, CDR is

```
movl 3(r6),r7.
```

To add two Lisp single-floats in r6 and r7, machine-number answer in r0,

```
addf3 -float-type(r6),-float-type(r7),r0
```

where *float-type* is the value of the type code of a single float.

There are a number of special assignments and special cases for the type codes. One of the most important is for fixnums. A pointer is a fixnum if the low two bits are 0. In effect, eight possible type code assignments are relegated to fixnums. The result is that NIL represents 30-bit fixnums without CONSing. Conversion to and from a machine number is done with a single arithmetic shift (ASHL) by −2 or 2. Addition and subtraction can be performed on the pointers directly, producing a pointer result. Multiplication needs to shift only one of the two arguments to produce a pointer result. Another result of this implementation of fixnums is that a fixnum index need only be added to the base address of a vector whose unit size is a longword such as a Common Lisp simple vector; it need not be shifted first.

The Vax user address space is loosely segmented into P0 (program) and P1 (stack) spaces. (These two make up one half of the Vax addressability. The other half is 'system' space.) The address field of a NIL pointer permits addressing the low half of P0 space. By selecting the type bits accordingly, one can, however, represent objects in other parts of the address space if the mask used to clear the type bits is different from the type code and if the appropriate high type bits are present in the type code itself. NIL represents 'stack vectors,' which are simple vectors allocated in the high half of P1 space where the NIL stack lives in the following way. There are two simple-vector type codes—one for heap-allocated vectors and one for stack-allocated vectors. The type code assignments are chosen so that there is a single mask that clears either one of the type codes, producing the correct address. (Stack vectors are important for a number of things, particularly for doing efficient &REST arguments without CONSing.)

The fact that 5 bits are used for type code means that there are 32 different primitive types; therefore a single longword mask can be used to represent the union of a number of these types. As a result, the computation of

```
(typep x '(or single-float double-float))
```

is identical to

```
(typep x '(or single-float double-float short-float long-float))
```

except for the mask used.

There is also an extended-number type, which implements BIGNUMs, ratios, and all the complex types.

2.7.2 *Function Call*

A compiled function is a typed pointer whose address points to a VAX procedure. It is called using the Vax CALL instructions. Function cells contain only the address, not the type bits, so getting to the function is done by 'evaluating' the function (identical to the way in which special variables are evaluated) and doing CALLS on the result. The procedure exits with the RET instruction.

The arguments to the function are passed on the stack in standard Vax style; in addition, three 'hidden' arguments are passed. As a result, the current NIL can pass a maximum of 252 Lisp arguments to any function.

The caller of the function does not need to know whether the called function takes &OPTIONAL and/or &REST arguments because all functions are called identically. When the function is entered, it may move arguments from the argument list into their eventual locations or 'homes.' For instance, PRIN1 with an argument list of

```
(object &optional stream)
```

has a home for the variable OBJECT in the argument list, and STREAM is in the local stack (like a LET-bound variable). Checking the number of arguments and moving some into their homes elsewhere on the stack is done by special out-of-line subroutines except in simple cases. At the primitive function-calling level, &REST arguments are passed as stack-allocated vectors that might later be copied into a list if necessary. &KEY passes off this vector to something else that, given a data structure describing the &KEY part of the lambda-list, parses the keyworded arguments into another locally-allocated stack-vector.

NIL functions are compiled as position-independent code. Functions are grouped together by the compiler into a single compiled-code module that contains a table of quoted constants and value cells. One of the function-entry actions is to load a register called FLP with the base address of this table. So a function

```
(defun foo () 'foo)
```

does

```
movl n(flp),ar1
```

to return the symbol FOO. This also means that there is no patching of the compiled code when the file is loaded—the code portion of the module is copied directly from the VASL (compiled NIL code) file. The FLP register is saved and restored around every function call by using the Vax procedure call entry-mask mechanism. The value saved in the highly structured Vax stack frame is used by the garbage collector to find the compiled code module so that it knows how to relocate saved PC's it finds on the stack.

2.7.3 *Storage Management*

NIL has just one amorphous heap from which everything is allocated. Garbage collection is by stop-and-copy.

2.7.4 *Generic Arithmetic*

The more common generic arithmetic functions are implemented as MACRO32 routines for efficiency. The arguments are checked for being numeric, and a special 'contagion code' is returned. A contagion code is a small integer assigned such that for multiple arguments, the maximum value of the contagion codes of the arguments defines what the type of the result will be. The routine (e.g., PLUS) dispatches to a piece of code that deals specifically with that type and runs each argument if necessary (as it is for floating point) through a special routine designed specifically for doing the conversion necessitated by contagion. Many of the types are not handled by the MACRO32 routines; for instance, most BIGNUM, rational, and complex arithmetic is written in Lisp. Some simple things like comparision or some logical operations on BIGNUMs are just done directly in the MACRO32 code, however. Some of these special subroutines are accessible to Lisp code—SIN and COS, for instance, are all written in Lisp. To deal with the varied floating-point types, special floating-point operators are used.

2.8 Spice Lisp

Spice Lisp is an implementation of Common Lisp written mostly in Common Lisp and partly in microcode. The initial implementation of Spice Lisp was done by the Spice Lisp Group at Carnegie-Mellon University (CMU) on the Perq, a user-microcodable machine built by Perq Systems Corporation.

2.8.1 *Data Types*

The Perq is a 16-bit machine, but the Lisp instruction set deals with 32-bit immediate and pointer objects. The typing scheme described here will probably be retained in other implementations of Spice Lisp. The most significant 5 bits of a 32 bit-object determine its type. Immediate objects (such as characters and fixnums) use the low-order bits to hold information.

Type (5)	Immediate Data (27)

Pointer objects (such as CONSes and arrays) have an additional 2-bit space field below the type field. All 32 bits are used as the virtual address of a piece of storage.

Type (5)	Space (2)	Other Address Bits (25)

Fixnums and short floats use two consecutive type codes each to encode positive and negative numbers. This yields 28 bits of precision. Fixnums look like this:

Type (4)	Two's Complement Integer (28)

And short floats like this:

Type (4)	Sign (1)	Exponent (8)	Mantissa (19)

CONSes are pointer types. Two consecutive words of storage at the virtual address specified by the pointer hold the CAR and CDR of the CONS.

There are several different kinds of arrays in Spice Lisp. General vectors (or G-vectors) are fixed-size, one-dimensional arrays of Lisp objects. The first word of a G-vector is a fixnum indicating its size in 32-bit words, the second word is element 0, the third word is element 1, and so on. Integer vectors (I-vectors) are fixed-size arrays of small integers. They range in size from 1 to 16 bits. The first word of an I-vector indicates its size in 32-bit words, and the second word indicates the size of each element and the number of elements; the entries are packed right to left in the words that follow. Strings are identical to I-vectors in format and have a fixed-element size of 8 bits.

The Spice Lisp instruction set on the Perq implements a stack architecture. The Perq Lisp instruction set does full runtime type checking, ensuring debuggability of compiled code. There are no type-specific instructions for arithmetic, just generic instructions that dispatch off of the types of their arguments. This frees the programmer from writing verbose declarations to get the compiler to emit the right instructions, but since the Perq hardware does not support type checking in parallel, it does incur a runtime penalty.

Because references to virtual memory are so expensive on the Perq, much can be gained by adding a few registers to the stack architecture. By keeping often-used arguments, local variables, constants, and special variables in registers, the number of memory references can be cut drastically. Adding instructions to manipulate four 32-bit registers and a compiler pass that endeavors to identify frequently used values to put in registers resulted in a 30% speedup for the PUZZLE benchmark.

2.8.2 *Function Calls*

There is no 'fast function call' in Spice Lisp—stack frames have a uniform format and contain enough information to debug compiled code, and functions may be redefined (or traced) at any time. Function call is done by the following:

1. Pushing a stack frame header, which contains the function to be called, the current stack frame, and other information. This new stack frame becomes the 'open frame.'

2. Pushing the arguments to the function.

3. Activating the frame by making the open frame the active frame, by stashing the next PC in the current function in the PC slot of the call frame, and by making the function that it contains the current function.

In the third step, the microcode checks to see that the function is being called with the proper number of arguments, and if the function can take different numbers of arguments, it selects an entry point. The called function then defaults any unsupplied optional arguments and bumps the stack pointer to allocate space for local variables. A call frame looks like this:

Frame Header
Function
Previous Active Frame
Previous Open Frame
Previous Binding Stack Pointer
Saved PC of Caller
Argument 0
Argument 1
. . .
Local 0
Local 1
. . .

If a function tries to return multiple values, the microcode looks at the stack frame's header word, which indicates whether or not the caller is expecting multiple values. If the caller is not expecting multiple values, only the first value is returned.

CATCH and THROW are implemented in much the same way as call and return (indeed, the microcoded instructions share a good deal of code). The CATCH instruction creates a catch frame, which looks much like a call frame except that the function that created the catch frame takes the place of the 'function to be called,' and the PC of the code to be executed when the catch frame is thrown to takes the place of the 'return PC.' A catch frame looks like this:

Frame Header
Function
Active Frame at Time of Catch
Open Frame at Time of Catch
Binding Stack Pointer at Time of Catch
Jump PC in Case of Throw
Previous Catch Frame
Throw Tag

The catch frames are linked through the 'previous catch frame' field, so when a throw is done, the microcode just traces through the previous catch frames looking for the given throw tag. When it finds such a frame, it 'returns into it.' The 'active catch frame' is kept in a register.

2.8.3 *Remarks*

The Perq has no hardware for virtual memory, but the Accent operating system (under which Spice Lisp runs) provides microcode to translate virtual addresses to physical addresses and Pascal code to service page faults. The language microcode on the Perq (one instruction set for Pascal, C, and Ada, and another for Lisp) caches a few recent virtual address translations in registers. This significantly reduces the number of times the microcode address translation routines need to be called. However, the time it takes to verify that a translation is correct and to construct a physical address from it almost quadruples the time it takes to access memory.

The performance degradation between TAK and TAKR shows the effect of these translation caches. The TAKR benchmark is intended to defeat the benefits of a cache memory (which the Perq does not have) but manages to defeat address translation caches as well.

Because Accent is intended to be a 'general purpose' operating system supporting many languages some things such as the the paging algorithms are not particularly tuned towards Lisp. As more functionality and performance enhancements have been added to the Accent kernel, the performance of Spice Lisp has improved. When code was added to write dirty pages out to the disk a whole track at a time, many of the CONS-intensive benchmarks shown here improved significantly.

The benchmarks were run on a Perq T2 with 2 megabytes of physical memory, a landscape (1280 by 1024 pixels) display, and a Micropolis 5.25 inch, 80 megabyte disk drive. Times reported are real time, with a resolution of one sixtieth second. The Perq microengine runs at approximately 170 nanoseconds per cycle. Memory is referenced up to 64 bits at a time in 680-nanosecond cycles.

The TPRINT benchmark was run with *Print-Pretty* set to NIL, and output directed to a Spice Typescript window 50 lines tall and 83 columns wide (approximately 8.5 by 9 inches).

2.9 Vax Common Lisp

Vax Common Lisp was the first Common Lisp implemented on stock hardware. It runs on all of the DEC Vax models under the VMS operating system.

2.9.1 *The Basic Strategy*

The basic strategy behind this implementation was to bring up a Common Lisp on the Vax rapidly by piggybacking on the Spice Lisp system. To do this, a postprocessor was written that takes the output of the Spice Lisp compiler and produces Vax instructions. This output is a sequence of Spice Lisp byte codes—a machine language for a stack-based Lisp machine. The postprocessor maps (translates) each byte code into a sequence of Vax instructions; each byte code expands into 1–5 Vax instructions and possibly a call to a Bliss routine that performs the operation specified by the byte code. Then a peephole processor optimizes the output from the mapper.

2.9.2 *The Vax Stack*

The Vax architecture supports a stack that occupies one half of the address space. Since Lisp requires both a large address space and a large stack, it is natural to try to use this stack.

There are some problems for Lisp with the architecturally supported stack. This stack is used by the call instructions that the Vax supports, and using that stack implies using those instructions. In the Vax Common Lisp, the function-call mechanism does not use CALLS or CALLG. This choice is also made by Portable Standard Lisp. A major problem with CALLS/CALLG is that these instructions place PCs with flag bits in the stack. This means that the garbage collector, which examines the stack, must be able to locate these objects. Usually that means that they must be marked or linked together, adding overhead to function-call.

2.9.2.1 *Vax Common Lisp Function Call*

All arguments and return values are passed on the stack. Frames, which contain sufficient information to reconstruct the dynamic and lexical environment of each call, are created on every function call. Lisp code is completely interruptable: Between any two instructions both the instructions themselves and the stacks may move (due to a GC). There is no more overhead for a function with &OPTIONAL

64

than there is for one without, and there is no runtime dispatching on the number of arguments for typical functions.

2.9.3 *Types*

2.9.3.1 *The Vax Common Lisp Hybrid Scheme.*

Vax Common Lisp uses a hybrid of BIBOP and tagging. A word on the Vax is 32 bits long. The two low bits are used to distinguish pointer (00), random (10), fixnum (01), and short-float (11). A random object is a short immediate object that is small enough for the object and subtype bits to inhabit the remaining 30 bits; character objects are an example of a random type. This has an advantage in that fixnums are immediate and type-checking them is fast and simple.

A BIBOP scheme is used for allocated objects (pointer objects), so determining the type of an allocated Lisp object consists of shifting to get a page index and looking at a table entry. Objects can be allocated in read-only, static, or dynamic spaces, and there's a table for that as well.

Determining the type of a pointer object requires clearing the top thirty bits, testing the bottom two, shifting the original pointer right to get a page address, and then comparing an indexed location in a table to a constant.

2.9.4 *Data Representations*

Fixnums are two's complement and 30 bits long within a 32-bit word; BIGNUMs are also two's complement and are allocated in longword chunks.

There are three floating point types corresponding to VAX F, G, and H types. Ratios are two cells. Complex numbers are not supported. CONSes are two cells. Simple-vectors are consecutive cells with a 1-longword header. Simple-strings and one-dimensional simple-arrays of fixnums elements are consecutive bytes with a 2-longword header. Multidimensional arrays have an array header. Array indices are always recalculated on each access and store.

2.9.5 *The Compiler*

As noted, the compiler is based on the CMU Spice compiler. The Vax Common Lisp compiler does not do any sophisticated register allocation, and none of the benchmarks were declared to have any in-line routines.

2.9.6 *Running the Benchmarks*

Each test was run in a separate Lisp with 3 megabytes dynamic space. Because a copying garbage collector is used, this leaves 1.5 megabytes available at any time. Fixnum or simple-vector declarations were added where appropriate, and the benchmarks were compiled for maximum speed and minimum safety.

The Vax 8600 is a pipelined ECL gate array Vax. During its development it was code-named 'Venus.'

2.10 Portable Standard Lisp

Portable Standard Lisp (PSL) is a 'LISP in LISP' that has been in development at the University of Utah since 1980 and at Hewlitt-Packard since 1982. It has its origins in Standard Lisp [Marti 1979] and in the Portable Lisp Compiler [Griss 1982]; both were used to implement an efficient Lisp interchange subset on a wide range of machines. The compiler has also been used by others as a basis for compilers for their own Lisps, (for example by Charles Hedrick for Elisp at Rutgers).

PSL was started as an experiment in writing a production-quality Lisp in Lisp itself as much as possible, with only minor amounts of code written by hand in assembly language or other systems languages. The key is the optimizing Lisp compiler, which compiles Lisp with machine-oriented extensions (bit, word and byte access, machine arithmetic, etc). The collection of these Lisp 'subprimitives' comprises a language called 'SYSLISP,' or 'System Lisp.' Many of the time-critical parts in the PSL system are written in SYSLISP—the garbage collector and inter-procedure-linkage functions, for instance. An early goal was efficient execution of the system as a base for large computer-aided graphics design, computer algebra, and computer-aided instruction programs.

Up to this point the PSL system has served a number of purposes:

1. An efficient portable Lisp for running large programs on a number of machines, it is in use on extended addressing DEC-20s, VAXes, CRAY-1s, various MC68000s (Apollos, HP9836s, and IBM 370s).

2. An experimental system testbed for easy testing of new binding models, garbage collectors, and evaluators.

3. A 'library' of modules to produce other Lisp-like systems. The PSL system provides a number of alternative modules for the same function (such as a compacting garbage collector and a copying collector). The DADO project at Columbia is extracting modules and using the compiler as a tool to explore a multiprocessor Lisp.

The PSL compiler has a number of passes, some of which were introduced to aid in the portability:

1. Lisp macros expanded, and the Lisp source decorated with type information.

2. Compilation of Lisp to an 'abstract' register machine whose instructions are called 'cmacros.' Redundant loads and stores are avoided by tracking register contents.

3. Essentially machine-independent optimization of the 'cmacro' form (jump optimizations, peephole, etc).

4. Expanding 'cmacros' into LAP for the target machine by using pattern-driven tables.

5. Some peephole optimization of the target machine LAP.

6. Output of LAP in a number of different forms: a) in-core assembly for direct execution, b) output as a FASL file for later fast loading, or c) output as symbolic assembly code for target machine assembler for bootstrapping.

A PSL implementation for a new machine consists of the following:

1. Choosing memory layout and tagging

2. Writing code generators and linkage routines to the systems language

3. Writing some IO primitives in assembly code or some other systems language (C, PASCAL, and FORTRAN have been used)

4. Testing primitives and code generators

5. Selecting an appropriate garbage collector

6. Cross-compiling a kernel ('mini-Lisp') to assembly code, assembling, and linking on the target machine

7. Finishing up and tuning

2.10.1 *Versions of PSL Mentioned in the Timing Tests*

PSL 3.1 This was the original version circulated from Utah; the kernel is written in RLisp syntax (an algebraic syntax). It forms the basis of the Apollo DOMAIN product and the IBM 370 version.

PSL 3.2 This is the current version available from Utah for DEC-20s, VAXes, and MC68000s.

PSL 3.3 This is the version at HP in which all of the kernel is written in Lisp syntax with no RLisp. The kernel is a complete 'mini-Lisp.'

PSL 3.4 This is the latest version at HP. Based on a 'microkernel' that is only enough of a Lisp to support a storage allocator and a fast-loader facility, it is cross-compiled, and the remainder of the system is loaded as compiled Lisp. New modules support a Common Lisp compatibility package. There are some improvements in function-linkage and in the storage allocator.

2.10.2 *Machines Mentioned in the Timing Tests*

HP 9836 This is actually a family of machines, which is officially called the HP9000, Series 200. It is Motorola MC68000-based; it is a nonpaging machine. It runs with a 12Mhz clock with 16Kbyte cache. Most of the timings were run on 3.5 megabytes to 4.5 megabytes of physical memory. The machine allows up to 8 megabytes of user memory. Each Lisp item is 32 bits, with the tag in the top 5 bits. No address masking is needed because it is an MC68000. Two different operating systems were used: PASCAL and HP-UX, the latter being HP's Bell System 3 Unix. In the charts, the PASCAL operating system times are denoted by 'PSL-HP200,' and the HP-UX operating system times are denoted by 'PSL-HP-UX.' These machines use a hand-coded compacting garbage collector, which is very fast.

CRAY-1 The final timings were run on a 2-processor Cray-XMP. The machine has 4 megawords of 64-bit-word physical memory. It has a 9.5 nanosecond cycle time; the memory time is 14.5 nanoseconds, but the actual times are unpredictable due to interference between the two processors. Each Lisp item is 64 bits; the tag is in the top 8 bits. No masking is needed to do memory reference. There are 24-bit addresses; 22 bits are actually used for data, and the extra bits are used by the compacting garbage collector. The operating system is CTSS, which is used by Los Alamos National Laboratory, Lawrence Livermore National Laboratory, and a couple of others. This is the only purely portable implementation (no tuning was done to improve performance). One aspect that could be improved is that there are four extra instructions for each procedure call (out of five) to allow compiled code to call interpreted code. If the compiler was told that the functions do not require the interpreted-option linkage, there would be significant speedup. There is a 300,000-item heap.

Vax 11/750 The Vax 11/750 used in the timings has 6 megabytes of memory, hardware floating-point, and cache. Each Lisp item is 32 bits, with the tag in the top 5 bits. Masking is required to reference objects. PSL runs both in VMS and BSD Unix, 4.x. There is a 400,000-item heap. A copying garbage collector is used.

Vax 11/780 This machine had the same configuration as the Vax 11/750s. There is no difference at all in the code.

DEC-20 This machine has 5 megabytes of physical memory, cache, and hardware floating-point. A Lisp item is 36 bits, and 6-bit tags are used (the extra bit is due to extended addressing). It runs the Tops-20 operating system. There is a 256,000-item heap. It uses a copying garbage collector.

70

Apollo Dn300 This is an MC68010-based (10 MHz) workstation with no local disk. Virtual memory paging is over a 10-megabit Ring network. The machine has 1.5 megabytes of physical memory. The PSL implementation is the same as that on the HP 9836. The operating system is the Aegis operating system, a Unix-like Apollo operating system. There is a 200,000-item heap. It uses a copying garbage collector.

Apollo Dn600 This is a dual MC68000-based (10 MHz) workstation; the second processor is used for paging (hence, this is a virtual memory machine). There is a 4 kilobyte cache, 2 megabytes of physical memory, a local disk, and a hardware floating-point processor. The PSL implementation is identical to that on the DN300.

Apollo Dn160 This workstation uses a bit-sliced (AMD2903) implementation of an MC68000 architecture machine. The bit-sliced CPU is microcoded to behave as an MC68000. It has fast floating-point, a 4-kilobyte instruction cache, a 16-kilobyte data cache, a 4-megabyte physical memory, and a local disk. The PSL implementation is identical to that on the DN300.

Sun The Sun timings were run on a Sun Workstation 2/120. It uses the MC68010 processor, runs with a 10Mhz clock, and has 3 megabytes of memory. It is a virtual memory machine allowing up to 16 megabytes per process. The operating system is BSD Unix 4.2. Each Lisp item in Sun PSL is 32 bits with the tag in the top 8 bits. A copying garbage collector is used.

IBM 3081 The 3081 timings were run on the IBM Palo Alto Scientific Center model D 3081. It has a 64 Kilobyte instruction cache, a 64 kilobyte data cache, and a 16 megabyte memory. The CPU runs at 4–8 MIPS Aside from a different use of tags during garbage collection, this implementation is PSL 3.2.

2.10.3 *Implementation Details*

The implementation is biased towards fast execution of programs consisting of many small compiled functions; debugging facilities and interpreter speed were less important design considerations. All implementations mentioned have explicitly tagged pointers with the tag in the high bits of the word. In some cases this means that the tags have to be stripped to access the referenced item.

2.10.4 *Data Types*

PSL has the following data types: ID (symbols), FIXNUM, BIGNUM, FLOAT, CODE, STRING, VECTOR (simple-vector), PAIR (CONSes), and IN-STANCE (for 'flavors'). Immediate numbers (INUMS) use a trick in that positive INUMs have a 0 tag, and negative INUMs have a -1 tag, which allows arithmetic to proceed without tag modifications.

CONS cells are represented as a pair of sequential items. A pair points to the CAR, and the CDR is the next word. Fixnums are a pointer to a 2-word heap element; the first says that it is a heap item and the second is the fixnum. Vectors are implemented in a similar manner with a 1-word heap item that contains the tag and the length of the vector and with an n-element contiguous block of heap. Arrays are simply vectors of vector pointers, so there is no packing. Floats are all double precision—once again with a 1-word heap item and two words of data.

The function types are:

> EXPR: fixed number of EVALed arguments, no checking for the correct number of arguments passed
>
> NEXPR: variable number of EVALed arguments collected in a list
>
> FEXPR: variable number of unEVALed arguments collected in a list
>
> MACRO: entire form passed to expansion function

Symbols have four cells: value, function, name, and property-list. The function cell contains either an executable instruction or a code address, depending on the implementation; the address or instruction goes either directly to the head of compiled code or to an auxiliary function for interpreted or missing functions.

2.10.5 *Function Call*

Compiled-to-compiled function-call consists of loading registers with the argument values and performing a CALL (or JUMP in tail-recursion-elimination situations) to the function cell. All implementations use five real registers for passing arguments; the rest go into the stack. The only other stack overhead is the return address.

Each function is responsible for saving its own parameters if needed. Some functions do all their computation from the registers and will need no stack at all; others allocate a small stack frame into which the compiler allocates temporaries as needed.

PSL is properly tail recursive.

2.11 Xerox D-Machine

All three members of the Xerox 1100 family are custom-microcoded processors. The INTERLISP-D virtual machine is built around a compact 8-bit byte code instruction set, the opcodes of which are implemented by a combination of microcode and macrocode. Not all byte codes are supported directly in each member by microcode; the alternative is a trap out to a standard Lisp function. Above the level of the instruction set, all three members of the family appear identical to the INTERLISP-D programmer. The implementation is such that a memory image can be compatibly run on any of the machines without any change.

2.11.1 Data Types

An INTERLISP pointer is an address in a 24-bit virtual address space; a quantum map indexed by the high bits of the address provides information for type decoding. Additionally, litatoms (symbols) and immediate numbers (integers in the range of -2_{16} to 2_{16-1}) live in a reserved portion of the address space; integers of larger magnitude (within the range -2_{31} to 2_{31-1}) are 'boxed'; floating-point numbers, which are in IEEE 32-bit format, are also boxed. All three machines have a 16-bit memory bus and 16-bit ALU; however, the byte codes tend to hide the actual word size from the programmer. The virtual address space is broken down into units of 512-byte pages, and the three machines have different degrees of hardware assist for virtual memory management and instruction fetch.

CONS cells are CDR-coded in a manner described in [Bobrow 1979]. A cell of 32 bits is used to store a CONS—typically 24 bits for the CAR and 8 bits for an encoding of the CDR. The encoding covers the four cases where (1) the CDR is NIL, or (2) the CDR is on the same page as the CONS cell, or (3) the CDR is contained in another cell on the same page as the CONS cell, or (4) the CONS cell is itself a full indirect pointer, which can address an ordinary two-cell slot on any page (the space normally used for the CAR is used to address a 64-bit cell elsewhere; this is to allow for RPLACD's when there are no more free cells on the same page as the cell being updated). All CONS cells, independent of how they are created, are CDR-coded, and as a consequence the 'average size' of such a cell is considerably less than 64 bits.

Strings and arrays are implemented as a fixed-length header with one field pointing to a variable-length memory chunk taken from an area that is separately managed. To run some of the benchmarks, we used INTERLISP's Common Lisp array utility package. Additionally, INTERLISP permits the user to define new first-class fixed-length data types with corresponding entries in the quantum map mentioned above; for example, a stream is implemented as a record structure with 19 pointer fields and assorted integer fields of 16 bits or less.

Garbage collection is patterned after that described in [Deutsch 1976]. A reference count is maintained for every collectible pointer (in addition to immediate pointers, litatoms are not reclaimed in INTERLISP-D). Updates to nonstack cells in data structures (i.e., the CAR slot of a CONS cell or the value cell of a global variable) require updates to the reference count. The reference counts are maintained separately from the objects in a hash table that is generally very sparse, and the updating is normally done within the microcode that effects the update operations. Reclamations are performed frequently. These involve scanning the stack area and augmenting the reference counts by a 'stackp' bit; then scanning the reference count table reclaiming any entry that has a count of 0 and no reference from the stack (and possibly additional pointers whose reference count goes to zero as a result of such a reclamation); and finally re-scanning the table to clear the 'stackp' bits. The scan through the reference count table looking for 0-count entries corresponds roughly to the scan of the marked-bits table in a Mark-and-Sweep collector; however, the scan of the stack is infinitesimal in time compared with a full 'mark' phase, and thus a reclamation typically runs in well under a second.

The internal architecture of the stack is a variant of the 'spaghetti stack' model described in [Bobrow 1973]. The stack area is currently limited to 128KB.

The particular configurations upon which the benchmarks were run are as follows:

> Xerox 1100 (Dolphin) 4k words of 40-bit microstore; microinstruction time 180ns; hardware assist for macroinstruction fetch; hardware memory map for up to 8MB of virtual space; hardware stack (for stack top); memory access is 1–4 words (64 bits) in about $2\mu s$. The particular unit used in the benchmarking runs had 1.8MB of real memory attached, but 2MB has been in standard delivery.

Xerox 1108 (DandeLion) 4k words of 48-bit microstore; microinstruction time 137ns; hardware assist for macroinstruction fetch;
hardware assist for virtual memory management (memory
map is kept in nonpaged real memory); memory access is
one nonmapped 16-bit word in 411ns, but a random 32-bit
cell access in about 1.2μs. The stack is held in real, nonmapped memory. The particular unit used in the benchmarking runs had 1.5MB of real memory attached.

Xerox 1132 (Dorado) 4k words of 34-bit high-speed ECL microstore;
microinstruction time 64ns; hardware instruction fetch
unit; hardware memory map for up to 32MB of virtual
space; 4k words of high-speed ECL memory cache permit
memory access of one 16-bit word in 64ns, and a cache-
reload of 256 bits takes about 1.8μs (additional details
on the cache and memory organization may be found in
[Clark 1981]. The particular unit used in the benchmarking runs had 2MB of real memory attached.

Note that the benchmarks were not run on the 1108-111 (DandeTiger), which
has considerably more memory and control store than the basic 1108 and which
also has a floating-point processor.

2.12 Data General Common Lisp

Data General Common Lisp is an implementation of Common Lisp that runs on the entire line of Data General MV-architecture computers. It runs under both the AOS/VS and MV/UX (hosted UNIX) operating systems. Future releases will also run under the DG/UX (native UNIX) operating system.

2.12.1 *Implementation Strategy*

In order to bring up a Common Lisp system quickly, a small, internal Lisp system was used to import much of the code from the Spice project at CMU. While a good deal of the code was used as it was, some important sections were changed significantly. For example:

1. a third pass was added to the compiler, and all code generation is delayed until then,

2. a LAP (Lisp Assembly Program) language was designed that was more appropriate for the MV machines than the Spice byte-codes originally emitted by the compiler,

3. the source-to-source transformation capabilities of the compiler were enhanced,

4. arrays, numbers, and I/O, among other things, were re-implemented.

2.12.2 *MV Memory Structure*

MV Memory Structure Memory on an MV is partitioned into 8 segments, or rings; these rings are used to implement a protection scheme. Code and data become more secure as they move to lower numbered rings; for example, the operating system kernel runs in ring 0, whereas typical user code runs in ring 7. Words on the MV are 32 bits long; half-words are 16 bits, and bytes are 8 bits. Pointers to memory are one word long, and may access memory in one of two granularities: half-words or bytes. In any word, bit 0 is the most significant bit and bit 31 is the least significant. Pointers to half-words are constructed as follows:

Ind (1)	Ring (3)	Offset within the named ring (28)

where **Ind** is an indirect indicator that is 0 if the pointer is not to be indirected and 1 if it is. Byte pointers are essentially half-word pointers shifted left one bit. That is, there is no indirect bit, the ring bits inhabit bits 0–2, and the offset is specified using bits 3–31. The per-ring available address space is 512 megabytes. The granularity of access depends upon the type of pointer used.

2.12.3 *Typing Scheme*

A 'pointer' in DG Common Lisp is 32 bits long and is used for one of two purposes: to actually point at a Lisp object (e.g., a CONS cell), or to encode an immediate datum. All Lisp objects are aligned on 32 bit boundaries, so half-word pointers provide a sufficient addressing mechanism. Pointers never have the indirect bit on.

DG Common Lisp uses the BIBOP typing scheme. While many implementations use tag bits in the pointer to differentiate between immediate and pointer objects and then use the BIBOP scheme to find the type of pointer objects, through the judicious use of the indirect and ring-selector bits, which are ignored by the hardware in certain situations, it is possible to use the BIBOP scheme for all objects. Furthermore, this scheme allows many objects (e.g. fixnums, short-floats, pointers) to be represented in a format that is directly usable by the machine. There is no decoding necessary when processing these objects: to follow a pointer, it is indirected through. To add two fixnums, the architectural ADD instruction is used on the objects directly.

The MV series of computers and their operating systems require that the type table used for BIBOP covers the entire address space. In order to keep the type table relatively small and to facilitate fast typing memory is partitioned into segments 32K words long; there are 64K such segments. To perform typing operations, all Lisp pointers (whether or not they are pointers or immediates) are treated as follows:

Segment (16)	Offset within segment (16)

To determine the type, the high order half-word of the pointer is used to index into the table. This style of BIBOP is often referred to as 'scattered memory.' A fixnum will be represented as the bits in the fixnum in the low order 28 bits, and the indirect bit and three ring-selector bits configured in a bit pattern which corresponds to the type 'fixnum.' Viewed as 32-bit addresses, all fixnums will start with the same first four bits, and thus they will appear as if they were located in a contiguous block of memory.

Note that the information in the type table will not change dynamically for any entries other than the real pointer entries. For example, all table entries for the ring that fixnums are mapped onto will return 'type-fixnum' when queried. Hence, a significant space savings can be realized by simply creating one page in the address space for each of the non-pointer types, and then mapping all pages of table entries for each non-pointer type onto its one physical page.

2.12.4 *Object Allocation and Garbage Collection*

All objects that need to be allocated come from a common heap. Many objects are not allocated, but are stored as immediate data. Examples of allocated objects are CONSes, STRINGs, and ARRAYs. Immediate objects include FIXNUMs, SHORT-FLOATs, and CHARACTERs. Object may be allocated in any one of the dynamic, static, or read-only spaces, as in the S-1 Lisp implementation.

The garbage collector is stop-and-copy. Along with using static and read-only spaces to help make collections faster, some heuristics are used to help determine a good time to collect.

2.12.5 *Function Call/Return*

The standard MV CALL sequence proves to be unusable for Lisp function-call for at least two reasons. First, the CALL instruction pushes the return addess after the actual parameters. With the complex interfaces possible in Common Lisp, this would force a rearrangement of the stack call frame by the callee in all but the simplest cases. That is, suppose that a function can take some number of optional arguments, and that some call to that function supplies none of these optional arguments. If the standard MV CALL were to be used, it would push the return address on the stack above the supplied required arguments. The compiler generates references to variables allocated on the stack—variables like the optionals—by using a display for the stack frame. References to variables will compile into constant displacements into the stack frame. If the optionals are defaulted, their calculated values will need to be installed on the stack exactly as if they were supplied by the calling function. However, the return address pushed on the stack by CALL will occupy a place reserved for such an optional argument. The return address pushed onto the stack will have to be moved, and the computed optionals moved down the supplied required arguments will have to be moved up, or else a more complicated and costly display management scheme will have to be used. This problem is the same as the one faced by implementors of Common Lisp on the Digital Equipment Corporation Vax series of computers with the CALLS and CALLG operations.

Second, the CALL instruction pushes flags and other status information that we would need to track in order to keep from confusing the garbage collector.

A call frame contains a return address, linkage to the previous frame, and the function that is being invoked. After this information is pushed, the arguments are evaluated and pushed. Control is then passed to the callee. Argument canonicalization, if any, is performed by the callee.

An empty function call/return—that is, a call to a function with no arguments and no body—takes less than 3.5 microseconds on an MV10000.

2.12.6 *Dynamic and Non-local Exit*

CATCH and targets of possible non-local exits (non-local GO or non-local RETURN) cause frames to be pushed onto the stack; these frames are linked together. When executing a THROW, a non-local GO, or a non-local RETURN, a search for the proper catch or non-local target frame is done. This operation is supported directly by the MV architecture.

2.12.7 *Closures*

Closures are implemented in such a way that access to any lexical variable that is free in body of the closure is always done by a sequence of two machine instructions.

2.12.8 *Remarks*

> 1. The MV family of computers currently has no microcode support for any Lisp operations.

2. The benchmark results contained herein were gathered by running DG Common Lisp on an MV10000 with 16 Mbytes of physical memory, an MV8000 with 4 Mbytes of memory, and an MV4000 with 8 Mbytes of memory.

3. Garbage collection was not disabled during the benchmarks. Any time spent in the collector is included in the total CPU time.

4. Type declarations were added to the benchmarks where appropriate.

Chapter 3

The Benchmarks

The sections in this chapter describe each benchmark. For each benchmark the following information is provided. The program itself is presented. The Common Lisp code always appears, and often the InterLisp code is presented. A description of what the benchmark does is given, along with statistics on the number of times each operation is performed by the benchmark. These statistics were obtained by creating an augmented version of the benchmark containing explicit operation-counting instructions. The result is that the counts are accurate and not estimated. Special instructions for people who may wish to translate the benchmarks to other Lisp dialects are provided under the heading **Translation Notes**.

The raw data is provided with each benchmark; this data is exactly as it exists in the data base, which was built over the period of the benchmark study. In the raw-data tables there are six columns, each of which contains either reported or computed times for various classes of timings for each benchmark. Implementation is the name of the implementation reported in that row; CPU is the CPU time; GC is the garbage collection time; Real is the real time; and Paging is the amount of paging time.

Some implementations report CPU+GC time only; some report real time only. In the raw-data tables, implementations that report only CPU+GC times are listed under Real time; these implementations are: InterLisp on the Vax 11/780 and Data General Common Lisp on the MV4000, MV8000, and MV10000 computers.

3.1 Tak

The TAK benchmark is a variant of the Takeuchi function that Ikuo Takeuchi of Japan used as a simple benchmark.[16] Because Tak is function-call-heavy, it is representative of many Lisp programs. On the other hand, because it does

---

[16] Historical note: When the Computer Science Department at Stanford University obtained the first two or three Xerox Dolphins, John McCarthy asked me to do a simple benchmark test with him. We sat down, and he tried to remember the Takeuchi function, which had had wide

little else but function calls (fixnum arithmetic is performed as well), it is not representative of the majority of Lisp programs. It is only a good test of function call and recursion, in particular.

3.1.1 *The Program*

Here is the code for this program:

```
(defun tak (x y z)
  (if (not (< y x))
      z
      (tak (tak (1- x) y z)
           (tak (1- y) z x)
           (tak (1- z) x y))))
```

We call this function as

```
(tak 18 12 6)
```

3.1.2 *Analysis*

When called on the above arguments, TAK makes 63,609 function calls and performs 47,706 subtractions by 1. The result of the function is 7. The depth of recursion is never greater than 18. No garbage collection takes place in the MacLisp version of this function because small fixnums are used.

The following table is typical of the tables that will be used to report the numbers of significant Lisp-level operations performed by the benchmark. The previous paragraph and the following table convey the same information:

Meter for Tak	
Item	**Count**
Calls to TAK	63609
1−'s	47706
Total	111315

---

circulation. Because it was simple and because there were many results for it in the literature, he felt that it would be a good initial test. Of course, John misremembered the function. But we did not realize it until I had gathered a great many numbers for it. Alas, we are stuck with this variant on Takeuchi.

3.1.3 *Translation Notes*

Because TAK returns a fixnum, the declarations that were used for this function declared TAK to return a fixnum and X, Y, and Z to be bound only to fixnums.

The function 1− takes a fixnum and subtracts 1 from it. When translating to INTERLISP, ILESSP is used for < and SUB1 is used for 1−.

3.1.4 *Comments*

Because TAK was the first benchmark and because it is a simple program, there are results for it on many machines and in several languages. They range from a slow speed of 47.6 seconds for Franz Lisp on a Vax 11/750, using generic arithmetic and doing slow function calls (a debugging setting) through a fast speed of .048 seconds for an initial implementation of PSL on a Cray-1 at Los Alamos National Laboratory. The fastest time for a full Lisp is on the S-1 Mark IIA running a near-Common Lisp. The time is .29 seconds.

An interesting exercise was to handcode TAK on the PDP-10 in assembly language and to compare that to Lisps on the PDP-10. To give an idea of the degree of hand-optimization, allocating space on the stack was done by direct addition to the register that holds the stack pointer; the variables x, y, and z were kept in registers where possible, and subtracting 1 was accomplished by the instruction MOVEI A,-1(A), which uses the addressing hardware to do the arithmetic (this requires knowing that A will never contain a number larger than 18 bits long); pushing three things on the stack was done with a double-word move and a single-word move; tail recursion was removed; and the termination test $(x \leq y)$ was performed before each recursive call.

On a DEC 2060 this version took .255 seconds—which is faster than the S-1 Mark IIA supercomputer running Lisp.

Here is a listing of the handcoded version:

```
tak1    caig a,(b)      ;x ≤ y quit
        popj p,
tak2    add fxp,[5,,5]   ;allocate 5 slots. 3 for args, 2 for temporaries
        dmovem a,-2(fxp) ;put a, b, c on the stack. add is push
        movem c,(fxp)    ;empty space, and the assumption of
                         ;a large enough stack is used here.
```

```
                          ;PUSH, ADJSP both do bounds
                          ;checking. DMOVEM saves an instruction fetch
                          ;and a decode.
     movei a,-1(a)        ;a ‗ a-1 using the address hardware.
                          Assumption is that 18 bit, non-negative arithmetic
                          is going on
     caile a,(b)          ;early quit? c already contains the right result.
                          ;this early quit just unwinds the first arm of
                          ;the conditional. Tak2 is the entry after that arm
     pushj p,tak2         ;no go on
     movem c,-4(fxp)      ;save result on fxp
     dmove a,-1(fxp)      ;get y,z
     move c,-2(fxp)       ;and x
     movei a,-1(a)        ;sub1
     caile a,(b)          ;early quit
     pushj p,tak2
     movem c,-3(fxp)      ;stash result
     move a,(fxp)         ;z
     dmove b,-2(fxp)      ;x,y
     movei a,-1(a)        ;sub1
     caile a,(b)
     pushj p,tak2
     dmove a,-4(fxp)      ;get first 2 results, the last already in c
                          ;notice how the choice of c as the results
                          ;register allowed us to hack the dmove's here
     sub fxp,[5,,5]       ;flush temporary space
     caig a,(b)           ;early quit on tail recursion?
     popj p,              ;qed
     jrst tak2            ;tail recursion
```

The original Takeuchi function, the one of which TAK is a variant, is

```
(defun takeuchi (x y z)
 (cond ((> x y)
        (takeuchi (takeuchi (1- x) y z)
                  (takeuchi (1- y) z x)
                  (takeuchi (1- z) x y) ))
       (t y)))
```

3.1.5 *Raw Data*

Raw Time Tak				
Implementation	**CPU**	**GC**	**Real**	**Paging**
SAIL	0.48	0.00	0.85	
Lambda	1.60			0.00
Lambda (MC)	0.19			0.00
3600	0.60			0.00
3600 + IFU	0.43			0.00
Dandelion	1.67	0.00		
Dolphin	3.84	0.00		
Dorado	0.52	0.00		
S-1			0.29	
PSL-SUN	1.44	0.00		
PSL-20	0.48	0.00		
PSL-3081	0.11	0.00		
PSL-Cray	0.04	0.00		
PSL-750	1.80	0.00		
PSL-750 (VMS)	1.37	0.00		
PSL-780	0.83	0.00		
PSL-DN300	1.62	0.00		
PSL-DN600	1.65	0.00		
PSL-DN160	1.95	0.00		
PSL-HP200	1.53	0.00		
PSL-HP-UX	1.51	0.00		
InterLispVax 780			3.08	
MV4000 CL			2.47	
MV8000 CL			1.89	
MV10000 CL			0.89	
3600 + FPA	0.43			0.00
750 NIL	4.16		4.16	
8600 CL	0.45	0.00		

Raw Time Tak				
Implementation	CPU	GC	Real	Paging
780 CL	1.83	0.00		
785 CL	1.18	0.00		
750 CL	2.69	0.00		
730 CL	10.55	0.00		
Perq			4.58	
750 Franz				
TrlOn & LclfYes	1.90	0.00		
TrlOn & LclfNo	3.30	0.00		
TrlOff & LclfYes	1.90	0.00		
TrlOff & LclfNo	14.80	0.00		
780 Franz				
TrlOn & LclfYes	1.09	0.00		
TrlOn & LclfNo	2.10	0.00		
TrlOff & LclfYes	1.09	0.00		
TrlOff & LclfNo	8.29	0.00		
Franz 68000				
TrlOn & LclfYes	2.37	0.00		
TrlOn & LclfNo	3.67	0.00		
TrlOff & LclfYes	2.35	0.00		
TrlOff & LclfNo	15.10	0.00		
InterLisp-10	2.08	0.00		
LM-2			2.90	

The Dolphin times are with the display turned off; with the display on, the
time is 5.23 seconds elapsed. Generally, there is 25%–30% speedup with the
display off over the time with the display on. The Dorado is shown with the
display off as well; with the display on the time is .564. The improvement is
generally around 7% on the Dorado. The DandeLion is shown with the display
on. The times for the 3600 and LM-2 were run with multiprocessing locked out
during the actual benchmarks.

In addition to the Lisp times, there are quite a few times for this benchmark
in other languages.

Tak Times	
Implementation	**Time**
On 11/750 in Franz generic arith (sfc)	47.6
On 11/780 in Franz generic arith (sfc)	27.6
On 11/750 in Franz generic arith	19.9
On 11/780 in Franz with generic (sfc)(TAKF)	15.8
On 11/750 in Franz fixnum arith (sfc)	14.1
On 2060 in INTERLISP (rc/swl)	13.288
On 2060 in INTERLISP (rc/swl)	12.7
On 11/750 in Franz generic arith (nfc)	11.6
On Dolphin in INTERLISP Nov 1981 (tr)	11.195
On 11/780 in Franz fixnum arith (sfc)	8.1
On 11/780 in Franz generic arith (nfc)	7.7
On 11/780 in Franz with generic arith (nfc)(TAKF)	7.5
On 11/750 in PSL, generic arith	7.1
On 11/750 in Franz with generic arith (nfc)(TAKF)	6.7
On MC (KL) in MacLisp (TAKF)	5.9
On Dolphin May 1982 generic arith	5.74
On Dolphin in INTERLISP Jan 1982 (tr)	5.71
On Dolphin May 1982 Inum arith (tr)	5.28
On Dolphin May 1982 generic arith (tr)	5.23
On 2060 in T/UCILISP (sfc)	4.801
On 2060 in INTERLISP (rc/nsw)	4.57

Tak Times	
On Symbolics LM-2	4.446
On 11/780 in Franz with fixnum arith (nfc)(TAKF)	4.3
On 11/780 in INTERLISP (load = 0)	4.24
On Dolphin May 1982 gen arth (d/o)	4.21
On 780 in NIL Aug 1983	4.16
On Foonly F2 in MacLisp	4.1
On Dolphin May 1982 Inum arth (d/o,tr)	3.88
On Dolphin May 1982 gen arth (d/o,tr)	3.84
On Apollo (MC68000) PASCAL	3.8
On 11/750 in Franz, Fixnum arith	3.6
On MIT CADR in ZetaLisp	3.16
On 2060 in R/UCILISP (sfc)	3.157
On MIT CADR in ZetaLisp	3.1
On MIT CADR in ZetaLisp (TAKF)	3.1
On Symbolics LM-2	2.905
On Apollo (MC68000) PSL SYSLISP	2.93
On 11/780 in NIL (TAKF)	2.8
On 11/780 in NIL	2.7
On SUN I in TAIL (tr)	2.6
On 11/750 in C	2.4
On 11/780 in Franz with fixnum arith (nfc)	2.13
On 11/780 (Diablo) in Franz with fixnum arith (nfc)	2.1
On 11/780 in Franz with fixnum arith (nfc)	2.1
On 11/780 in Franz fixnum arith (nfc)	2.1
On 2060 in INTERLISP (bc)	2.153
On 2060 in INTERLISP (bc)	2.04

Tak Times	
On 11/780 DEC Common Lisp	1.96
On 68000 in C	1.9
On 11/750 in Franz fixnum arith (lfc)	1.9
On Apollo PSL (10Mz/1Mb/Cache)	1.679
On Utah-20 in PSL Generic arith	1.672
On DandeLion Normal	1.67
On 11/750 in PSL INUM arith	1.4
On LMI Lambda	1.4
On 11/780 (Diablo) in C	1.35
On 11/780 in Franz with fixnum arith (lfc)	1.13
On UTAH-20 in Lisp 1.6	1.1
On 11/780 in Franz fixnum arith (lfc)	1.1
On UTAH-20 in PSL Inum arith	1.077
On 2060 in Elisp (nfc)	1.063
On 2060 in R/UCILISP (nfc)	.969
On 2060 in T/UCILISP (nfc)	.930
On SAIL (KL) in MacLisp	.832
On SAIL in bummed MacLisp	.795
On MC (KL) in MacLisp (TAKF,dcl)	.789
On 68000 in machine language	.7
On MC (KL) in MacLisp (dcl)	.677
On Symbolics 3600 (no-peep,no-ifu)	.633
On SAIL in bummed MacLisp (dcl)	.616
On Symbolics 3600 (peep,no-ifu)	.590
On SAIL (KL) in MacLisp (dcl)	.564
On Dorado in INTERLISP Feb 1983 (tr)	.526
On UTAH-20 in SYSLISP arith	.526

Tak Times	
On SAIL (KLB) in MacLisp (dcl)	.489
On LMI Lambda (Microcompiled)	.45
On Symbolics 3600 (peep,ifu)	.430
On S-1 Mark IIA (Common Lisp) 12/02/83	.410
On S-1 Mark IIA (Common Lisp) 3/23/84	.320
On S-1 Mark IIA (Common Lisp) 3/23/84	.295
On SAIL in machine language (wholine)	.255
On SAIL in machine language (ebox)	.184
On SCORE (2060) in machine language (ebox)	.162
On S-1 Mark I in machine language	.114
On Cray-1, PSL	.044

(tr) means that tail recursion removal was done by the compiler. (d/o) means that the display was turned off during the timing run; this applies to the Xerox D-machines (Dolphin, DandeLion, and Dorado) only. (sfc) means 'slow function call.' In Franz, this is a debugging setting. (nfc) means 'normal function call.' In Franz, this is the normal setting. (lfc) means 'local function call.' In Franz, this is a fast function call.

In the table above, (nfc) corresponds to 'TrlOn' and (SFC) to 'TrlOff' above; (LCF) corresponds to 'LclfYes.'

(bc) means that the function was block compiled in INTERLISP. (rc) means that the function was not block compiled in INTERLISP, but compiled normally. (swl) means that the swapping space in INTERLISP-10 was set low. (nsw) means that there was no swapping space used in INTERLISP-10. (dcl) means that there was heavy use of declarations in MacLisp. This typically means that the types of all variables and return values for functions were declared.

U/UCILISP is the University of Texas (Austin) version of UCILisp. At the time of the benchmarking it was maintained by Mabry Tyson. R/UCILISP is the Rutgers University version of UCILisp. It is maintained by Charles Hedrick.

It is interesting to note that some implementations have more than one entry at different benchmark dates. This shows how the performance can be tuned by the implementors. S-1 Lisp is a good example. The increase in performance on TAK of S-1 Lisp is due to three things: 1) improving function call by removing pipeline turbulence from the calling sequence; 2) using simpler addressing modes at function entry; 3) introducing a new function call mechanism for functions that call themselves (this is different from tail recursion removal).

(KLB) refers to the Model B KL-10 CPU, which is the designation for the CPU in a DEC 2060. SAIL is a KL-10 running the WAITS operating system. During the time of the benchmarking, SAIL was upgraded from a KL-10A CPU to a KL-10 CPU. There was nearly a 20% improvement in most things with the KL-10B CPU.

TAKF is an alternative TAK formulation proposed by George Carrette, who was working on the Vax NIL project at MIT when the benchmark study was started.

```
;;; Here are the definitions of TAKF as provided by GJC.
;;; #-NIL means except in NIL, #+NIL means for NIL.
(defun takf (x y z)
  (takfsub #'takfsub x y z))

#-NIL
(defun takfsub (f x y z)
  (if (not (< y x))
      z
      (funcall f f (funcall f f (1- x) y z)
                   (funcall f f (1- y) z x)
                   (funcall f f (1- z) x y))))
#+NIL
(defun takfsub ((&function f) x y z)
  ;; lexical scoping of function bindings allows this.
  (if (not (< y x))
      z
      (f #'f (f #'f (1- x) y z)
             (f #'f (1- y) z x)
             (f #'f (1- z) x y))))
```

This style of function call is measured in the data driven symbolic derivative benchmark (DDERIV).

In TAKF, changing the variable F to FF
speeded up the function by a factor of 5.
That is because F is a built-in variable and FF is not.

— Charles Hedrick, *discussing a now non-existent*
problem, in TIMING.MSG[TIM,LSP] (May 2, 1982)

It doesn't sound plausible at first glance,
though of course anything is possible.

— Charles Hedrick, *responding to a request for permission to quote*
him as above. (April 24, 1985)

People in general seem to think that this is a worthless benchmark
because it is so small and tests such a small and specific set of features,
although I think that it is still worth something
despite that fact.

— Daniel Weinreb, *discussing TAK* (November 14, 1981)

3.2 Stak

STAK is a variant of TAK; it uses special binding to pass arguments rather than the normal argument-passing mechanism. Here is the code:

3.2.1 *The Program*

```
(defvar x)
(defvar y)
(defvar z)

(defun stak (x y z)
  (stak-aux))
(defun stak-aux ()
  (if (not (< y x))
      z
      (let ((x (let ((x (1- x))
                     (y y)
                     (z z))
                 (stak-aux)))
            (y (let ((x (1- y))
                     (y z)
                     (z x))
                 (stak-aux)))
            (z (let ((x (1- z))
                     (y x)
                     (z y))
                 (stak-aux))))
        (stak-aux))))
```

3.2.2 *Analysis*

If everything else is equal, this benchmark will show slower times for deep-bound Lisps than for shallow-bound Lisps; the less efficient the implementation of deep binding, the slower the time will be. The S-1 Lisp caches lookups of such variables, but not at the optimal points in a function (special variables are cached at the contours that contain references to them). As a result, S-1 Lisp performs badly on this benchmark. Moreover, the special lookup code is implemented as a 'fast' internal function call that translates into a jump instruction; jump instructions often cause a wrong branch prediction to occur in pipelined machines.

Deep binding is a useful technique in multiprocessing settings or in settings in which the stacks being used are often switched.

In Vax NIL, there appears to be excessive saving and restoring of registers, which is the cause of the slowness of NIL as compared with the Vax 750 Common Lisp.

STAK does 47,709 special binds, 63,609 <'s, 63,609 function calls to STAK, and 47,709 1−'s.

Meter for Stak	
Item	**Count**
Calls to STAK	63609
<'s	63609
Binds	47709
1−'s	47706
Total	222633

3.2.3 *Translation Notes*

STAK-AUX is declared to return a fixnum, and X, Y, and Z are declared to be bound only to fixnums.

The function 1− takes a fixnum and subtracts 1 from it. When translating to INTERLISP, ILESSP is used for < and SUB1 is used for 1−.

In INTERLISP, X, Y, and Z are declared SPECVARS. TAK and STAK form a block with TAK as the entry point. The functions are block compiled. The INTERLISP code is

```
(RPAQQ STAKCOMS ((FNS TAK STAK)
                 (BLOCKS
                  (STAKBLOCK TAK STAK
                             (ENTRIES TAK)))
                 (SPECVARS X Y Z)))
```

```
(DEFINEQ
(TAK
  (LAMBDA (X Y Z)
    (DECLARE (SPECVARS X Y Z))
     (STAK)))
(STAK
  (LAMBDA NIL
          (DECLARE (SPECVARS   T))
    (COND
      ((NOT (ILESSP Y X))
        Z)
      (T (PROG ((X (PROG ((X (SUB1 X))
                          (Y Y)
                          (Z Z))
                         (RETURN (STAK))))
                (Y (PROG ((X (SUB1 Y))
                          (Y Z)
                          (Z X))
                         (RETURN (STAK))))
                (Z (PROG ((X (SUB1 Z))
                          (Y X)
                          (Z Y))
                         (RETURN (STAK)))))
               (RETURN (STAK)))))))

(DECLARE: DOEVAL@COMPILE DONTCOPY
          (SPECVARS X Y Z))
```

3.2.4 *Raw Data*

Raw Time Stak				
Implementation	CPU	GC	Real	Paging
SAIL	3.50	0.00	4.42	
Lambda	6.50			0.00
Lambda (MC)	5.35			0.00
3600	2.58			0.00
3600 + IFU	2.30			0.00
Dandelion	4.66	0.00		
Dolphin	12.40	0.00		
Dorado	1.89	0.00		
S-1			4.31	
PSL-SUN	16.06	0.00		
PSL-20	2.69	0.00		
PSL-3081	1.69	0.00		
PSL-Cray	1.13	0.00		
PSL-750	17.78	0.00		
PSL-750 (VMS)	19.73	0.00		
PSL-780	7.10	0.00		
PSL-DN300	19.44	0.00		
PSL-DN600	18.68	0.00		
PSL-DN160	11.30	0.00		
PSL-HP200	11.71	0.00		
PSL-HP-UX	12.51	0.00		
InterLispVax 780			9.72	
MV4000 CL			9.35	
MV8000 CL			6.76	
MV10000 CL			3.09	
3600 + FPA	2.30			0.00
750 NIL	23.14		23.24	
8600 CL	1.41	0.00		

Raw Time Stak				
Implementation	CPU	GC	Real	Paging
780 CL	4.11	0.00		
785 CL	2.40	0.00		
750 CL	6.21	0.00		
730 CL	20.96	0.00		
Perq			12.30	
750 Franz				
TrlOn & LclfYes	5.05	0.00		
TrlOn & LclfNo	11.18	0.00		
TrlOff & LclfYes	5.01	0.00		
TrlOff & LclfNo	25.98	0.00		
780 Franz				
TrlOn & LclfYes	3.17	0.00		
TrlOn & LclfNo	6.32	0.00		
TrlOff & LclfYes	3.15	0.00		
TrlOff & LclfNo	17.75	0.00		
Franz 68000				
TrlOn & LclfYes	8.25	0.00		
TrlOn & LclfNo	10.00	0.00		
TrlOff & LclfYes	8.27	0.00		
TrlOff & LclfNo	25.12	0.00		
InterLisp-10	6.37	0.00		
LM-2			7.83	

As Peter Deutsch has pointed out, this is a crummy benchmark,
which was implemented by relatively unenlightened programming on the CADR.
I made it almost 50% faster in 5 minutes ....

— Bruce Edwards, *discussing an unknown benchmark* (February 27, 1981)

Seems to me benchmarking generates more debate than information.

— Vaughan Pratt, *TIMING.MSG[TIM,LSP]* (October 19, 1981)

3.3 Ctak

CTAK is a variant of TAK that uses CATCH and THROW to return values
rather than the function-return mechanism. Not all Lisps have CATCH/THROW
functionality; INTERLISP can mimic the behavior of CATCH/THROW with its
much more powerful spaghetti stack. The times for INTERLISP on this benchmark
are quite slow, but the implementation doubles the number of function calls, as
we shall see.

3.3.1 *The Program*

```
(defun ctak (x y z)
  (catch 'ctak (ctak-aux x y z)))

(defun ctak-aux (x y z)
  (cond ((not (< y x))
         (throw 'ctak z))
        (t (ctak-aux
             (catch 'ctak
               (ctak-aux (1- x)
                         y
                         z))
             (catch 'ctak
               (ctak-aux (1- y)
                         z
                         x))
             (catch 'ctak
               (ctak-aux (1- z)
                         x
                         y))))))
```

3.3.2 *Analysis*

This benchmark is similar to TAK, but has both CATCH and THROW. The
use of CATCH and THROW here is somewhat trivial because the THROW always
throws to the nearest enclosing CATCH frame. Typically, CATCH and THROW
are implemented in the following manner: whenever a CATCH is evaluated, a
catch frame is placed on the stack. In the catch frame is a pointer to the next
enclosing catch frame, so that we end up with a linked list of catch frames. When
a THROW is evaluated, it determines which tag it will search for, and it will
search up this threaded list of catch frames, checking whether the tags are EQ. In
CTAK, this search only goes as far as the first catch frame. The length of time

that THROW uses is linear in the number of enclosing catch frames before the one that is required.

Meter for Ctak	
Item	**Count**
<'s	63609
Calls to CTAK-AUX	63609
Throw's	47707
Catch's	47707
1−'s	47706
Total	270338

3.3.3 *Translation Notes*

INTERLISP does not support CATCH and THROW directly, but it does support the more powerful spaghetti stack mechanism. To use that mechanism in CTAK we need to introduce an auxiliary function, TAKCALLER. TAKCALLER provides the name from which the RETFROM returns. Thus, the function TAK-CALLER serves the role of the CATCH frame and tag in the Common Lisp CATCH, and RETFROM serves the role of THROW. When evaluating the performance of CTAK on INTERLISP implementations, keep in mind that there are twice as many function calls taking place as in most Common Lisp dialects. Here is the INTERLISP code:

```
(RPAQQ CTAKCOMS ((FNS TAK TAK1 TAKCALLER)))
(DEFINEQ
(TAK
  (LAMBDA (X Y Z)
    (TAKCALLER X Y Z)))
(TAK1
  (LAMBDA (X Y Z)
    (COND
      ((NOT (ILESSP Y X))
        (RETFROM (QUOTE TAKCALLER)
                 Z))
      (T (TAK1 (TAKCALLER (SUB1 X)
                          Y Z)
               (TAKCALLER (SUB1 Y)
                          Z X)
               (TAKCALLER (SUB1 Z)
                          X Y)))))))
(TAKCALLER
  (LAMBDA (X Y Z)
    (TAK1 X Y Z)))
)
```

3.3.4 *Raw Data*

Raw Time Ctak				
Implementation	CPU	GC	Real	Paging
SAIL	2.85	0.00	4.18	
Lambda	4.39			0.00
Lambda (MC)				
3600	7.65			0.00
3600 + IFU	5.04			0.00
Dandelion	63.20	0.00		
Dolphin	140.00	0.00		
Dorado	18.00	0.00		
S-1			0.82	
PSL-SUN	10.11	0.00		
PSL-20	2.97	0.00		
PSL-3081	0.82	0.00		
PSL-Cray	0.59	0.00		
PSL-750	13.58	0.00		
PSL-750 (VMS)	12.08	0.00		
PSL-780	5.38	0.00		
PSL-DN300	12.43	0.00		
PSL-DN600	12.25	0.00		
PSL-DN160	6.63	0.00		
PSL-HP200	9.33	0.00		
PSL-HP-UX	9.49	0.00		
InterLispVax 780			31.63	
MV4000 CL			5.08	
MV8000 CL			3.37	
MV10000 CL			1.79	
3600 + FPA	5.04			0.00
750 NIL	9.91		9.91	
8600 CL	2.32	0.00		

Raw Time Ctak				
Implementation	CPU	GC	Real	Paging
780 CL	8.09	0.00		
785 CL	5.65	0.00		
750 CL	13.86	0.00		
730 CL	34.86	0.00		
Perq			7.63	
750 Franz				
TrlOn & LclfYes	18.75	0.00		
TrlOn & LclfNo	18.33	0.00		
TrlOff & LclfYes	18.25	0.00		
TrlOff & LclfNo	27.05	0.00		
780 Franz				
TrlOn & LclfYes	10.68	0.00		
TrlOn & LclfNo	12.05	0.00		
TrlOff & LclfYes	10.70	0.00		
TrlOff & LclfNo	17.80	0.00		
Franz 68000				
TrlOn & LclfYes	16.60	0.00		
TrlOn & LclfNo	17.80	0.00		
TrlOff & LclfYes	16.60	0.00		
TrlOff & LclfNo	24.17	0.00		
InterLisp-10	44.67	0.00		
LM-2			10.43	

It measures EBOX milliseconds.

You might possibly be getting charged for somebody else's spacewar or interrupt level.

I don't really remember.

You get charged for some amount of context switching and scheduling (possibly even figuring out that it should just run you again next).

— Jeff Rubin, *answering how the KL10 reports runtime* (October 19, 1981)

3.4 Takl

TAKL is very much like TAK, but it does not perform any explicit arithmetic.

3.4.1 *The Program*

```
(defun listn (n)
  (if (not (= 0 n))
      (cons n (listn (1- n)))))
(defvar 18l (listn 18.)) ;note that these are potential numbers
(defvar 12l (listn 12.))
(defvar  6l (listn 6.))
(defun mas (x y z)
  (if (not (shorterp y x))
      z
      (mas (mas (cdr x)
                y z)
           (mas (cdr y)
                z x)
           (mas (cdr z)
                x y))))
(defun shorterp (x y)
  (and y (or (null x)
             (shorterp (cdr x)
                       (cdr y)))))
```

3.4.2 *Analysis*

TAK mostly measures function call, but it also measures some amount of numeric operations, namely subtraction by 1 and the less-than relation. 47,706 such subtractions by 1 are done as well as 63,609 less-than relation tests. To separate out this computation, and to make this benchmark more of a purely symbol-manipulating program, Larry Masinter suggested that we use a unary representation of numbers instead of the usual machine representations. In TAKL, N is represented by the list $(n, n-1, n-2, \ldots, 1)$.

The function $<$ is implemented by SHORTERP, which tests whether one list is shorter than the other. We use the global variables 18L, 12L, and 6L to represent the constants 18, 12, and 6.

Notice that SHORTERP is defined recursively; implementations that do tail recursion will do much better on this benchmark than implementations that don't.

Because of the average size of the lists being compared with SHORTERP, approximately ten times as many calls are made to SHORTERP than to MAS itself.

When a capitalized word appears under ITEM in this table and in all subsequent ones, that is the entry for the number of calls made to the function with that name. So, LISTN refers to the number of times that LISTN was called.

Meter for Listn	
Item	**Count**
LISTN	39
='s	39
Cons's	36
1-'s	36
Total	150

Meter for Mas	
Item	**Count**
MAS	63609
Cdr's	47706
Total	111315

Meter for Shorterp	
Cdr's	818900
Null's	425352
SHORTERP	473059
Total	1717311

3.4.3 *Translation Notes*

S-1 Lisp function calls are quite expensive, and the S-1 suffers from *pipeline turbulence*. Pipeline turbulence occurs when one instruction in an instruction stream depends on a value produced by an earlier instruction. If the earlier instruction has not placed this value in a place that the second instruction can get when the second instruction needs that value, the pipeline blocks and performance degrades.

Also, S-1 Lisp does not do any tail recursion removal, although it does do the analysis that would allow it to do that removal. Therefore, SHORTERP is somewhat slow on the S-1. If SHORTERP is defined as

```
(defun shorterp (x y)
      (do ((x x (cdr x))
           (y y (cdr y)))
          ((null x) (not (null y)))
          (cond ((null y) (return '())))))
```

then the time for the S-2 is 1.18 seconds instead of 2.92. This demonstrates that a knowledge of the implementation can go a long way when tuning a program for performance. INTERLISP does do tail recursion removal, as does PSL.

3.4.4 *Raw Data*

Raw Time Takl				
Implementation	CPU	GC	Real	Paging
SAIL	2.81	0.00	4.02	
Lambda	10.70			0.00
Lambda (MC)	5.31			0.00
3600	6.44			0.00
3600 + IFU	4.95			0.00
Dandelion	14.00	0.00		
Dolphin	45.60	0.00		
Dorado	3.62	0.00		
S-1			2.92	
PSL-SUN	9.91	0.00		
PSL-20	2.52	0.00		
PSL-3081	0.61	0.00		
PSL-Cray	0.30	0.00		
PSL-750	15.45	0.00		
PSL-750 (VMS)	12.36	0.00		
PSL-780	5.27	0.00		
PSL-DN300	12.90	0.00		
PSL-DN600	10.92	0.00		
PSL-DN160	3.98	0.00		
PSL-HP200	5.73	0.00		
PSL-HP-UX	6.39	0.00		
InterLispVax 780			9.87	
MV4000 CL			17.93	
MV8000 CL			10.80	
MV10000 CL			5.52	
3600 + FPA	4.95			0.00
750 NIL	39.13		39.27	
8600 CL	2.03	0.00		

Raw Time Takl				
Implementation	CPU	GC	Real	Paging
780 CL	7.34	0.00		
785 CL	5.26	0.00		
750 CL	12.35	0.00		
730 CL	34.15	0.00		
Perq			21.73	
750 Franz				
TrlOn & LclfYes	12.60	0.00		
TrlOn & LclfNo	18.40	0.00		
TrlOff & LclfYes	12.37	0.00		
TrlOff & LclfNo	47.02	0.00		
780 Franz				
TrlOn & LclfYes	6.17	0.00		
TrlOn & LclfNo	9.72	0.00		
TrlOff & LclfYes	6.18	0.00		
TrlOff & LclfNo	24.67	0.00		
Franz 68000				
TrlOn & LclfYes	12.82	66.64		
TrlOn & LclfNo	16.00	67.14		
TrlOff & LclfYes	12.82	46.05		
TrlOff & LclfNo	43.12	46.38		
InterLisp-10	3.78	0.00		
LM-2			25.90	

It is a known bug that arrays larger than the size of main memory
don't work very well,
in particular they have to be paged in at least twice to create them.
— David Moon, *discussing LM-2 Performance* (December 11, 1981)

3.5 Takr

3.5.1 *The Program*

```
(defun tak0 (x y z)
  (cond ((not (< y x)) z)
        (t (tak1 (tak37 (1- x) y z)
                 (tak11 (1- y) z x)
                 (tak17 (1- z) x y)))))

(defun tak18 (x y z)
  (cond ((not (< y x)) z)
        (t (tak19 (tak3 (1- x) y z)
                  (tak9 (1- y) z x)
                  (tak23 (1- z) x y)))))
```

3.5.2 *Analysis*

TAKR is a function that was defined to thwart the effectiveness of cache memories. TAKR comprises 100 copies of TAK, each with a different name. Where TAK recursively calls itself, TAKR will call a predetermined, but random, copy of itself. In the program above, TAK18 calls TAK19, TAK3, TAK9, and TAK23.

Unfortunately, the cache on many machines is large enough to keep most of the 100 functions in the cache. For small machines with a cache, there will be a difference in runtime between TAK and TAKR.

SAIL used to be a KL-10A CPU with a 2K-word 200-nanosecond cache memory and a main memory consisting of a 2-megaword 1.5-μsec memory and a 256K-word .9-μsec memory. Currently SAIL is a KL-10B CPU, which is identical to a DEC 2060 CPU—it is 20% faster than the KL-10A CPU. On SAIL, the cache memory allows a very large, but slow, physical memory to behave reasonably well.

This benchmark was run with no load and the result was

```
CPU time = 0.595
elapsed time = 0.75
wholine time = 0.75
gc time = 0.0
load average before = 0.020
load average after  = 0.026
```

where CPU time is the EBOX time (no memory reference time included), elapsed
time is real time, wholine time is EBOX + MBOX (memory reference) times, GC
time is garbage collector time, and the load averages are given before and after
the timing run. All times are in seconds, and the load average is the exponentially
weighted, over time, average of the number of jobs in all runnable queues. With
no load, wholine and elapsed times are the same.

On TAKR with no load the result on SAIL (KL-10A) was

```
CPU time = 0.602
elapsed time = 1.02
wholine time = 1.02
gc time = 0.0
load average before = 0.27
load average after  = 0.28
```

which shows a 36% degradation. The question is how well these 100 functions
destroy the effect of the cache on SAIL. The answer is that it does not destroy the
effect very much. This makes sense because the total number of instructions for
100 copies of the function is about 3800, and the cache holds about 2000 words.
Here is the result for the single function TAK' run on SAIL with the cache shut
off:

```
CPU time = 0.6
elapsed time = 6.95
wholine time = 6.9
gc time = 0.0
load average before = 0.036
load average after  = 0.084
```

which shows a factor of 9.2 degradation. The 100-function version ran in the same
time within a few percent.

Hence, in order to destroy the effect of a cache, one must increase the size of
the code significantly beyond the size of the cache. Also, the distribution of the
locus of control must be roughly uniform or random.

More important to most implementations, though, is that the tail recursion is
no longer guaranteed to be a call from a function to itself, and many implementations do not do tail recursion removal when the call is not to that same function.
That is, often a compiler will implement tail recursion removal by transforming a
function that calls itself to one that does a GO to the head of the function. Of
course, the function has to be converted to a PROG equivalent of itself as well.

Meter for Tak0	
TAK0	817
1—'s	522
Total	1339

Meter for Tak18	
TAK18	683
1—'s	453
Total	1136

Each function is called an average of 636.09 times with a standard deviation of 8.2.

3.5.3 *Raw Data*

Raw Time Takr				
Implementation	CPU	GC	Real	Paging
SAIL	0.48	0.00	1.18	
Lambda	1.80			0.19
Lambda (MC)				
3600	0.60			0.00
3600 + IFU	0.43			0.00
Dandelion	1.75	0.00		
Dolphin	3.42	0.00		
Dorado	0.67	0.00		
S-1			0.58	
PSL-SUN	1.42	0.00		
PSL-20	0.59	0.00		
PSL-3081	0.12	0.00		
PSL-Cray	0.06	0.00		
PSL-750	2.82	0.00		
PSL-750 (VMS)	2.13	0.00		
PSL-780	1.17	0.00		
PSL-DN300	1.75	0.00		
PSL-DN600	2.13	0.00		
PSL-DN160	3.20	0.00		
PSL-HP200	1.76	0.00		
PSL-HP-UX	1.55	0.00		
InterLispVax 780			4.95	
MV4000 CL			2.60	
MV8000 CL			2.40	
MV10000 CL			1.20	
3600 + FPA	0.43			0.00
750 NIL	5.71		5.71	
8600 CL	0.81	0.00		

Raw Time Takr				
Implementation	CPU	GC	Real	Paging
780 CL	3.42	0.00		
785 CL	1.75	0.00		
750 CL	4.39	0.00		
730 CL	15.63	0.00		
Perq			8.40	
750 Franz				
TrlOn & LclfYes	2.70	0.00		
TrlOn & LclfNo	5.08	0.00		
TrlOff & LclfYes	2.70	0.00		
TrlOff & LclfNo	19.17	0.00		
780 Franz				
TrlOn & LclfYes	1.70	0.00		
TrlOn & LclfNo	3.62	0.00		
TrlOff & LclfYes	1.70	0.00		
TrlOff & LclfNo	13.26	0.00		
Franz 68000				
TrlOn & LclfYes				
TrlOn & LclfNo				
TrlOff & LclfYes				
TrlOff & LclfNo				
InterLisp-10	2.16	0.00		
LM-2			2.87	

Of course, all could, in principle, be tuned ....
— Richard Fateman, *discussing Franz performance* (February 19, 1982)

3.6 Boyer

Here is what Bob Boyer said about the Boyer Benchmark:

J Moore and I wrote the REWRITE program as quick means of guessing how fast our theorem-proving program would run if we translated it into some other Lisp system. Roughly speaking, it is a rewrite-rule-based simplifier combined with a very dumb tautology-checker, which has a three-place IF as the basic logical connective.

3.6.1 *The Program*

```
(defvar unify-subst)
(defvar temp-temp)
(defun add-lemma (term)
  (cond ((and (not (atom term))
              (eq (car term)
                  (quote equal))
              (not (atom (cadr term))))
         (setf (get (car (cadr term)) (quote lemmas))
               (cons term (get (car (cadr term))
                               (quote lemmas)))))
        (t (error "~%ADD-LEMMA did not like term:  ~a" term))))
(defun add-lemma-lst (lst)
  (cond ((null lst)
         t)
        (t (add-lemma (car lst))
           (add-lemma-lst (cdr lst)))))
(defun apply-subst (alist term)
  (cond ((atom term)
         (cond ((setq temp-temp (assq term alist))
                (cdr temp-temp))
               (t term)))
        (t (cons (car term)
                 (apply-subst-lst alist (cdr term))))))
(defun apply-subst-lst (alist lst)
  (cond ((null lst)
         nil)
        (t (cons (apply-subst alist (car lst))
                 (apply-subst-lst alist (cdr lst))))))
```

```
(defun falsep (x lst)
  (or (equal x (quote (f)))
      (member x lst)))
(defun one-way-unify (term1 term2)
  (progn (setq unify-subst nil)
         (one-way-unify1 term1 term2)))
(defun one-way-unify1 (term1 term2)
  (cond ((atom term2)
         (cond ((setq temp-temp (assq term2 unify-subst))
                (equal term1 (cdr temp-temp)))
               (t (setq unify-subst (cons (cons term2 term1)
                                          unify-subst))
                  t)))
        ((atom term1)
         nil)
        ((eq (car term1)
             (car term2))
         (one-way-unify1-lst (cdr term1)
                             (cdr term2)))
        (t nil)))
(defun one-way-unify1-lst (lst1 lst2)
  (cond ((null lst1)
         t)
        ((one-way-unify1 (car lst1)
                         (car lst2))
         (one-way-unify1-lst (cdr lst1)
                             (cdr lst2)))
        (t nil)))
(defun rewrite (term)
  (cond ((atom term)
         term)
        (t (rewrite-with-lemmas
             (cons (car term)
                   (rewrite-args (cdr term)))
             (get (car term)
                  (quote lemmas))))))
(defun rewrite-args (lst)
  (cond ((null lst)
         nil)
        (t (cons (rewrite (car lst))
                 (rewrite-args (cdr lst))))))
```

```
(defun rewrite-with-lemmas (term lst)
  (cond ((null lst)
         term)
        ((one-way-unify term (cadr (car lst)))
         (rewrite
          (apply-subst unify-subst (caddr (car lst)))))
        (t (rewrite-with-lemmas term (cdr lst)))))
(defun setup ()
  (add-lemma-lst
    (quote ((equal (compile form)
                   (reverse (codegen (optimize form)
                                     (nil))))
            (equal (eqp x y)
                   (equal (fix x)
                          (fix y)))
            (equal (greaterp x y)
                   (lessp y x))
            (equal (lesseqp x y)
                   (not (lessp y x)))
            (equal (greatereqp x y)
                   (not (lessp x y)))
            (equal (boolean x)
                   (or (equal x (t))
                       (equal x (f))))
            (equal (iff x y)
                   (and (implies x y)
                        (implies y x)))
            (equal (even1 x)
                   (if (zerop x)
                       (t)
                       (odd (1- x))))
            (equal (countps- l pred)
                   (countps-loop l pred (zero)))
            (equal (fact- i)
                   (fact-loop i 1))
            (equal (reverse- x)
                   (reverse-loop x (nil)))
            (equal (divides x y)
                   (zerop (remainder y x)))
            (equal (assume-true var alist)
                   (cons (cons var (t))
                         alist))
```

```
(equal (assume-false var alist)
       (cons (cons var (f))
             alist))
(equal (tautology-checker x)
       (tautologyp (normalize x)
                   (nil)))
(equal (falsify x)
       (falsify1 (normalize x)
                 (nil)))
(equal (prime x)
       (and (not (zerop x))
            (not (equal x (add1 (zero))))
            (prime1 x (1- x))))
(equal (and p q)
       (if p (if q (t)
                   (f))
             (f)))
(equal (or p q)
       (if p (t)
             (if q (t)
                   (f))
             (f)))
(equal (not p)
       (if p (f)
             (t)))
(equal (implies p q)
       (if p (if q (t)
                   (f))
             (t)))
(equal (fix x)
       (if (numberp x)
           x
           (zero)))
(equal (if (if a b c)
           d e)
       (if a (if b d e)
             (if c d e)))
(equal (zerop x)
       (or (equal x (zero))
           (not (numberp x))))
(equal (plus (plus x y)
             z)
       (plus x (plus y z)))
```

```
(equal (equal (plus a b)
              (zero))
       (and (zerop a)
            (zerop b)))
(equal (difference x x)
       (zero))
(equal (equal (plus a b)
              (plus a c))
       (equal (fix b)
              (fix c)))
(equal (equal (zero)
              (difference x y))
       (not (lessp y x)))
(equal (equal x (difference x y))
       (and (numberp x)
            (or (equal x (zero))
                (zerop y))))
(equal (meaning (plus-tree (append x y))
                a)
       (plus (meaning (plus-tree x)
                      a)
             (meaning (plus-tree y)
                      a)))
(equal (meaning (plus-tree (plus-fringe x))
                a)
       (fix (meaning x a)))
(equal (append (append x y)
               z)
       (append x (append y z)))
(equal (reverse (append a b))
       (append (reverse b)
               (reverse a)))
(equal (times x (plus y z))
       (plus (times x y)
             (times x z)))
(equal (times (times x y)
              z)
       (times x (times y z)))
(equal (equal (times x y)
              (zero))
       (or (zerop x)
           (zerop y)))
```

```
(equal (exec (append x y)
             pds envrn)
       (exec y (exec x pds envrn)
             envrn))
(equal (mc-flatten x y)
       (append (flatten x)
               y))
(equal (member x (append a b))
       (or (member x a)
           (member x b)))
(equal (member x (reverse y))
       (member x y))
(equal (length (reverse x))
       (length x))
(equal (member a (intersect b c))
       (and (member a b)
            (member a c)))
(equal (nth (zero)
            i)
       (zero))
(equal (exp i (plus j k))
       (times (exp i j)
              (exp i k)))
(equal (exp i (times j k))
       (exp (exp i j)
            k))
(equal (reverse-loop x y)
       (append (reverse x)
               y))
(equal (reverse-loop x (nil))
       (reverse x))
(equal (count-list z (sort-lp x y))
       (plus (count-list z x)
             (count-list z y)))
(equal (equal (append a b)
              (append a c))
       (equal b c))
(equal (plus (remainder x y)
             (times y (quotient x y)))
       (fix x))
(equal (power-eval (big-plus1 l i base)
                   base)
       (plus (power-eval l base)
             i))
```

```
(equal (power-eval (big-plus x y i base)
                   base)
       (plus i (plus (power-eval x base)
                     (power-eval y base)))))
(equal (remainder y 1)
       (zero))
(equal (lessp (remainder x y)
              y)
       (not (zerop y)))
(equal (remainder x x)
       (zero))
(equal (lessp (quotient i j)
              i)
       (and (not (zerop i))
            (or (zerop j)
                (not (equal j 1)))))
(equal (lessp (remainder x y)
              x)
       (and (not (zerop y))
            (not (zerop x))
            (not (lessp x y))))
(equal (power-eval (power-rep i base)
                   base)
       (fix i))
(equal (power-eval (big-plus (power-rep i base)
                             (power-rep j base)
                             (zero)
                             base)
                   base)
       (plus i j))
(equal (gcd x y)
       (gcd y x))
(equal (nth (append a b)
            i)
       (append (nth a i)
               (nth b (difference i (length a)))))
(equal (difference (plus x y)
                   x)
       (fix y))
(equal (difference (plus y x)
                   x)
       (fix y))
(equal (difference (plus x y)
                   (plus x z))
       (difference y z))
```

```
(equal (times x (difference c w))
       (difference (times c x)
                   (times w x)))
(equal (remainder (times x z)
                  z)
       (zero))
(equal (difference (plus b (plus a c))
                   a)
       (plus b c))
(equal (difference (add1 (plus y z))
                   z)
       (add1 y))
(equal (lessp (plus x y)
              (plus x z))
       (lessp y z))
(equal (lessp (times x z)
              (times y z))
       (and (not (zerop z))
            (lessp x y)))
(equal (lessp y (plus x y))
       (not (zerop x)))
(equal (gcd (times x z)
            (times y z))
       (times z (gcd x y)))
(equal (value (normalize x)
              a)
       (value x a))
(equal (equal (flatten x)
              (cons y (nil)))
       (and (nlistp x)
            (equal x y)))
(equal (listp (gopher x))
       (listp x))
(equal (samefringe x y)
       (equal (flatten x)
              (flatten y)))
(equal (equal (greatest-factor x y)
              (zero))
       (and (or (zerop y)
                (equal y 1))
            (equal x (zero))))
(equal (equal (greatest-factor x y)
              1)
       (equal x 1))
```

```
(equal (numberp (greatest-factor x y))
       (not (and (or (zerop y)
                     (equal y 1))
                 (not (numberp x)))))
(equal (times-list (append x y))
       (times (times-list x)
              (times-list y)))
(equal (prime-list (append x y))
       (and (prime-list x)
            (prime-list y)))
(equal (equal z (times w z))
       (and (numberp z)
            (or (equal z (zero))
                (equal w 1))))
(equal (greatereqpr x y)
       (not (lessp x y)))
(equal (equal x (times x y))
       (or (equal x (zero))
           (and (numberp x)
                (equal y 1))))
(equal (remainder (times y x)
                  y)
       (zero))
(equal (equal (times a b)
              1)
       (and (not (equal a (zero)))
            (not (equal b (zero)))
            (numberp a)
            (numberp b)
            (equal (1- a)
                   (zero))
            (equal (1- b)
                   (zero))))
(equal (lessp (length (delete x l))
              (length l))
       (member x l))
(equal (sort2 (delete x l))
       (delete x (sort2 l)))
(equal (dsort x)
       (sort2 x))
```

```
(equal (length
        (cons
         x1
         (cons
          x2
          (cons
           x3
           (cons
            x4
            (cons
             x5
             (cons x6 x7)))))))
       (plus 6 (length x7)))
(equal (difference (add1 (add1 x))
                   2)
       (fix x))
(equal (quotient (plus x (plus x y))
                 2)
       (plus x (quotient y 2)))
(equal (sigma (zero)
              i)
       (quotient (times i (add1 i))
                 2))
(equal (plus x (add1 y))
       (if (numberp y)
           (add1 (plus x y))
           (add1 x)))
(equal (equal (difference x y)
              (difference z y))
       (if (lessp x y)
           (not (lessp y z))
           (if (lessp z y)
               (not (lessp y x))
               (equal (fix x)
                      (fix z)))))
(equal (meaning (plus-tree (delete x y))
                a)
       (if (member x y)
           (difference (meaning (plus-tree y)
                                a)
                       (meaning x a))
           (meaning (plus-tree y)
                    a)))
```

```
(equal (times x (add1 y))
       (if (numberp y)
           (plus x (times x y))
           (fix x)))
(equal (nth (nil)
            i)
       (if (zerop i)
           (nil)
           (zero)))
(equal (last (append a b))
       (if (listp b)
           (last b)
           (if (listp a)
               (cons (car (last a))
                     b)
               b)))
(equal (equal (lessp x y)
              z)
       (if (lessp x y)
           (equal t z)
           (equal f z)))
(equal (assignment x (append a b))
       (if (assignedp x a)
           (assignment x a)
           (assignment x b)))
(equal (car (gopher x))
       (if (listp x)
           (car (flatten x))
           (zero)))
(equal (flatten (cdr (gopher x)))
       (if (listp x)
           (cdr (flatten x))
           (cons (zero)
                 (nil))))
(equal (quotient (times y x)
                 y)
       (if (zerop y)
           (zero)
           (fix x)))
(equal (get j (set i val mem))
       (if (eqp j i)
           val
           (get j mem)))))))
```

```
(defun tautologyp (x true-lst false-lst)
  (cond ((truep x true-lst)
         t)
        ((falsep x false-lst)
         nil)
        ((atom x)
         nil)
        ((eq (car x)
             (quote if))
         (cond ((truep (cadr x)
                       true-lst)
                (tautologyp (caddr x)
                        true-lst false-lst))
               ((falsep (cadr x)
                        false-lst)
                (tautologyp (cadddr x)
                        true-lst false-lst))
               (t (and (tautologyp (caddr x)
                                   (cons (cadr x)
                                         true-lst)
                                   false-lst)
                       (tautologyp (cadddr x)
                                   true-lst
                                   (cons (cadr x)
                                         false-lst))))))
        (t nil)))
(defun tautp (x)
  (tautologyp (rewrite x)
              nil nil))
```

128

```lisp
(defun test ()
  (prog (ans term)
        (setq term
              (apply-subst
                (quote ((x f (plus (plus a b)
                                   (plus c (zero))))
                        (y f (times (times a b)
                                    (plus c d)))
                        (z f (reverse (append (append a b)
                                              (nil))))
                        (u equal (plus a b)
                           (difference x y))
                        (w lessp (remainder a b)
                           (member a (length b)))))
                (quote (implies (and (implies x y)
                                     (and (implies y z)
                                          (and (implies z u)
                                               (implies u w))))
                                (implies x w)))))
        (setq ans (tautp term))))
(defun trans-of-implies (n)
  (list (quote implies)
        (trans-of-implies1 n)
        (list (quote implies)
              0 n)))
(defun trans-of-implies1 (n)
  (cond ((eql n 1)
         (list (quote implies)
               0 1))
        (t (list (quote and)
                 (list (quote implies)
                       (1- n)
                       n)
                 (trans-of-implies1 (1- n))))))
(defun truep (x lst)
       (or (equal x (quote (t)))
           (member x lst)))
(eval-when (compile load eval)
  (setup))
;;; make sure you've run (setup) then call:  (test)
```

3.6.2 *Analysis*

This benchmark, which has been distributed by Robert Boyer for several years, has formed the basis of many comparisons between Lisp implementations. It is essentially a theorem-proving benchmark.

SETUP is called to initialize the system; the initialization simply places a number of axioms in a data base of such axioms. The quoted list in the function SETUP is a representation for this list of axioms. Take, for example, the second element of that list:

```
(equal (greaterp x y)
       (lessp y x))
```

This axiom is placed on the property list of the symbol greaterp. It states that the truth value of the statement

```
(greaterp x y)
```

is equivalent to that of

```
(lessp x y)
```

The basic operation of the benchmark is to prove that a particular logical statement is a tautology. The statement is

$$(x \supset y \wedge (y \supset z \wedge (z \supset u \wedge u \supset w))) \supset (x \supset w)$$

where

$$x = \mathrm{f}((a + b) + (c + 0))$$

$$y = \mathrm{f}(\mathrm{reverse}(\mathrm{append}(\mathrm{append}(a, b), \mathrm{nil})))$$

$$z = (a + b) = (x - y))$$

$$w = \mathrm{remainder}(a, b) < \mathrm{member}(a, \mathrm{length}(b))$$

To prove this is a tautology, the program first rewrites the statement into canonical form, which is as nested IF statements. To do this rewriting process, the program uses the axioms stored in the data base as production rules. In the sample axiom above, the action of the rewriter would be to substitute occurrences of

        (greaterp x y)

with

        (lessp y x)

The greaterp form is matched (1-way unified) to bind the variables x and y. The bindings are then substituted into a copy of the lessp form. This rewriting phase is a simplication and canonicalization phase.

Once the sentence has been rewritten, the tautology-checker is invoked. This checker is quite simple; it maintains a list of true statements and a list of false statements. A sentence is a tautology if it is in the list of true sentences; it is not a tautology if it is in the list of false sentences; it is false if it is not in either of these lists and if it is not an IF statement.

An IF statement is of the form

        (if a b c)

A sentence of this form is a tautology if one of the following three things is the case: 1) if **a** is true and **b** is a tautology; 2) if **a** is false and **c** is a tautology; or 3) if **a** is added to the list of true sentences and **b** can be shown to be a tautology, and if **a** is added to the list of false sentences and **c** can be shown to be a tautology.

Besides a fair number of function calls, by far the largest number of operations that this benchmark performs are list operations—mostly CARs, CDRs, NULL and ATOM tests, and about a quarter of a million CONSs. The breakdown is about three quarters of a million CARs and a half million each of CDRs, NULLs, and ATOMs.

One would have to say that this benchmark is a good mixture of typical list-structure-manipulating operations with a normal number of function calls. There are also about 80,000 GETs, which is a typical mix if property lists are used.

Meter for Add-Lemma during SETUP	
Car's	424
Atom's	212
Null's	107
ADD-LEMMA-LST	107
Cdr's	106
Get's	106
Cons's	106
Putprop's	106
Eq's	106
ADD-LEMMA	106
TRUEP	0
Sub1's	0
TRANS-OF-IMPLIES1	0
TRANS-OF-IMPLIES	0
TAUTP	0
TAUTOLOGYP	0
REWRITE-WITH-LEMMAS	0
REWRITE-ARGS	0
REWRITE	0
ONE-WAY-UNIFY1-LST	0
ONE-WAY-UNIFY1	0
ONE-WAY-UNIFY	0
Member's	0
Equal's	0
FALSEP	0
APPLY-SUBST-LST	0
APPLY-SUBST	0
Total	1486

Meter for Add-Lemma during TEST	
Car's	788408
Cdr's	462652
Null's	434133
Atom's	419284
Cons's	226464
ONE-WAY-UNIFY1	171145
REWRITE-ARGS	169804
REWRITE-WITH-LEMMAS	152280
Eq's	128879
ONE-WAY-UNIFY1-LST	100601
REWRITE	91024
Get's	79742
ONE-WAY-UNIFY	73499
APPLY-SUBST-LST	11448
APPLY-SUBST	9512
Equal's	1403
Member's	272
TRUEP	207
FALSEP	150
TAUTOLOGYP	111
TAUTP	1
Sub1's	0
TRANS-OF-IMPLIES1	0
TRANS-OF-IMPLIES	0
ADD-LEMMA-LST	0
Putprop's	0
ADD-LEMMA	0
Total	3321019

3.6.3 *Raw Data*

Raw Time Boyer				
Implementation	CPU	GC	Real	Paging
SAIL	6.47	11.60	23.50	
Lambda	31.70			7.20
Lambda (MC)	10.60			4.60
3600	11.99			2.93
3600 + IFU	9.40			1.77
Dandelion	74.60	44.40		
Dolphin	101.10	31.30		
Dorado	17.08	13.20		
S-1			10.03	
PSL-SUN	31.26	14.99		
PSL-20	11.96	11.60		
PSL-3081	2.34	2.26		
PSL-Cray	1.85	1.50		
PSL-750	43.38	40.71		
PSL-750 (VMS)	45.65	17.33		
PSL-780	21.30	19.97		
PSL-DN300	46.92	48.58		
PSL-DN600	43.70	41.18		
PSL-DN160	25.66	15.34		
PSL-HP200	25.52	0.00		
PSL-HP-UX	25.19	7.34		
InterLispVax 780			53.28	
MV4000 CL			86.07	
MV8000 CL			66.74	
MV10000 CL			29.30	
3600 + FPA	9.40			1.77
750 NIL	81.33		83.78	
8600 CL	12.18	14.29		

Raw Time Boyer				
Implementation	CPU	GC	Real	Paging
780 CL	46.79	40.90		
785 CL	27.50	23.20		
750 CL	69.38	79.30		
730 CL	258.98	180.82		
Perq			125.43	
750 Franz				
TrlOn & LclfYes	34.35	50.98		
TrlOn & LclfNo	60.55	50.90		
TrlOff & LclfYes	34.67	35.03		
TrlOff & LclfNo	224.03	34.69		
780 Franz				
TrlOn & LclfYes	20.58	31.08		
TrlOn & LclfNo	40.17	31.33		
TrlOff & LclfYes	21.00	21.35		
TrlOff & LclfNo	144.98	21.32		
Franz 68000				
TrlOn & LclfYes	37.94	66.64		
TrlOn & LclfNo	55.85	67.14		
TrlOff & LclfYes	38.46	46.05		
TrlOff & LclfNo	216.22	46.38		
InterLisp-10	25.45	27.47		
LM-2			45.00	

Perhaps the people who did the other timings
did not do a WITHOUT-INTERRUPTS?

— Howard Cannon, *discussing timing variations* (February 26, 1982)

SUBRCALL can be used in interpreted code, since
trampolines can be consed up on-the-fly to jump to the interpreter.
This technique is used in NIL,
which is one reason why the NIL timings for FUNCALL
are so good.

— George Carrette, *discussing performance arcana* (March 3, 1982)

3.7 Browse

3.7.1 *The Program*

```
;;; BROWSE -- Benchmark to create and browse through
;;; an AI-like data base of units.
;;; n is # of symbols
;;; m is maximum amount of stuff on the plist
;;; npats is the number of basic patterns on the unit
;;; ipats is the instantiated copies of the patterns
(defvar rand 21.)
(defmacro char1 (x) '(char (string ,x) 0))
(defun init (n m npats ipats)
  (let ((ipats (copy-tree ipats)))
    (do ((p ipats (cdr p)))
        ((null (cdr p)) (rplacd p ipats)))
    (do ((n n (1- n))
         (i m (cond ((= i 0) m)
                    (t (1- i))))
         (name (gensym) (gensym))
         (a ()))
        ((= n 0) a)
      (push name a)
      (do ((i i (1- i)))
          ((= i 0))
        (setf (get name (gensym)) nil))
      (setf (get name 'pattern)
            (do ((i npats (1- i))
                 (ipats ipats (cdr ipats))
                 (a ()))
                ((= i 0) a)
              (push (car ipats) a)))
      (do ((j (- m i) (1- j)))
          ((= j 0))
        (setf (get name (gensym)) nil)))))
(defun browse-random ()
  (setq rand (mod (* rand 17.) 251.)))
```

```
(defun randomize (l)
  (do ((a ()))
      ((null l) a)
    (let ((n (mod (browse-random) (length l))))
      (cond ((= n 0)
              (push (car l) a)
              (setq l (cdr l)))
            (t
              (do ((n n (1- n))
                   (x l (cdr x)))
                  ((= n 1)
                   (push (cadr x) a)
                   (rplacd x (cddr x)))))))))
(defun match (pat dat alist)
  (cond ((null pat)
          (null dat))
        ((null dat) ())
        ((or (eq (car pat) '?)
             (eq (car pat)
                 (car dat)))
          (match (cdr pat) (cdr dat) alist))
        ((eq (car pat) '*)
          (or (match (cdr pat) dat alist)
              (match (cdr pat) (cdr dat) alist)
              (match pat (cdr dat) alist)))
        (t (cond
             ((atom (car pat))
              (cond
                ((eq (char1 (car pat)) #\?)
                 (let ((val (assoc (car pat) alist)))
                   (cond (val (match
                                (cons (cdr val)
                                      (cdr pat))
                               dat
                               alist))
                         (t (match
                              (cdr pat)
                              (cdr dat)
                              (cons (cons (car pat)
                                          (car dat))
                                    alist))))))))
```

```
                        ((eq (char1 (car pat)) #\*)
                         (let ((val (assoc (car pat) alist)))
                          (cond (val (match
                                        (append (cdr val)
                                                (cdr pat))
                                      dat
                                      alist))
                   (t
                    (do ((l () (nconc l (cons (car d) nil)))
                         (e (cons () dat) (cdr e))
                         (d dat (cdr d)))
                        ((null e) ())
                      (cond ((match
                                (cdr pat)
                                d
                                (cons (cons (car pat) l)
                                     alist))
                             (return t))))))))))))
                  (t (and
                        (not (atom (car dat)))
                        (match (car pat)
                               (car dat) alist)
                        (match (cdr pat)
                               (cdr dat) alist)))))))))
(defun browse ()
  (investigate (randomize
                 (init
                  100.
                  10.
                  4.
                  '((a a a b b b b a a a a a b b a a a)
                    (a a b b b b a a
                     (a a)(b b))
                    (a a a b (b a) b a b a))))
                '((*a ?b *b ?b a *a a *b *a)
                  (*a *b *b *a (*a) (*b))
                  (? ? * (b a) * ? ?)))))
(defun investigate (units pats)
  (do ((units units (cdr units)))
      ((null units))
    (do ((pats pats (cdr pats)))
        ((null pats))
      (do ((p (get (car units) 'pattern)
              (cdr p)))
          ((null p))
        (match (car pats) (car p) ())))))
;;; call: (browse)
```

3.7.2 *Analysis*

This program is intended to perform many of the operations that a simple expert system might perform. There is a simple pattern matcher that uses the form of a symbol to determine its role within a pattern, and the data base of 'units' or 'frames' is implemented as property lists. In some ways this benchmark duplicates some of the operations in Boyer, but it is designed to perform a mixture of operations in proportions more nearly like those in real expert systems.

The basic operation of the benchmark is to search a data base of objects, identifying all of those objects that satisfy some predicate. The objects contain *descriptors*, which are patterns. The predicate is that a set of search patterns matches the descriptors. The matching is done exhaustively—all search patterns are matched against all descriptors regardless of the outcome of any of the individual matches.

The property lists are placed on symbols created for this purpose. The content of the unit—as they are called—is a list of data. The content is stored under the indicator PATTERN (an unfortunate choice of terms). For example, one of the data items stored in the list placed under the indicator PATTERN is

```
(a a b b b b a a
  (a a)(b b))
```

The symbol will have other entries in order to complicate the property list operations. In this benchmark, each symbol has ten entries—one is the PATTERN entry and the other nine are the 'filler.' The PATTERN entry is uniformly distributed among the other nine entries. That is, it is as often the case that the PATTERN entry is the first entry on the property list as it is the second, as it is the third, etc. This means that the benchmark does not discriminate between implementations that add new properties at the head and those that add new properties at the end. For example, if a property list is of the form $[i_1\ v_1\ i_2\ v_2]$, when one adds the value v under the indicator i in MacLisp, one gets $[i\ v\ i_1\ v_1\ i_2\ v_2]$, and in INTERLISP one gets $[i_1\ v_1\ i_2\ v_2\ i\ v]$.

The first thing the benchmark does is to initialize its data base. INIT takes 4 arguments: 1) the number of entries in the data base; 2) the total number of objects, including the intended entry, on the property list of each symbol; 3) the number of patterns on a unit; and 4) the data against which the patterns will be matched—this is a list of instantiated patterns.

The symbol names are GENSYMed; the list of data that is stored on the symbols is copied and turned into a circular list to aid with the task of placing n of them on each symbol's property list. The remainder of the initialization is scanning down lists, GENSYMing symbols, and manipulating their property lists. A fair amount of CONSing is done as well; some arithmetic is done, too. This code is all in INIT.

INIT returns a list of the symbols—the list of all of the items in the data base. Because the initialization in INIT could have created the property lists in such a way that paging and cache operations would be coincidentally improved in performance, the property lists have been localized, and RANDOMIZE is called to transform the list of symbols into a randomly permuted list.

There is a random number generator provided that operates identically on all 2's complement machines that support at least 8-bit arithmetic. The generator uses the updator

$$n \leftarrow 17n \quad (\text{mod } 251)$$

Notice that 17 and 251 are relatively prime. Another way to have accomplished this would been to have supplied a list of numbers that could be recirculated. However, the operations performed by the random-number-generating process are similar to many operations done in compilers, AI systems, and other large systems—they all have state-preserving generators. In the generator here, the global variable *rand* holds the current random number, and the state of the random number generator is precisely this number. The function BROWSE-RANDOM globally assigns to this variable. *rand* starts out as 21.

RANDOMIZE takes a list, L, and produces a permutation of it as follows: Let L be the length of L. n is set to:

$$\text{RAND} \quad (\text{mod L}),$$

where RAND is updated before n is computed. Then the n_{th} element of L is removed from L and placed (CONSed) at the head of the permutation list. The removal is achieved using RPLACD.

The main part of the benchmark is now done. For every symbol in the permuted list, for every pattern on a predetermined list of patterns, for every data item in the list of data items on the property list of that symbol, the pattern is matched against the data item by using a pattern matcher.

The pattern matcher matches patterns that are tree structures containing atoms, numbers, and pattern variables at the leaves against tree structures containing atoms and numbers at the leaves. Here is one of the patterns:

```
(*a ?b *b ?b a *a a *b *a)
```

Pattern variables can be '?,' which matches any node in the tree, '*,' which matches 0 or more elements in a list, a symbol of the form '?-<var>,' which matches any node in the tree with multiple instances of this symbol matching the same (EQ) node, and a symbol of the form '*-<var>,' which matches 0 or more elements in list with multiple instances of this symbol matching EQUAL lists. *-variables can, therefore, cause backtracking to occur.

For example, in order to test whether a symbol is of the form '?-<var>,' the first character in the print name is extracted. In Common Lisp this is done by getting the first character out of the string that represents that print name.

There are a lot of list-structure-manipulating operations in this benchmark.

Meter for Init	
='s	1901
1−'s	1591
Gensym's	1101
Putprop's	1100
Car's	800
Cons's	500
Cdr's	405
Intern's	101
Null's	3
Rplacd's	1
INIT	1
Total	7504

Meter for Randomize	
='s	2573
Cdr's	2475
1−'s	2375
Null's	101
Cons's	100
Length's	100
Rplacd's	98
Car's	4
RANDOMIZE	1
Total	7827

Meter for Seed	
SEED	1
Total	1

Meter for Random	
RANDOM	100
Total	100

Meter for Match	
Car's	1319800
Eq's	755700
Null's	504100
Cdr's	483400
Cons's	239200
Char1	226800
MATCH	213600
Nconc's	69000
Return's	600
Total	3812200

Meter for Investigate	
Car's	2700
Null's	2001
Cdr's	1600
Get's	300
Total	6601

Note that the entry for PUTPROP in the table above refers to instances of

```
(SETF (GET X Y) Z)
```

3.7.3 *Translation Notes*

This benchmark is trivially translated to other Lisp dialects. Obtaining the first character in the print name of a symbol is the significant problem to be solved in the translation.

3.7.4 *Raw Data*

Raw Time Browse				
Implementation	**CPU**	**GC**	**Real**	**Paging**
SAIL	13.64	39.52	82.68	
Lambda	29.20			10.30
Lambda (MC)	19.70			18.58
3600	30.80			3.13
3600 + IFU	21.43			2.51
Dandelion	174.00	126.00		
Dolphin	249.00	82.60		
Dorado	52.50	41.90		
S-1			10.20	
PSL-SUN	61.94	16.85		
PSL-20	23.81	4.89		
PSL-3081	3.84	2.46		
PSL-Cray	4.70	3.66		
PSL-750	75.49	16.08		
PSL-750 (VMS)	95.70	8.02		
PSL-780	41.15	9.12		
PSL-DN300				
PSL-DN600				
PSL-DN160				
PSL-HP200	39.84	4.61		
PSL-HP-UX	42.99	6.61		
InterLispVax 780			111.53	
MV4000 CL			181.54	
MV8000 CL			136.20	
MV10000 CL			57.91	
3600 + FPA	21.43			2.51
750 NIL	1099.84		1226.53	
8600 CL	38.69	30.37		

Raw Time Browse				
Implementation	CPU	GC	Real	Paging
780 CL	118.51	86.50		
785 CL	53.40	43.30		
750 CL	195.11	164.05		
730 CL	540.58	380.50		
Perq			310.28	
750 Franz				
TrlOn & LclfYes	117.20	137.93		
TrlOn & LclfNo	212.48	132.53		
TrlOff & LclfYes	122.67	138.45		
TrlOff & LclfNo	254.43	134.92		
780 Franz				
TrlOn & LclfYes	73.02	88.97		
TrlOn & LclfNo	135.70	77.30		
TrlOff & LclfYes	78.25	92.00		
TrlOff & LclfNo	155.53	77.83		
Franz 68000				
TrlOn & LclfYes	63.68	167.35		
TrlOn & LclfNo	66.22	168.38		
TrlOff & LclfYes	92.40	159.79		
TrlOff & LclfNo	113.10	160.79		
InterLisp-10	70.32	26.98		
LM-2			70.21	

My face is red.
I think what is going on here is that
INTERN is a big loser.

— Glenn Burke *explaining a poor showing.* (August 5, 1983.)

3.8 Destructive

3.8.1 *The Program*

```
;;; DESTRU -- Destructive operation benchmark
(defun destructive (n m)
  (let ((l (do ((i 10. (1- i))
                (a () (push () a)))
               ((= i 0) a))))
    (do ((i n (1- i)))
        ((= i 0))
      (cond ((null (car l))
             (do ((l l (cdr l)))
                 ((null l))
               (or (car l)
                   (rplaca l (cons () ())))
               (nconc (car l)
                      (do ((j m (1- j))
                           (a () (push () a)))
                          ((= j 0) a)))))
            (t
             (do ((l1 l (cdr l1))
                  (l2 (cdr l) (cdr l2)))
                 ((null l2))
               (rplacd (do ((j (floor (length (car l2)) 2)
                               (1- j))
                            (a (car l2) (cdr a)))
                           ((zerop j) a)
                         (rplaca a i))
                       (let ((n (floor (length (car l1)) 2)))
                         (cond ((= n 0) (rplaca l1 ())
                                (car l1))
                               (t
                                (do ((j n (1- j))
                                     (a (car l1) (cdr a)))
                                    ((= j 1)
                                     (prog1 (cdr a)
                                            (rplacd a ())))
                                  (rplaca a i)))))))))))))
;;; call:  (destructive 600. 50.)
```

3.8.2 *Analysis*

Destructive benchmarks the 'destructive' (hence the name) list utilities. It does this by constructing a tree that is a list of lists and then destructively modifying its elements. This manipulation proceeds by means of a fairly elaborate iterative control structure.

Destructive builds a list of lists, ten long, called L. Each element in this list is set to a list of m ()'s by using RPLACA. Then the following operations are performed n times: If the first element in L is empty, it is replenished by another list of m ()'s. If it is not empty, then the following operations are performed on each element of the list L but the first element. The middle of each sublist in the list L is found. The sublist is chopped off at that point, and another part of the existing structure is placed there instead. The middle of the sublist is determined by dividing the length of the sublist by 2. Then the sublist is scanned to find that spot, and while doing this, each element of the sublist is replaced with an integer, i, which is the outside loop index. The part of the structure that is spliced onto the end of the current sublist—which is the middle of the original list—is the second half of the sublist that preceeds this one in L. The same operations are performed on this preceding sublist as on this one to find the middle.

Suppose L is

$$(\dots(a_1\dots a_n\dots a_{2n})(b_1\dots b_m\dots b_{2m}),$$

and we are at iteration i. Then after one step of iteration this part of the list will look like

$$(\dots(a_1\dots a_n)(i\dots ia_{n+1}\dots a_{2n})$$

If parts of the lists run out, they are replenished by m ()'s. This sample alteration assumes that the sublists are of even length.

Here is a tabulation of the number of operations performed by this benchmark:

148

Meter for Destructive	
Rplacd's	9167
Nconc's	860
Rplaca's	84550
Cons's	43105
='s	142635
1-'s	127980
Cdr's	99537
Quotient's	9252
Length's	9252
Car's	20824
Null's	6686
Total	553848

3.8.3 *Translation Notes*

In the MacLisp version, the FIXSW flag is set. This forces all the generic arithmetic functions to assume fixnum arguments. The translation to Common Lisp required that QUOTIENT be replaced with an explicit integer divide using FLOOR, since the / function could return a rational result.

Here is the INTERLISP code:

```
(DEFINEQ
 (DESTRUCTIVE
  (LAMBDA (n m)
    (PROG ((l (COLLECTN 10)))
     (for i from n by -1 to 1
      do (if (NULL (CAR l))
          then (for L on l
                do (OR (CAR L)
                       (RPLACA L (LIST NIL)))
                   (NCONC (CAR L)
                      (COLLECTN m)))
          else (for l1 on l as l2 on (CDR l)
                do
                  (RPLACD
                   (for j from (IQUOTIENT
                                 (FLENGTH (CAR l2))
                                 2)
                     by -1 to 1 as a on (CAR l2) do (RPLACA a i)
                     finally (RETURN a))
                   (PROG ((n (IQUOTIENT (FLENGTH (CAR l1))
                                        2)))
                    (RETURN (if (ZEROP n)
                             then (RPLACA l1 NIL)
                                  (CAR l1)
                             else
                             (for j from n by -1 to 2 as a
                              on (CAR l1)
                              do (RPLACA a i)
                              finally
                               (RETURN
                                (PROG1 (CDR a)
                                       (RPLACD a NIL)))))
                   ))))))
     (RETURN l)))))
```

And here is a simple macro:

```
(PUTPROPS COLLECTN MACRO
  ((N)
  (PROG (VAL)
        (FRPTQ N (PUSH VAL NIL)) (RETURN VAL))))
```

Notice that 'fast' versions of operations like FLENGTH were used. This code was written for the D-machines in which FRPLACA and FRPLACD are exactly the same as RPLACA and RPLACD.

150

3.8.4 *Raw Data*

Raw Time Destructive				
Implementation	CPU	GC	Real	Paging
SAIL	2.16	5.38	8.41	
Lambda	4.00			1.09
Lambda (MC)	2.67			0.43
3600	3.03			0.43
3600 + IFU	2.18			0.26
Dandelion	17.58	9.27		
Dolphin	27.00	7.97		
Dorado	3.77	3.41		
S-1			0.91	
PSL-SUN	7.46	0.00		
PSL-20	2.38	0.00		
PSL-3081				
PSL-Cray	0.44	0.00		
PSL-750	7.22	0.00		
PSL-750 (VMS)	8.40	0.00		
PSL-780	3.87	0.00		
PSL-DN300	10.16	0.00		
PSL-DN600	10.59	0.00		
PSL-DN160	7.43	0.00		
PSL-HP200	4.25	0.00		
PSL-HP-UX	4.69	0.00		
InterLispVax 780			5.44	
MV4000 CL			18.27	
MV8000 CL			12.99	
MV10000 CL			6.15	
3600 + FPA	2.18			0.26
750 NIL	8.95		8.96	
8600 CL	2.10	0.00		

Raw Time Destructive				
Implementation	CPU	GC	Real	Paging
780 CL	6.38	0.00		
785 CL	4.27	0.00		
750 CL	11.30	0.00		
730 CL	26.41	0.00		
Perq			17.46	
750 Franz				
TrlOn & LclfYes	8.79	6.90		
TrlOn & LclfNo	11.40	7.72		
TrlOff & LclfYes	8.66	6.95		
TrlOff & LclfNo	11.02	7.65		
780 Franz				
TrlOn & LclfYes	5.20	6.63		
TrlOn & LclfNo	6.96	6.70		
TrlOff & LclfYes	6.95	6.78		
TrlOff & LclfNo	6.95	6.77		
Franz 68000				
TrlOn & LclfYes	9.57	0.00		
TrlOn & LclfNo	9.54	0.00		
TrlOff & LclfYes	11.88	2.65		
TrlOff & LclfNo	11.88	2.68		
InterLisp-10	9.20	1.42		
LM-2			8.54	

Very few programs that I have been associated with
abuse the numeric features of Lisp as much as these test programs.
If you were to give a paper including only these results,
I would protest that this was not typical
of Lisp programs....

— Anonymous, *criticizing my methodology.* (May 11, 1982.)

3.9 Traverse

3.9.1 *The Program*

```
;;; TRAVERSE --  Benchmark that creates and traverses
;;;             a tree structure.
(defstruct node
  (parents ())
  (sons ())
  (sn (snb))
  (entry1 ())
  (entry2 ())
  (entry3 ())
  (entry4 ())
  (entry5 ())
  (entry6 ())
  (mark ()))
(defvar *sn* 0)
(defvar *rand* 21.)
(defvar *count* 0)
(defvar *marker* nil)
(defvar *root*)
(defun snb ()
  (setq *sn* (1+ *sn*)))
(defun seed ()
  (setq *rand* 21.))
(defun traverse-random () (setq *rand* (mod (* *rand* 17.)
                                       251.)))
```

```
(defun traverse-remove (n q)
  (cond ((eq (cdr (car q)) (car q))
         (prog2 () (caar q) (rplaca q ())))
        ((= n 0)
         (prog2 () (caar q)
                (do ((p (car q) (cdr p)))
                    ((eq (cdr p) (car q))
                     (rplaca q
                             (rplacd p (cdr (car q)))))))))
        (t (do ((n n (1- n))
                (q (car q) (cdr q))
                (p (cdr (car q)) (cdr p)))
               ((= n 0) (prog2 () (car q) (rplacd q p)))))))
(defun traverse-select (n q)
  (do ((n n (1- n))
       (q (car q) (cdr q)))
      ((= n 0) (car q))))
(defun add (a q)
  (cond ((null q)
         `(,(let ((x `(,a)))
              (rplacd x x) x)))
        ((null (car q))
         (let ((x `(,a)))
           (rplacd x x)
           (rplaca q x)))
        (t (rplaca q
                   (rplacd (car q) `(,a .,(cdr (car q))))))))
```

```
(defun create-structure (n)
  (let ((a '(,(make-node))))
    (do ((m (1- n) (1- m))
         (p a))
        ((= m 0) (setq a '(,(rplacd p a)))
         (do ((unused a)
              (used (add (traverse-remove 0 a) ()))
              (x) (y))
             ((null (car unused))
              (find-root (traverse-select 0 used) n))
           (setq x (traverse-remove
                     (mod (traverse-random) n)
                     unused))
           (setq y (traverse-select
                     (mod (traverse-random) n)
                     used))
           (add x used)
           (setf (node-sons y) '(,x .,(node-sons y)))
           (setf (node-parents x) '(,y .,(node-parents x))) ))
      (push (make-node) a))))
(defun find-root (node n)
  (do ((n n (1- n)))
      ((= n 0) node)
    (cond ((null (node-parents node))
           (return node))
          (t (setq node (car (node-parents node)))))))
(defun travers (node mark)
  (cond ((eq (node-mark node) mark) ())
        (t (setf (node-mark node) mark)
           (setq *count* (1+ *count*))
           (setf (node-entry1 node) (not (node-entry1 node)))
           (setf (node-entry2 node) (not (node-entry2 node)))
           (setf (node-entry3 node) (not (node-entry3 node)))
           (setf (node-entry4 node) (not (node-entry4 node)))
           (setf (node-entry5 node) (not (node-entry5 node)))
           (setf (node-entry6 node) (not (node-entry6 node)))
           (do ((sons (node-sons node) (cdr sons)))
               ((null sons) ())
             (travers (car sons) mark)))))
(defun traverse (root)
  (let ((*count* 0))
    (travers root (setq *marker* (not *marker*)))
    *count*))
```

```
(defmacro init-traverse()
  (prog2 (setq *root* (create-structure 100.)) ()))
(defmacro run-traverse ()
  (do ((i 50. (1- i)))
      ((= i 0))
    (traverse *root*)
    (traverse *root*)
    (traverse *root*)
    (traverse *root*)
    (traverse *root*)))
;;; to initialize, call:  (init-traverse)
;;; to run traverse, call:  (run-traverse)
```

3.9.2 *Analysis*

Traverse is split into two parts: the initialization and the actual traversal. This benchmarks tries to measure the performance that can be expected from the abstract data structure systems provided by the various Lisp dialects.

The basic idea is to build a directed graph of nodes and then to traverse it. The nodes contain ten slots: one contains backpointers to parents, one contains pointers to sons, one is a serial number (a fixed-point number), one is a 'mark' bit, and six are available for random information.

The initialization phase of the benchmark is building the random graph. For this purpose there is a random number generator provided that operates identically on all 2's complement machines that support at least 8-bit arithmetic. The generator uses the updator

$$n \leftarrow 17n \pmod{251}$$

A detailed discussion of this generator is given in the section describing the Browse benchmark.

Similarly, there is a serial number generator, which uses the global variable *snb*.

CREATE-STRUCTURE is called to produce a 100-node directed graph. First, this program creates 100 nodes without linking them together. The

100 nodes are formed into a circular list; two circular lists are kept—a circular list of used nodes (*used*) and a circular list of unused nodes (*unused*). The program ADD adds items to a circular list, and REMOVE removes the n_{th} item from a circular list and travels around the list more than once if necessary.

In CREATE-STRUCTURE, there is a loop that builds the random graph. This is done by selecting two random numbers, n and m. Let

$$x = \text{unused}_n \quad (\text{mod length(unused)})$$

and

$$y = \text{used}_m \quad (\text{mod length(used)})$$

x is removed from *unused* and it is made a son of y. The loop continues until *unused* is empty.

The graph is directed, and a root is found. All nodes are in the graph, which can be proved by induction. A node is placed in *used* at the start of the loop. This node has neither sons nor parents; it is a single connected component. At any stage of the iteration, if *unused* is empty, we are done and there is one connected component in *used*. If *unused* is not empty, then a node in it is connected to the single connected component in *used*, and the resulting new graph in *used* has one connected component. The induction is complete.

Because directed arcs are added to existing nodes in *used*, the graph has a single root, and a procedure is used to find that root by tracing back along parent arcs. This is not necessary because it is easy to prove that the root must be the node that was first placed in *used*. However, this step adds a little to the runtime of the benchmark.

At this stage, the remainder of the benchmark is to mark the graph, starting at the root. There is a process that traverses the graph. At any node it does one of two things: If that node has already been marked, then the process is done with that node. If the node has not been marked, the process 'flips' the sense of each entry (sets the contents of the entry to NOT of the entry—the entries flip between NIL and T), and for each node in the sons of that node, it traverses that

158

node. The number of nodes visited by the traverser is counted by using a special variable.

The marking is done 250 times to the graph.

The interesting aspect of this benchmark is that it uses DEFSTRUCT in Common Lisp, so that it tests the quality of the abstract data structuring facilities of the Lisp system, as much as anything.

Meter for Snb	
1+'s	100
Total	100

Meter for Remove	
Cdr's	1093372
='s	553818
1−'s	529455
Car's	66207
Eq's	17281
Rplacd's	12231
Rplaca's	100
Total	2272464

Meter for Select	
='s	541492
1−'s	529260
Cdr's	529260
Car's	24464
Total	1624476

Meter for Add	
Car's	36693
Null's	24463
Rplacd's	12232
Rplaca's	12231
Conses	12231
Cdr's	12231
Total	110081

Meter for Create-Structure	
Setf's	24462
RANDOM	24462
ADD	12232
REMOVE	12232
Null's	12232
Car's	12232
SELECT	12232
PARENTS	12231
SONS	12231
Cons's	12331
1−'s	100
='s	100
Rplacd's	1
FIND-ROOT	1
Total	147079

Meter for Travers	
MARK	3083000
Null's	3082750
Cdr's	3057750
Eq's	3058000
TRAVERS	3057750
Car's	3057750
Setf's	175000
1+'s	25000
ENTRY1	25000
ENTRY2	25000
ENTRY3	25000
ENTRY4	25000
ENTRY5	25000
ENTRY6	25000
Total	18747000

Meter for Find-Root	
='s	1
PARENTS	1
Null's	1
1−'s	0
Car's	0
Total	3

3.9.3 *Translation Notes*

In INTERLISP, a DATATYPE is created to represent the nodes in the graph. Here is the INTERLISP code

```
(RPAQQ TRAVERSECOMS
 ((RECORDS NODE)
  (FNS SNB SEED RANDOM TREMOVE TSELECT TADD CREATE-STRUCTURE
   FIND-ROOT TRAVERS TRAVERSE TIMIT)
  (BLOCKS
   (TRAVERSE
    SNB SEED RANDOM TREMOVE TSELECT TADD CREATE-STRUCTURE
    FIND-ROOT TRAVERS TRAVERSE TIMIT-10)
   (ENTRIES TRAVERSE CREATE-STRUCTURE TIMIT-10))
  (VARS (SN 0)
        (RAND 21.0)
        (COUNT 0)
        (MARKER NIL))
  (GLOBALVARS RAND SN MARKER ROOT)
  (PROP GLOBALVAR ROOT)
  (SPECVARS COUNT)))
[DECLARE: EVAL@COMPILE
(DATATYPE NODE ((PARENTS POINTER)
               (SONS POINTER)
               (SN WORD)
               (ENTRY1 FLAG)
               (ENTRY2 FLAG)
               (ENTRY3 FLAG)
               (ENTRY4 FLAG)
               (ENTRY5 FLAG)
               (ENTRY6 FLAG)
               (MARK FLAG))
              SN ,(SNB))
```

```
(/DECLAREDATATYPE
 (QUOTE NODE)
 (QUOTE (POINTER POINTER WORD FLAG FLAG FLAG FLAG
         FLAG FLAG FLAG)))
(DEFINEQ
(SNB
  (LAMBDA NIL
    (SETQ SN (ADD1 SN))))
(SEED
  (LAMBDA NIL
    (SETQ RAND 21)))
(RANDOM
  (LAMBDA NIL
    (SETQ RAND (IMOD (ITIMES RAND 17.0)
                     251))))
(TREMOVE
  (LAMBDA (N Q)
    (COND
      ((EQ (CDR (CAR Q))
           (CAR Q))
        (PROG2 NIL (CAAR Q)
               (RPLACA Q NIL)))
      ((ZEROP N)
        (PROG2 NIL (CAAR Q)
               (bind (P ,(CAR Q)) until (EQ (CDR P)
                                            (CAR Q))
                   do (pop P)
                   finally (RETURN
                             (RPLACA
                              Q
                              (RPLACD
                               P
                               (CDR (CAR Q))))))))
      (T (for N (Q ,(CAR Q))
              (P ,(CDR (CAR Q))) from N by -1
                                 until (ZEROP N)
              do (pop Q)
                 (pop P)
              finally (RETURN (PROG2 NIL (CAR Q)
                                     (RPLACD Q P)))))))))
```

```
(TSELECT
  (LAMBDA (N Q)
    (for N (Q ,(CAR Q)) from N by -1
         until (ZEROP N) do (pop Q)
         finally (RETURN (CAR Q))))))
(TADD
  (LAMBDA (A Q)
    (COND
      ((NULL Q)
        (PROG ((X (LIST A)))
              (RPLACD X X)
              (RETURN (LIST X))))
      ((NULL (CAR Q))
        (PROG ((X (LIST A)))
              (RPLACD X X)
              (RETURN (RPLACA Q X))))
      (T (RPLACA Q (RPLACD (CAR Q)
                           (CONS A (CDR (CAR Q)))))))))))
(CREATE-STRUCTURE
 (LAMBDA (N)
  (PROG ((A (LIST (create NODE))))
   (RETURN
    (for M (P , A) from (SUB1 N) by -1
     until (ZEROP M) do (push A (create NODE))
     finally (PROGN (SETQ A (LIST (RPLACD P A)))
                (RETURN
                 (bind (UNUSED , A)
                       (USED ,(TADD (TREMOVE 0 A)
                                    NIL))
                     X Y
                  until (NULL (CAR UNUSED))
                  do (SETQ X
                       (TREMOVE (IMOD (RANDOM) N)
                                UNUSED))
                     (SETQ Y (TSELECT (IMOD (RANDOM) N)
                                      USED))
                     (TADD X USED)
                     (push (fetch SONS of Y) X)
                     (push (fetch PARENTS of X) Y)
                  finally
                   (RETURN
                    (FIND-ROOT
                     (TSELECT 0 USED) N)))))))))))
```

```
(FIND-ROOT
  (LAMBDA (NODE N)
    (for N from N by -1
         until (ZEROP N)
         do (COND
              ((NULL (fetch PARENTS of NODE))
               (RETURN NODE))
              (T (SETQ NODE
                   (CAR (fetch PARENTS of NODE)))))
         finally (RETURN NODE))))
(TRAVERS
  (LAMBDA (NODE MARK)
    (COND
      ((EQ (fetch MARK of NODE)
           MARK)
        NIL)
      (T (replace MARK of NODE with MARK)
         (SETQ COUNT (ADD1 COUNT))
         (replace ENTRY1 of NODE with
                 (NOT (fetch ENTRY1 of NODE)))
         (replace ENTRY2 of NODE with
                 (NOT (fetch ENTRY2 of NODE)))
         (replace ENTRY3 of NODE with
                 (NOT (fetch ENTRY3 of NODE)))
         (replace ENTRY4 of NODE with
                 (NOT (fetch ENTRY4 of NODE)))
         (replace ENTRY5 of NODE with
                 (NOT (fetch ENTRY5 of NODE)))
         (replace ENTRY6 of NODE with
                 (NOT (fetch ENTRY6 of NODE)))
         (for SONS on (fetch SONS of NODE)
          do (TRAVERS (CAR SONS) MARK))))))
(TRAVERSE
  (LAMBDA (ROOT1)
    (PROG ((COUNT 0))
          (DECLARE (SPECVARS COUNT)
                   (GLOBALVARS MARKER))
          (TRAVERS ROOT1 (SETQ MARKER (NOT MARKER)))
          (RETURN COUNT))))
```

```
(TIMIT
  (LAMBDA NIL
    (TIMEALL (SETQ ROOT (CREATE-STRUCTURE 100)))
    (TIMEALL (FRPTQ 50 (TRAVERSE ROOT)
                       (TRAVERSE ROOT)
                       (TRAVERSE ROOT)
                       (TRAVERSE ROOT)
                       (TRAVERSE ROOT)))))
(TIMIT-10
  (LAMBDA NIL
    (PRINT (TIME (SETQ ROOT (CREATE-STRUCTURE 100)) 1 3))
    (PRINT (TIME (FRPTQ 50 (TRAVERSE ROOT)
                       (TRAVERSE ROOT)
                       (TRAVERSE ROOT)
                       (TRAVERSE ROOT)
                       (TRAVERSE ROOT)) 1 3))))
```

3.9.4 *Raw Data*

Raw Time Traverse Initialization				
Implementation	CPU	GC	Real	Paging
SAIL	6.69	45.14	51.82	
Lambda	18.70			1.20
Lambda (MC)	11.50			0.14
3600	8.62			0.33
3600 + IFU	6.37			0.25
Dandelion	48.00	1.16		
Dolphin	100.00	1.25		
Dorado	20.50	0.49		
S-1			1.93	
PSL-SUN	30.07	0.00		
PSL-20	7.59	0.00		
PSL-3081	1.80	0.00		
PSL-Cray				
PSL-750	35.53	0.00		
PSL-750 (VMS)	31.20	0.00		
PSL-780	15.06	0.00		
PSL-DN300				
PSL-DN600				
PSL-DN160	29.84	0.00		
PSL-HP200	13.54	0.00		
PSL-HP-UX	14.89	0.00		
InterLispVax 780			24.78	
MV4000 CL			96.26	
MV8000 CL			74.39	
MV10000 CL			27.77	
3600 + FPA	6.37			0.25
750 NIL	38.92		39.71	
8600 CL	6.12	0.00		

Raw Time Traverse Initialization				
Implementation	CPU	GC	Real	Paging
780 CL	20.76	0.00		
785 CL	13.10	0.00		
750 CL	35.44	0.00		
730 CL	94.77	0.00		
Perq			46.53	
750 Franz				
TrlOn & LclfYes	32.98	19.30		
TrlOn & LclfNo	35.44	19.72		
TrlOff & LclfYes	33.17	20.75		
TrlOff & LclfNo	51.23	21.03		
780 Franz				
TrlOn & LclfYes	18.47	11.80		
TrlOn & LclfNo	20.42	11.77		
TrlOff & LclfYes	18.70	12.73		
TrlOff & LclfNo	29.61	12.82		
Franz 68000				
TrlOn & LclfYes	43.32	21.17		
TrlOn & LclfNo	44.98	21.10		
TrlOff & LclfYes	55.16	24.52		
TrlOff & LclfNo	70.64	24.48		
InterLisp-10	37.62	6.09		
LM-2			41.23	

Raw Time Traverse				
Implementation	CPU	GC	Real	Paging
SAIL	23.96	0.00	23.96	
Lambda	138.60			0.00
Lambda (MC)	48.40			4.24
3600	49.95			0.00
3600 + IFU	35.34			0.00
Dandelion	181.00	0.00		
Dolphin	299.00	0.00		
Dorado	63.90	0.00		
S-1			30.10	
PSL-SUN	125.00	0.00		
PSL-20	43.88	0.00		
PSL-3081	9.89	0.00		
PSL-Cray				
PSL-750	185.65	0.00		
PSL-750 (VMS)	146.62	0.00		
PSL-780	72.35	0.00		
PSL-DN300				
PSL-DN600				
PSL-DN160	56.16	0.00		
PSL-HP200	108.69	0.00		
PSL-HP-UX	102.36	0.00		
InterLispVax 780			255.76	
MV4000 CL			134.68	
MV8000 CL			90.12	
MV10000 CL			45.86	
3600 + FPA	35.34			0.00
750 NIL	273.25		273.32	
8600 CL	40.65	0.00		

Raw Time Traverse				
Implementation	CPU	GC	Real	Paging
780 CL	161.68	0.00		
785 CL	86.60	0.00		
750 CL	217.21	0.00		
730 CL	804.02	0.00		
Perq			442.70	
750 Franz				
TrlOn & LclfYes	132.62	0.00		
TrlOn & LclfNo	244.01	0.00		
TrlOff & LclfYes	132.60	0.00		
TrlOff & LclfNo	911.20	0.00		
780 Franz				
TrlOn & LclfYes	82.98	0.00		
TrlOn & LclfNo	156.20	0.00		
TrlOff & LclfYes	83.03	0.00		
TrlOff & LclfNo	559.58	0.00		
Franz 68000				
TrlOn & LclfYes	129.12	0.00		
TrlOn & LclfNo	201.98	0.00		
TrlOff & LclfYes	129.25	0.00		
TrlOff & LclfNo	903.48	0.00		
InterLisp-10	85.86	0.00		
LM-2			215.68	

While I was editing UCADR,
I decided to microcode a two-argument NCONC.
With this microcoded NCONC,
the SCCPP benchmark radically improved.

— David L. Andre *talking about an abandoned benchmark.* (August 4, 1982.)

This test seems to suffer from
an incredibly cretinously written NCONC.

— David L. Andre *an earlier remark about NCONC.* (August 4, 1982.)

3.10 Derivative

3.10.1 *The Program*

```
;;; DERIV -- This is the Common Lisp version of a symbolic
;;; derivative benchmark written by Vaughan Pratt.
;;; It uses a simple subset of Lisp and does a lot of
;;; CONSing.
(defun deriv-aux (a) (list '/ (deriv a) a))

(defun deriv (a)
  (cond
    ((atom a)
     (cond ((eq a 'x) 1) (t 0)))
    ((eq (car a) '+)
     (cons '+ (mapcar #'deriv (cdr a))))
    ((eq (car a) '-)
     (cons '- (mapcar #'deriv
                      (cdr a))))
    ((eq (car a) '*)
     (list '*
           a
           (cons '+ (mapcar #'deriv-aux (cdr a)))))
    ((eq (car a) '/)
     (list '-
           (list '/
                 (deriv (cadr a))
                 (caddr a))
           (list '/
                 (cadr a)
                 (list '*
                       (caddr a)
                       (caddr a)
                       (deriv (caddr a))))))
    (t 'error))))
(defun run ()
  (declare (fixnum i))  ;improves the code a little
  (do ((i 0 (1+ i)))
      ((= i 1000.))      ;runs it 5000 times
    (deriv '(+ (* 3 x x) (* a x x) (* b x) 5))
    (deriv '(+ (* 3 x x) (* a x x) (* b x) 5))
    (deriv '(+ (* 3 x x) (* a x x) (* b x) 5))
    (deriv '(+ (* 3 x x) (* a x x) (* b x) 5))
    (deriv '(+ (* 3 x x) (* a x x) (* b x) 5))))

;;; call:  (run)
```

3.10.2 *Analysis*

This benchmark performs a simple symbolic derivative in which the data representation is the usual S-expression representation for functions. The main driving function, DERIV, simply dispatches off a built-in table of operators to a function that knows how to take the derivative of a form that is that operator applied to some subforms. Thus, if one were to take the derivative of

    (TIMES form1 form2)

a special program that knew about how to take derivatives of multiplications would be invoked. This table is simply a large COND whose clauses are sequentially tried. Aside from executing the control structure, the program CONSes a lot because the derivative is constructed as the algorithm proceeds.

The derivative of $3x^2 + ax^2 + bx + 5$ is taken 5000 times with this program. This is done with a loop in which the derivative is taken 5 times. This benchmark is CONS and function-call heavy.

Meter for Der1	
Cons's	120000
DER1	40000
Total	160000

Meter for Deriv	
Cons's	160000
Eq's	95000
DERIV	65000
Car's	50000
Cdr's	20000
Mapcar's	20000
Total	410000

Meter for Run	
='s	1001
1+'s	1000
Total	2001

3.10.3 *Translation Notes*

In every Lisp, this benchmark is very straightforwardly written.

3.10.4 *Raw Data*

Raw Time Deriv				
Implementation	**CPU**	**GC**	**Real**	**Paging**
SAIL	1.81	17.09	30.23	
Lambda	6.40			3.70
Lambda (MC)	3.62			3.80
3600	5.12			1.40
3600 + IFU	3.79			0.99
Dandelion	23.90	52.20		
Dolphin	40.30	39.40		
Dorado	15.70	6.80		
S-1			4.99	
PSL-SUN	13.77	3.99		
PSL-20	5.64	1.23		
PSL-3081	1.06	1.17		
PSL-Cray	1.30	1.16		
PSL-750	15.36	3.87		
PSL-750 (VMS)	20.65	2.66		
PSL-780	8.58	2.10		
PSL-DN300				
PSL-DN600	26.69	5.31		
PSL-DN160	14.11	1.70		
PSL-HP200	14.82	0.00		
PSL-HP-UX	15.66	2.97		
InterLispVax 780			23.10	
MV4000 CL			28.22	
MV8000 CL			19.10	
MV10000 CL			5.60	
3600 + FPA	3.79			0.99
750 NIL	22.69		24.63	
8600 CL	4.27	9.34		

Raw Time Deriv				
Implementation	**CPU**	**GC**	**Real**	**Paging**
780 CL	13.76	26.20		
785 CL	10.30	13.70		
750 CL	24.50	49.63		
730 CL	62.54	116.96		
Perq			64.45	
750 Franz				
TrlOn & LclfYes	13.86	22.20		
TrlOn & LclfNo				
TrlOff & LclfYes				
TrlOff & LclfNo				
780 Franz				
TrlOn & LclfYes	11.00	16.00		
TrlOn & LclfNo				
TrlOff & LclfYes	8.29	16.90		
TrlOff & LclfNo				
Franz 68000				
TrlOn & LclfYes	14.37	7.93		
TrlOn & LclfNo	17.03	8.04		
TrlOff & LclfYes	18.97	10.60		
TrlOff & LclfNo	45.80	10.70		
InterLisp-10	40.21	7.74		
LM-2			23.90	

174

*The benchmark should solve a problem
whose computer solution is frequently
called for.
The programming style used
should be one that helps make programs
more writable, readable, maintainable, and portable.
The benchmark should implement
an efficient solution to the problem it solves.*

— Vaughan Pratt *philosophizing about benchmarks.* (October 20, 1981.)

3.11 Data-Driven Derivative

3.11.1 *The Program*

```
;;; DDERIV -- The Common Lisp version of a
;;; symbolic derivative benchmark, written by Vaughan Pratt.
;;;
;;; This benchmark is a variant of the simple symbolic
;;; derivative program (DERIV). The main change is that it is
;;; 'table-driven.' Instead of using a large COND that branches
;;; on the CAR of the expression, this program finds the code
;;; that will take the derivative on the property list of the
;;; atom in the CAR position. So, when the expression is (+
;;; <rest>), the code stored under the atom '+ with indicator
;;; DERIV will take <rest> and return the derivative for '+. The
;;; way that MacLisp does this is with the special form: (DEFUN
;;; (FOO BAR) ...). This is exactly like DEFUN with an atomic
;;; name in that it expects an argument list and the compiler
;;; compiles code, but the name of the function with that code
;;; is stored on the property list of FOO under the indicator
;;; BAR, in this case.
(defun dderiv-aux (a)
  (list '/ (dderiv a) a))
(defun +dderiv (a)
  (cons '+ (mapcar 'dderiv a)))
(defun -dderiv (a)
  (cons '- (mapcar 'dderiv a)))
(defun *dderiv (a)
  (list '* (cons '* a)
        (cons '+ (mapcar 'dderiv-aux a))))
(defun /dderiv (a)
  (list '-
        (list '/
              (dderiv (car a))
              (cadr a))
        (list '/
              (car a)
              (list '*
                    (cadr a)
                    (cadr a)
                    (dderiv (cadr a))))))
(mapc
 #'(lambda (op fun)
     (setf
      (get op 'dderiv)
      (symbol-function fun)))
 '((+ +dderiv)(- -dderiv)(* *dderiv)(/ /dderiv)))
```

```
(defun dderiv (a)
  (cond
    ((atom a)
     (cond ((eq a 'x) 1) (t 0)))
    (t (let ((dderiv (get (car a) 'dderiv)))
         (cond (dderiv (funcall dderiv (cdr a)))
               (t 'error))))))
(defun run ()
  (declare (fixnum i))
  (do ((i 0 (1+ i)))
      ((= i 1000.))
    (dderiv '(+ (* 3 x x) (* a x x) (* b x) 5))
    (dderiv '(+ (* 3 x x) (* a x x) (* b x) 5))
    (dderiv '(+ (* 3 x x) (* a x x) (* b x) 5))
    (dderiv '(+ (* 3 x x) (* a x x) (* b x) 5))
    (dderiv '(+ (* 3 x x) (* a x x) (* b x) 5))))

call: (run)
```

3.11.2 *Analysis*

This benchmark is exactly like DERIV except that functions taking derivatives of specific operators are located on the property list of the operator rather than buried in a piece of code. So, instead of a COND clause to do the dispatch, a GET and a FUNCALL are used. This is referred to as the 'data driven' version of DERIV.

Meter for Dderiv-Aux	
Conses	120000
DDERIV-AUX	40000
Total	160000

Meter for +Dderiv	
Cons's	50000
Mapcar's	5000
+DDERIV	5000
Total	60000

Meter for *Dderiv	
Cons's	180000
Mapcar's	15000
*DDERIV	15000
Total	210000

Meter for −Dderiv	
Mapcars	0
Conses	0
−DDERIV	0
Total	0

Meter for /Dderiv	
Car's	0
Cons's	0
/DDERIV	0
Total	0

Meter for Dderiv	
DERIV	65000
Eq's	45000
Cdr's	20000
Funcall's	20000
Car's	20000
Get's	20000
Total	190000

3.11.3 *Translation Notes*

Some Lisp dialects do not support FUNCALL and need to use APPLY instead. In this case, an extra CONS per FUNCALL is performed.

3.11.4 *Raw Data*

Raw Time Dderiv				
Implementation	**CPU**	**GC**	**Real**	**Paging**
SAIL	2.83	18.28	38.62	
Lambda	7.10			4.10
Lambda (MC)	5.92			3.10
3600	5.24			1.51
3600 + IFU	3.89			1.06
Dandelion	33.30	59.50		
Dolphin	56.60	43.60		
Dorado	17.70	6.80		
S-1			3.27	
PSL-SUN	15.67	4.01		
PSL-20	6.00	2.07		
PSL-3081	1.22	1.11		
PSL-Cray	1.44	1.16		
PSL-750	19.44	3.89		
PSL-750 (VMS)	24.51	2.41		
PSL-780	10.23	2.10		
PSL-DN300	28.95	6.24		
PSL-DN600	27.29	5.22		
PSL-DN160	14.97	1.79		
PSL-HP200	16.03	0.00		
PSL-HP-UX	16.78	2.90		
InterLispVax 780			29.96	
MV4000 CL			33.63	
MV8000 CL			23.96	
MV10000 CL			8.11	
3600 + FPA	3.89			1.06
750 NIL	26.90		29.00	
8600 CL	6.58	9.85		

Raw Time Dderiv				
Implementation	**CPU**	**GC**	**Real**	**Paging**
780 CL	19.00	21.60		
785 CL	12.40	13.90		
750 CL	32.90	45.80		
730 CL				
Perq			72.52	
750 Franz				
TrlOn & LclfYes				
TrlOn & LclfNo				
TrlOff & LclfYes				
TrlOff & LclfNo				
780 Franz				
TrlOn & LclfYes	9.79	17.58		
TrlOn & LclfNo				
TrlOff & LclfYes	13.52	17.28		
TrlOff & LclfNo				
Franz 68000				
TrlOn & LclfYes	16.95	92.50		
TrlOn & LclfNo	20.53	96.27		
TrlOff & LclfYes	21.62	92.80		
TrlOff & LclfNo	50.88	96.48		
InterLisp-10	28.06	9.12		
LM-2			23.67	

180

> *I find it rather startling*
> *that increasing memory size by 33%*
> *adds 300% in speed.*

— Peter Friedland *discussing a performance experiment.* (November 10, 1982.)

3.12 Another Data-Driven Derivative

3.12.1 *The Program*

The following program is a variant of DDERIV. It optimizes FUNCALL by
using a FUNCALL-like function that assumes it is being handed compiled code.
Because this is mainly a MacLisp optimization, the program is shown in MacLisp:

```
(declare (mapex t))

(defun der1 (a) (list 'quotient (deriv a) a))
(defun (plus deriv deriv) (a)
       (cons 'plus (mapcar 'deriv a)))
(defun (difference deriv deriv) (a)
       (cons 'difference (mapcar 'deriv
                                      a)))
(defun (times deriv deriv) (a)
        (list 'times (cons 'times a)
              (cons 'plus (mapcar 'der1 a))))
(defun (quotient deriv deriv) (a)
       (list 'difference
             (list 'quotient
                   (deriv (car a))
                   (cadr a))
             (list 'quotient
                   (car a)
                   (list 'times
                         (cadr a)
                         (cadr a)
                         (deriv (cadr a)))))))
 (defun deriv (a)
        (cond
         ((atom a)
          (cond ((eq a 'x) 1) (t 0)))
         (t (let ((deriv (get (car a) 'deriv)))
                 (cond (deriv (subrcall t deriv (cdr a)))
                       (t 'error))))))
(defun run ()
 (declare (fixnum i))
 (do ((i 0 (1+ i)))
     ((= i 1000.))
     (deriv '(plus (times 3 x x) (times a x x) (times b x) 5))
     (deriv '(plus (times 3 x x) (times a x x) (times b x) 5))
     (deriv '(plus (times 3 x x) (times a x x) (times b x) 5))
     (deriv '(plus (times 3 x x) (times a x x) (times b x) 5))
     (deriv '(plus (times 3 x x) (times a x x) (times b x) 5))))
```

182

3.12.2 *Analysis*

This benchmark is exactly like DDERIV, but it uses the fact that the derivative-taking functions are compiled. That is, in MacLisp, FUNCALL internally tests whether the function it has been handed as its first argument is compiled or interpreted and does different things in each case; it also checks whether it has been handed a LAMBDA expression.

In this MacLisp-specific benchmark, SUBRCALL is used in place of FUNCALL. SUBRCALL avoids the checks mentioned.

Meter for Der1	
Cons's	120000
DER1	40000
Total	160000

Meter for Plus-Deriv	
Cons's	50000
Mapcar's	5000
PLUS-DERIV	5000
Total	60000

Meter for Times-Deriv	
Cons's	300000
Mapcar's	15000
TIMES-DERIV	15000
Total	330000

Meter for Difference-Deriv	
Mapcar's	0
Cons's	0
DIFFERENCE-DERIV	0
Total	0

Meter for Quotient-Deriv	
Car's	0
Cons's	0
QUOTIENT-DERIV	0
Total	0

Meter for Deriv	
DERIV	65000
Eq's	45000
Get's	40000
Cdr's	20000
SUBRcall's	20000
Car's	20000
Total	210000

3.12.3 *Translation Notes*

Only NIL, MacLisp, and ZetaLisp on the Symbolics LM-2 machine report times for this benchmark.

3.12.4 *Raw Data*

Raw Time Fdderiv				
Implementation	CPU	GC	Real	Paging
SAIL	2.15	18.28	34.62	
Lambda				
Lambda (MC)				
3600				
3600 + IFU				
Dandelion				
Dolphin				
Dorado				
S-1				
PSL-SUN				
PSL-20				
PSL-3081				
PSL-Cray				
PSL-750				
PSL-750 (VMS)				
PSL-780				
PSL-DN300				
PSL-DN600				
PSL-DN160				
PSL-HP200				
PSL-HP-UX				
InterLispVax 780				
MV4000 CL				
MV8000 CL				
MV10000 CL				
3600 + FPA				
750 NIL	26.45		28.29	
8600 CL				

Raw Time Fdderiv				
Implementation	CPU	GC	Real	Paging
780 CL				
785 CL				
750 CL				
730 CL				
Perq				
750 Franz				
TrlOn & LclfYes				
TrlOn & LclfNo				
TrlOff & LclfYes				
TrlOff & LclfNo				
780 Franz				
TrlOn & LclfYes				
TrlOn & LclfNo				
TrlOff & LclfYes				
TrlOff & LclfNo				
Franz 68000				
TrlOn & LclfYes				
TrlOn & LclfNo				
TrlOff & LclfYes				
TrlOff & LclfNo				
InterLisp-10				
LM-2			25.20	

The point is that
we are concerned about what will happen when real users
use the thing for program development,
not what happens when the implementors
optimize performance.

— Charles Hedrick *philosophizing on benchmarking.* (May 30, 1983.)

3.13 Division by 2

3.13.1 *The Program*

```
;;; DIV2 -- Benchmark that divides by 2 using lists of n NIL's.
;;; This file contains a recursive as well as an iterative test.
(defun create-n (n)
  (do ((n n (1- n))
       (a () (push () a)))
      ((= n 0) a)))

(defvar ll (create-n 200.))
(defun iterative-div2 (l)
  (do ((l l (cddr l))
       (a () (push (car l) a)))
      ((null l) a)))
(defun recursive-div2 (l)
  (cond ((null l) ())
        (t (cons (car l) (recursive-div2 (cddr l))))))
(defun test-1 (l)
  (do ((i 300. (1- i)))
      ((= i 0))
    (iterative-div2 l)
    (iterative-div2 l)
    (iterative-div2 l)
    (iterative-div2 l)))
(defun test-2 (l)
  (do ((i 300. (1- i)))
      ((= i 0))
    (recursive-div2 l)
    (recursive-div2 l)
    (recursive-div2 l)
    (recursive-div2 l)))
    for the iterative test call: (test-1 ll)
    for the recursive test call: (test-2 ll)
```

3.13.2 *Analysis*

In this benchmark, numbers are represented in unary form: n is represented as a list of n ()'s. The benchmark divides numbers in this representation by 2 by returning a list of every other () in the original list. There are two versions of this program: One is the simple recursive definition, and the other is an iterative definition. The test is to divide 200 by 2 1200 times for each version.

As is apparent from the metering, these benchmarks simply CONS, take CAR and CDR, and do some function calling or GO'ing.

These benchmarks were proposed by a computer scientist at Bell Laboratories. He thought that they best epitomized what his programs did—function-calls, CONS, CAR, CDR, and iteration. He wanted to find out how Franz Lisp on a Vax 11/780 did vis-à-vis other implementations. He was surprised to find out that the iterative version ran slower than the recursive one on the Vax 11/780. After some investigation, we found out that the iterative version had a number of sequential MOVL instructions in a row—more than the recursive version. At that time (1982), the Vax 11/780 did very poorly on MOVL's, and by counting cycle times we were able to justify the results we saw. Since then, the problem has been corrected on Vaxes and possibly in Franz itself.

Meter for Iterative Div2		Meter for Recursive Div2	
Cdr's	240000	Cdr's	240000
Null's	121200	Null's	121200
Cons's	120200	RECURSIVE-DIV2	121200
Car's	120000	Cons's	120200
ITERATIVE-DIV2	1200	Car's	120000
='s	201	1−'s	200
1−'s	200	='s	201
CREATE-N	1	CREATE-N	1
Total	603002	Total	723002

3.13.3 *Translation Notes*

The INTERLISP versions are straightforward:

```
(DEFINEQ
(DIV2
  (LAMBDA (l)
    (for L A on l by (CDDR L) do (push A (CAR L))
     finally (RETURN A))))

(DV2
  (LAMBDA (l)
    (if (NULL l)
        then NIL
      else (CONS (CAR l)
                 (DV2 (CDDR l)))))))
```

3.13.4 *Raw Data*

Raw Time Iterative Div2				
Implementation	CPU	GC	Real	Paging
SAIL	0.84	8.45	17.25	
Lambda	3.80			3.60
Lambda (MC)	2.90			3.00
3600	1.85			1.04
3600 + IFU	1.51			0.71
Dandelion	23.80	8.50		
Dolphin	19.90	16.70		
Dorado	3.43	8.54		
S-1			0.82	
PSL-SUN	6.95	0.00		
PSL-20	2.30	0.00		
PSL-3081	0.45	0.00		
PSL-Cray	0.57	0.00		
PSL-750	8.02	2.09		
PSL-750 (VMS)	9.98	0.00		
PSL-780	3.80	1.09		
PSL-DN300				
PSL-DN600	13.20	2.62		
PSL-DN160	6.60	0.88		
PSL-HP200	6.34	0.00		
PSL-HP-UX	6.58	0.00		
InterLispVax 780			3.76	
MV4000 CL			8.83	
MV8000 CL			6.54	
MV10000 CL			2.86	
3600 + FPA	1.85			1.04
750 NIL	9.44		9.94	
8600 CL	1.65	0.00		

Raw Time Iterative Div2				
Implementation	CPU	GC	Real	Paging
780 CL	5.00	0.00		
785 CL	3.20	0.00		
750 CL	14.32	24.85		
730 CL	18.21	0.00		
Perq			27.30	
750 Franz				
TrlOn & LclfYes	5.50	20.22		
TrlOn & LclfNo	5.37	20.47		
TrlOff & LclfYes	5.57	21.18		
TrlOff & LclfNo	5.60	21.28		
780 Franz				
TrlOn & LclfYes	3.35	16.83		
TrlOn & LclfNo	3.20	16.77		
TrlOff & LclfYes	3.33	16.70		
TrlOff & LclfNo	3.45	16.75		
Franz 68000				
TrlOn & LclfYes	6.52	38.15		
TrlOn & LclfNo	6.43	38.15		
TrlOff & LclfYes	6.47	38.37		
TrlOff & LclfNo	6.75	38.16		
InterLisp-10	131.85	5.02		
LM-2			8.63	

Raw Time Recursive Div2				
Implementation	CPU	GC	Real	Paging
SAIL	1.28	8.90	18.08	
Lambda	5.60			3.50
Lambda (MC)	2.80			3.30
3600	2.89			1.03
3600 + IFU	2.50			0.71
Dandelion	24.80	8.50		
Dolphin	22.40	17.30		
Dorado	4.08	8.66		
S-1			1.49	
PSL-SUN	6.42	0.00		
PSL-20	2.34	0.00		
PSL-3081	0.42	0.00		
PSL-Cray	0.60	0.00		
PSL-750	7.29	2.78		
PSL-750 (VMS)	10.03	2.78		
PSL-780	3.75	1.06		
PSL-DN300				
PSL-DN600	6.70	2.63		
PSL-DN160	3.26	0.88		
PSL-HP200	5.87	0.00		
PSL-HP-UX	5.95	0.00		
InterLispVax 780			8.44	
MV4000 CL			13.14	
MV8000 CL			8.91	
MV10000 CL			4.48	
3600 + FPA	2.89			1.03
750 NIL	14.70		15.15	
8600 CL	2.52	4.61		

Raw Time Recursive Div2				
Implementation	CPU	GC	Real	Paging
780 CL	9.84	12.85		
785 CL	5.38	8.91		
750 CL	9.07	0.00		
730 CL	43.89	56.48		
Perq			32.92	
750 Franz				
TrlOn & LclfYes	5.75	20.53		
TrlOn & LclfNo	11.30	20.58		
TrlOff & LclfYes	5.57	21.47		
TrlOff & LclfNo	40.42	21.32		
780 Franz				
TrlOn & LclfYes	3.55	16.78		
TrlOn & LclfNo	7.68	16.97		
TrlOff & LclfYes	3.47	16.75		
TrlOff & LclfNo	28.88	17.17		
Franz 68000				
TrlOn & LclfYes	6.93	38.50		
TrlOn & LclfNo	9.82	38.71		
TrlOff & LclfYes	6.92	38.53		
TrlOff & LclfNo	38.94	38.98		
InterLisp-10	68.20	4.95		
LM-2			12.38	

192

*If naive users write cruddy code,
the compiler should fix it up for them, yes?
I'd say that most Stanford PhD's in Computer Science
qualify as 'naive users.'*

— Anonymous Implementor Working for a Major
Lisp Vendor *waxing cynical.* (July 18, 1983.)

3.14 FFT

3.14.1 *The Program*

```
;;; FFT -- This is an FFT benchmark written by Harry Barrow.
;;; It tests a variety of floating point operations,
;;; including array references.
(defvar re (make-array
            1025.
            :element-type 'single-float
            :initial-element 0.0))
(defvar im (make-array
            1025.
            :element-type 'single-float
            :initial-element 0.0))
(defun fft (areal aimag)
 ;;; fast fourier transform
 ;;; areal = real part
 ;;; aimag = imaginary part
  (prog
    (ar ai i j k m n le le1 ip nv2 nm1 ur ui wr wi tr ti)
    ;;; initialize
    (setq ar areal
          ai aimag   n (array-dimension ar 0)
          n (1- n)   nv2 (floor n 2)
          ;;; compute m = log(n)
          nm1 (1- n) m 0
          i 1)
 11 (cond ((< i n) (setq m (1+ m) i (+ i i)) (go 11)))
    (cond ((not (equal n (expt 2 m)))
           (princ "error ... array size not a power of two.")
           (read) (return (terpri))))
    ;;; interchange elements in bit-reversed order
    (setq j 1 i 1)
 13 (cond ((< i j)
           (setq tr (aref ar j) ti (aref ai j))
           (setf (aref ar j) (aref ar i))
           (setf (aref ai j) (aref ai i))
           (setf (aref ar i) tr)
           (setf (aref ai i) ti)))
    (setq k nv2)
```

```
16 (cond ((< k j)
          (setq j (- j k) k (/ k 2))
          (go 16)))
   (setq j (+ j k)
         i (1+ i))
   (cond ((< i n)
          (go 13)))
   ;;; loop thru stages
   (do ((l 1 (1+ l)))
       ((> l m))
       (setq le (expt 2 l)
             le1 (floor le 2) ur 1.0
             ui 0.                wr (cos (/ pi (float le1)))
             wi (sin (/ pi (float le1))))
       ;;; loop thru butterflies
       (do ((j 1 (1+ j)))
           ((> j le1))
           ;;; do a butterfly
           (do ((i j (+ i le)))
               ((> i n))
               (setq ip (+ i le1)
                     tr (- (* (aref ar ip) ur)
                           (* (aref ai ip) ui))
                     ti (+ (* (aref ar ip) ui)
                           (* (aref ai ip) ur)))
               (setf (aref ar ip) (- (aref ar i) tr))
               (setf (aref ai ip) (- (aref ai i) ti))
               (setf (aref ar i) (+ (aref ar i) tr))
               (setf (aref ai i) (+ (aref ai i) ti)))
       (setq tr (- (* ur wr) (* ui wi))
             ti (+ (* ur wi) (* ui wr))
             ur tr ui ti))
   (return t)))
;;; the timer, which does 10 calls on fft
(defmacro fft-bench ()
  '(do ((ntimes 0 (1+ ntimes)))
      ((= ntimes 10.))
    (fft re im)))
;;; call:  (fft-bench)
```

3.14.2 *Analysis*

This is a 1024-point complex FFT written by Harry Barrow. As can be seen, the programming style is FORTRAN-like. The data is all 0.0's.

Meter for FFT	
Flonum Array Hacking	2087680
Floating *'s	245720
Flonum Array Accesses	224640
Flonum Array Stores	224640
Floating +'s	163830
Floating −'s	163830
>'s	71870
<'s	40930
1+'s	20660
Integer /'s	10240
FLOAT's	200
Floating /'s	200
Exponentiation's	110
SIN	100
COS	100
1−'s	20
Get's	20
Return's	10
Equal's	10
Total	3254810

3.14.3 *Translation Notes*

The INTERLISP code presented uses a Common Lisp array package written
by Jonl White. Common Lisp arrays as implemented by this package are faster
than the standard INTERLISP arrays.

```
(RPAQQ FFTCOMS
       ((FILES (SYSLOAD FROM LISPUSERS)
               CMLARRAY)
        (FNS FFT)
        (VARS (RE (MAKEARRAY 1025 (QUOTE INITIALELEMENT)
                             0.0))
              (IM (MAKEARRAY 1025 (QUOTE INITIALELEMENT)
                             0.0)))
        (MACROS IEXPT)))
(DEFINEQ
 (FFT
  (LAMBDA (AREAL AIMAG)
    (PROG (AR AI PI I J K M N LE LE1 IP NV2
           NM1 UR UI WR WI TR TI)
          (SETQ AR AREAL)
          (SETQ AI AIMAG)
          (SETQ PI 3.141593)
          (SETQ N (ARRAYDIMENSION AR 0))
          (add N -1)
          (SETQ NV2 (LRSH N 1))
          (SETQ NM1 (SUB1 N))
          (SETQ M 0)
          (SETQ I 1)
      L1  (until (NOT (ILESSP I N))
              do (* Compute M = log (N))
                 (add M 1)
                 (add I I))
```

```
        (if (NOT (IEQP N (IEXPT 2 M)))
            then
             (PRINC
              "Error ... array size not a power of two.")
             (READ)
             (RETURN (TERPRI)))
        (SETQ J 1)  (* Interchange elements)
        (SETQ I 1)  (* in bit-reversed order)
L3   (repeatuntil (NOT (ILESSP I N))
        do (if (ILESSP I J)
               then (SETQ TR (PAREF AR J))
                    (SETQ TI (PAREF AI J))
                    (PASET (PAREF AR I)
                           AR J)
                    (PASET (PAREF AI I)
                           AI J)
                    (PASET TR AR I)
                    (PASET TI AI I))
           (SETQ K NV2)
           L6
           (until (NOT (ILESSP K J))
              do (SETQ J (IDIFFERENCE J K))
                 (SETQ K (LRSH K 1)))
           (SETQ J (IPLUS J K))
           (add I 1))
        (for L to M
          do  (* Loop thru stages)
             (SETQ LE (IEXPT 2 L))
             (SETQ LE1 (LRSH LE 1))
             (SETQ UR 1.0)
             (SETQ UI 0.0)
             (SETQ WR (COS (FQUOTIENT PI (FLOAT LE1))))
             (SETQ WI (SIN (FQUOTIENT PI (FLOAT LE1))))
```

```
                          (for J to LE1
                           do   (* Loop thru butterflies)
                              (for I from J by LE until (IGREATERP I N)
                                do (* Do a butterfly)
                                    (SETQ IP (IPLUS I LE1))
                                    (SETQ TR
                                          (FDIFFERENCE
                                             (FTIMES (PAREF AR IP)
                                                     UR)
                                             (FTIMES (PAREF AI IP)
                                                     UI)))
                                    (SETQ TI
                                          (FPLUS
                                             (FTIMES (PAREF AR IP)
                                                     UI)
                                                (FTIMES (PAREF AI IP)
                                                        UR)))
                                    (PASET (FDIFFERENCE (PAREF AR I)
                                                        TR)
                                           AR IP)
                                    (PASET (FDIFFERENCE (PAREF AI I)
                                                        TI)
                                           AI IP)
                                    (PASET (FPLUS (PAREF AR I)
                                                  TR)
                                           AR I)
                                    (PASET (FPLUS (PAREF AI I)
                                                  TI)
                                           AI I))
                               (SETQ TR (FDIFFERENCE (FTIMES UR WR)
                                                     (FTIMES UI WI)))
                               (SETQ TI (FPLUS (FTIMES UR WI)
                                               (FTIMES UI WR)))
                               (SETQ UR TR)
                               (SETQ UI TI)))
                 (RETURN T))))
      )
      (RPAQ RE (MAKEARRAY 1025 (QUOTE INITIALELEMENT)
                          0.0))
      (RPAQ IM (MAKEARRAY 1025 (QUOTE INITIALELEMENT)
                          0.0))
```

```
(DECLARE: EVAL@COMPILE
(PUTPROPS IEXPT MACRO (X
  (PROG ((N (CAR (CONSTANTEXPRESSIONP (CAR X))))
         (E (CADR X)))
        (RETURN (if (AND (FIXP N)
                         (POWEROFTWOP N))
                    then (if (NEQ 2 N)
                           then
                             (SETQ
                               E
                               (BQUOTE
                                 (ITIMES
                                   ,(SUB1 (INTEGERLENGTH N))
                                   ,E))))
                         (BQUOTE (MASK.1'S , E 1))
                    else (BQUOTE
                           (EXPT (IPLUS O , (CAR X))
                                 (IPLUS O , (CADR X)))))))))))
```

3.14.4 *Raw Data*

Raw Time FFT				
Implementation	CPU	GC	Real	Paging
SAIL	4.00	2.91	9.38	
Lambda	15.90			0.07
Lambda (MC)	13.90			0.23
3600	4.75			0.01
3600 + IFU	3.87			0.03
Dandelion	44.20	10.10		
Dolphin	13.20	21.70		
Dorado	1.57	3.03		
S-1			1.44	
PSL-SUN	139.12	27.89		
PSL-20	35.44	10.76		
PSL-3081	7.30	4.02		
PSL-Cray				
PSL-750	141.71	28.08		
PSL-750 (VMS)	127.82	13.59		
PSL-780	60.55	13.44		
PSL-DN300				
PSL-DN600				
PSL-DN160				
PSL-HP200	132.94	8.58		
PSL-HP-UX	131.10	12.29		
InterLispVax 780			22.79	
MV4000 CL			159.10	
MV8000 CL			124.73	
MV10000 CL			62.78	
3600 + FPA	3.87			0.03
750 NIL	35.59		38.17	
8600 CL	9.08	15.65		

Raw Time FFT				
Implementation	CPU	GC	Real	Paging
780 CL	32.69	35.56		
785 CL	24.40	29.00		
750 CL	131.59	101.84		
730 CL	293.46	240.56		
Perq			89.00	
750 Franz TrlOn & LclfYes TrlOn & LclfNo TrlOff & LclfYes TrlOff & LclfNo				
780 Franz TrlOn & LclfYes TrlOn & LclfNo TrlOff & LclfYes TrlOff & LclfNo				
Franz 68000 TrlOn & LclfYes TrlOn & LclfNo TrlOff & LclfYes TrlOff & LclfNo				
InterLisp-10	12.60	0.00		
LM-2			39.07	

202

This is not to say Franz's compiler could not be
hacked to do fast arithmetic.
We offered to take money from <a company> and other
places to support a Franz numeric-compiler project.
They did not respond.

— Richard J. Fateman *talking about the FFT benchmark.* (July 7, 1982.)

3.15 Puzzle

3.15.1 *The Program*

```
;;; PUZZLE -- Forest Baskett's Puzzle benchmark,
;;; originally written in Pascal.
(eval-when (compile load eval)
  (defconstant size 511.)
  (defconstant classmax 3.)
  (defconstant typemax 12.))
(defvar *iii* 0)
(defvar *kount* 0)
(defvar *d* 8.)
(defvar piececount
        (make-array (1+ classmax) :initial-element 0))
(defvar class
        (make-array (1+ typemax) :initial-element 0))
(defvar piecemax
        (make-array (1+ typemax) :initial-element 0))
(defvar puzzle (make-array (1+ size)))
(defvar p (make-array (list (1+ typemax) (1+ size))))
(defun fit (i j)
  (let ((end (aref piecemax i)))
    (do ((k 0 (1+ k)))
        ((> k end) t)
      (cond ((aref p i k)
             (cond ((aref puzzle (+ j k))
                    (return nil))))))))
```

```
(defun place (i j)
  (let ((end (aref piecemax i)))
    (do ((k 0 (1+ k)))
        ((> k end))
      (cond ((aref p i k)
             (setf (aref puzzle (+ j k)) t))))
    (setf (aref piececount (aref class i))
          (- (aref piececount (aref class i)) 1))
    (do ((k j (1+ k)))
        ((> k size)
         (terpri)
         (princ "Puzzle filled")
         0)
      (cond ((not (aref puzzle k))
             (return k))))))
(defun puzzle-remove (i j)
  (let ((end (aref piecemax i)))
    (do ((k 0 (1+ k)))
        ((> k end))
      (cond ((aref p i k)
             (setf (aref puzzle (+ j k)) nil))))
    (setf (aref piececount (aref class i))
          (+ (aref piececount (aref class i)) 1))))
(defun trial (j)
  (let ((k 0))
    (do ((i 0 (1+ i)))
        ((> i typemax) (setq *kount* (1+ *kount*))   nil)
      (cond
        ((not
          (= (aref piececount (aref class i)) 0))
         (cond
           ((fit i j)
            (setq k (place i j))
            (cond
              ((or (trial k)
                   (= k 0))
               (format
                t
                "~%Piece ~4D at ~4D." (+ i 1) (+ k 1))
               (setq *kount* (+ *kount* 1))
               (return t))
              (t (puzzle-remove i j)))))))))))
```

```
(defun definepiece (iclass ii jj kk)
  (let ((index 0))
    (do ((i 0 (1+ i)))
        ((> i ii))
      (do ((j 0 (1+ j)))
          ((> j jj))
        (do ((k 0 (1+ k)))
            ((> k kk))
          (setq index  (+ i (* *d* (+ j (* *d* k)))))
          (setf (aref p *iii* index)  t))))
    (setf (aref class *iii*) iclass)
    (setf (aref piecemax *iii*) index)
    (cond ((not (= *iii* typemax))
           (setq *iii* (+ *iii* 1))))))
(defun start ()
  (do ((m 0 (1+ m)))
      ((> m size))
    (setf (aref puzzle m) t))
  (do ((i 1 (1+ i)))
      ((> i 5))
    (do ((j 1 (1+ j)))
        ((> j 5))
      (do ((k 1 (1+ k)))
          ((> k 5))
        (setf
         (aref puzzle (+ i (* *d* (+ j (* *d* k)))))
         nil))))
  (do ((i 0 (1+ i)))
      ((> i typemax))
    (do ((m 0 (1+ m)))
        ((> m size))
      (setf (aref p i m)  nil)))
  (setq *iii* 0)
  (definePiece 0 3 1 0)
  (definePiece 0 1 0 3)
  (definePiece 0 0 3 1)
  (definePiece 0 1 3 0)
  (definePiece 0 3 0 1)
  (definePiece 0 0 1 3)
  (definePiece 1 2 0 0)
  (definePiece 1 0 2 0)
  (definePiece 1 0 0 2)
  (definePiece 2 1 1 0)
```

```
(definePiece 2 1 0 1)
(definePiece 2 0 1 1)
(definePiece 3 1 1 1)
(setf (aref pieceCount 0) 13.)
(setf (aref pieceCount 1) 3)
(setf (aref pieceCount 2) 1)
(setf (aref pieceCount 3) 1)
(let ((m (+ 1 (* *d* (+ 1 *d*))))
      (n 0)(*kount* 0))
  (cond ((fit 0 m) (setq n (place 0 m)))
        (t (format t "~%Error.")))
  (cond ((trial n)
         (format t "~%Success in ~4D trials." *kount*))
        (t (format t "~%Failure.")))))
;;; call: (start)
```

3.15.2 *Analysis*

Puzzle is a benchmark written by Forest Baskett. It solves a search problem that is a block-packing puzzle invented by John Conway. Given a 5x5x5 cube and some pieces of various sizes, find a packing of those pieces into the cube. There are four types of pieces: a) 13 4x2x1 pieces, b) 3 3x1x1 pieces, c) 1 2x2x1 piece, and d) 1 2x2x2 piece.

In Conway's original conception of the puzzle, there is an insight that allows it to be solved easily by hand; without this insight, it is fairly difficult. Solutions only exist for two positions of the small 2x2x2 cube, and once this cube is placed, the 2x2x1 piece is uniquely placed.

The puzzle benchmark program does not take advantage of these insights, but it does place one of the 4x2x1 pieces in the corner at the outset. There are eight corners in the 5x5x5 cube and only five other pieces, so three 4x2x1 pieces occupy corner positions.

There are five arrays used by the benchmark. PUZZLE is a one-dimensional array that represents the 5x5x5 cube. This one-dimensional array is used rather than a three-dimensional array, and the three-dimensional to one-dimensional array indexing arithmetic is performed explicitly.

P is a two-dimensional array that stores the piece patterns. The first dimension represents pieces, and the second dimension locates filled-in parts of the piece.

Suppose we want to place piece i in PUZZLE at point j. Then for $0 \le k \le l(i)$ if (P i k) contains TRUE, then (PUZZLE (+ j k)) is filled in. $l(i)$ is a maximum index for the second component of P for each piece, and this is a function of i. The one-dimensional array PIECEMAX represents that function.

The type of piece that is stored in (P i *) is stored in the one-dimensional array CLASS. And the number of pieces of type i is stored in the one-dimensional array PIECECOUNT. (PIECECOUNT i) is the number of pieces of type i left to fit.

The basic strategy is to do a depth-first search by placing a piece in PUZZLE and trying to solve the subproblem of filling the rest of PUZZLE with the rest of the pieces. To backtrack, the pieces are removed from PUZZLE using the inverse operation to placing the piece.

The various functions in the benchmark will now be explained. FIT takes a piece and an origin in PUZZLE, and it returns TRUE if and only if the piece can be placed at that point in PUZZLE.

PLACE places a piece at a certain point in PUZZLE. If PUZZLE is not filled after that piece has been placed, then PLACE returns the first empty index into PUZZLE; if PUZZLE is filled, then PLACE returns 0. PIECECOUNT is updated by this function.

REMOVE is the inverse of PLACE.

TRIAL is the main search routine. It takes an index in PUZZLE and tries to complete the puzzle by starting at that index. It finds the first available piece type and tries to fit a piece of that piece at the index supplied. If the piece FIT's, it is PLACE'd, and TRIAL is called recursively to complete the puzzle using the index returned by PLACE as the starting point.

If the puzzle cannot be completed with the recursive call, then the piece is REMOVE'd and the next piece is tried. If the piece did not FIT, the next piece is tried.

In P, all of the symmetries of the pieces are explicitly stored, so no computation is needed to rotate pieces; the rotations are stored explicitly.

During the search, the first eight pieces placed are placed correctly. After that, the search tree becomes quite bushy, attaining a maximum average branching factor of 5 at depth 10 and declining after that. The tree that is actually searched has 977 leaves and 2005 nodes. A solution is found at depth 18.

Meter for Puzzle	
>'s	824530
1+'s	795877
References to (p i j)	759987
References to (puzzle x)	75253
References to (class x)	33901
References to (piececount (class x))	29909
='s	27918
Stores into (puzzle x)	24102
References to (piecemax x)	19331
FIT	15339
Stores into (p i j)	6733
Stores into (piececount (class x))	3992
Return's	2021
TRIAL	2005
PLACE	2005
REMOVE	1987
Stores into (piecemax x)	13
Stores into (class x)	13
DEFINEPIECE	13
Total	2624929

3.15.3 *Translation Notes*

The INTERLISP version uses the Common Lisp array package as well. 16ASET
and 16AREF, which manipulate 16-bit byte arrays, do not error-check.

```
(RPAQQ PUZZLECOMS
        ((FILES (SYSLOAD FROM <RPG>)
          CMLARRAY)
         (CONSTANTS SIZE TYPEMAX D CLASSMAX)
         (FNS FIT PLACE REMOVE! TRIAL DEFINEPIECE
          START FRESHPUZZLES)
         (BLOCKS
          (PUZZLEBLOCK
            FIT PLACE REMOVE! TRIAL DEFINEPIECE START FRESHPUZZLES
          (SPECVARS KOUNT)
          (ENTRIES
           START FRESHPUZZLES)))
         (MACROS CLASS PIECEMAX PUZZLE P PIECECOUNT)
         (INITVARS (CLASS NIL)
                   (PIECEMAX NIL)
                   (PUZZLE NIL)
                   (P NIL)
                   (PIECECOUNT NIL)
                   (PUZZLETRACEFLG NIL))
         (GLOBALVARS CLASS PIECEMAX PUZZLE P PIECECOUNT III PUZZLETRACEFLG)
         (SPECVARS KOUNT)
         (P (FRESHPUZZLES))))
(RPAQQ SIZE 511)
(RPAQQ TYPEMAX 12)
(RPAQQ D 8)
(RPAQQ CLASSMAX 3)
```

```
(CONSTANTS SIZE TYPEMAX D CLASSMAX))
(DEFINEQ
(FIT
  (LAMBDA (I J)
    (NOT
      (find K from 0 to (PIECEMAX I)
       suchthat
        (AND (P I K)
             (PUZZLE (IPLUS J K))))))))
(PLACE
  (LAMBDA (I J)
    (for K from 0 to (PIECEMAX I) do
         (if (P I K)
             then (PASET T PUZZLE (IPLUS J K))))
    (16ASET (SUB1 (PIECECOUNT (CLASS I)))
            PIECECOUNT
            (CLASS I))
    (OR (find K from J to SIZE suchthat (NOT (PUZZLE K)))
        0)))
(REMOVE!
  (LAMBDA (I J)
    (for K from 0 to (PIECEMAX I) do
         (if (P I K)
             then (PASET NIL PUZZLE (IPLUS J K))))
    (16ASET (ADD1 (PIECECOUNT (CLASS I)))
            PIECECOUNT
            (CLASS I))))
```

```
(TRIAL
  (LAMBDA (J)
    (bind (K , 0) for I from 0 to TYPEMAX
       do (if (AND (NEQ 0 (PIECECOUNT (CLASS I)))
                   (FIT I J))
             then
               (SETQ K (PLACE I J))
               (if (OR (TRIAL K)
                       (ZEROP K))
                  then
                    (AND PUZZLETRACEFLG
                         (printout
                          NIL
                          T
                          "Piece" .TAB "at" .TAB (ADD1 K)))
                    (add KOUNT 1)
                    (RETURN T)
                  else (REMOVE! I J)))
       finally (PROGN (add KOUNT 1)
                      NIL))))
(DEFINEPIECE
  (LAMBDA (ICLASS II JJ KK)
    (PROG ((INDEX 0))
      (for I from 0 to II
        do (for J from 0 to JJ
             do (for K from 0 to KK
                  do (SETQ
                       INDEX
                       (IPLUS I
                              (ITIMES D
                                      (IPLUS J
                                             (ITIMES D K)))))
                     (PASET T P III INDEX))))
      (16ASET ICLASS CLASS III)
      (16ASET INDEX PIECEMAX III)
      (if (NEQ III TYPEMAX)
          then (add III 1)))))
```

```
(START
 (LAMBDA NIL
  (for M from 0 to SIZE do (PASET T PUZZLE M))
   (for I from 1 to 5 do
    (for J from 1 to 5
     do (for K from 1 to 5
         do (PASET
             NIL
             PUZZLE
             (IPLUS
              T
              (ITIMES
               D
               (IPLUS
                J
                (ITIMES D K)))))))
   )
        (for I from 0 to TYPEMAX
         do (for M from 0 to SIZE
             do (PASET NIL P I M)))
        (SETQ III 0)
        (DEFINEPIECE 0 3 1 0)
        (DEFINEPIECE 0 1 0 3)
        (DEFINEPIECE 0 0 3 1)
        (DEFINEPIECE 0 1 3 0)
        (DEFINEPIECE 0 3 0 1)
        (DEFINEPIECE 0 0 1 3)
        (DEFINEPIECE 1 2 0 0)
        (DEFINEPIECE 1 0 2 0)
        (DEFINEPIECE 1 0 0 2)
        (DEFINEPIECE 2 1 1 0)
        (DEFINEPIECE 2 1 0 1)
        (DEFINEPIECE 2 0 1 1)
        (DEFINEPIECE 3 1 1 1)
        (16ASET 13 PIECECOUNT 0)
        (16ASET 3 PIECECOUNT 1)
        (16ASET 1 PIECECOUNT 2)
        (16ASET 1 PIECECOUNT 3)
        (PROG ((M (IPLUS 1 (ITIMES D (IPLUS 1 D))))
               (N 0)
               (KOUNT 0))
              (if (FIT 0 M)
                  then (SETQ N (PLACE 0 M))
                else (printout NIL T "Error"))
              (if (TRIAL N)
                  then (printout NIL T "Success in " KOUNT " trials.")
                else (printout NIL T "Failure."))
              (TERPRI))))
```

```
(FRESHPUZZLES
  (LAMBDA NIL
    (SETQ CLASS (MAKEARRAY (ADD1 TYPEMAX)
                           (QUOTE ELEMENTTYPE)
                           (QUOTE (MOD 65536)))))
    (SETQ PIECEMAX (MAKEARRAY (ADD1 TYPEMAX)
                              (QUOTE ELEMENTTYPE)
                              (QUOTE (MOD 65536))))
    (SETQ PUZZLE (MAKEARRAY (IPLUS SIZE 2)))
    (SETQ P (MAKEARRAY (LIST (ADD1 TYPEMAX)
                             (IPLUS SIZE 2))))
    (SETQ PIECECOUNT (MAKEARRAY (IPLUS CLASSMAX 2)
                                (QUOTE ELEMENTTYPE)
                                (QUOTE (MOD 65536))))
    NIL))
)
(DECLARE: EVAL@COMPILE
(PUTPROPS CLASS MACRO ((I . REST)
  (16AREF CLASS I . REST)))
(PUTPROPS PIECEMAX MACRO ((I . REST)
  (16AREF PIECEMAX I . REST)))
(PUTPROPS PUZZLE MACRO ((I . REST)
  (PAREF PUZZLE I . REST)))
(PUTPROPS P MACRO ((I . REST)
  (PAREF P I . REST)))
(PUTPROPS PIECECOUNT MACRO ((I . REST)
  (16AREF PIECECOUNT I . REST)))
)
(RPAQ? CLASS NIL)
(RPAQ? PIECEMAX NIL)
(RPAQ? PUZZLE NIL)
(RPAQ? P NIL)
(RPAQ? PIECECOUNT NIL)
(RPAQ? PUZZLETRACEFLG NIL)
(DECLARE: DOEVAL@COMPILE DONTCOPY

(ADDTOVAR GLOBALVARS CLASS PIECEMAX PUZZLE P PIECECOUNT
          III PUZZLETRACEFLG)
)
(DECLARE: DOEVAL@COMPILE DONTCOPY
(SPECVARS KOUNT)
)
(FRESHPUZZLES)
```

214

3.15.4 *Raw Data*

Raw Time Puzzle				
Implementation	CPU	GC	Real	Paging
SAIL	7.87	0.00	11.83	
Lambda	28.80			0.50
Lambda (MC)	24.20			0.15
3600	13.89			0.00
3600 + IFU	11.04			0.04
Dandelion	50.20	0.00		
Dolphin	91.00	0.00		
Dorado	14.00	0.00		
S-1			1.82	
PSL-SUN	26.29	0.00		
PSL-20	15.92	0.00		
PSL-3081	1.47	0.00		
PSL-Cray	1.00	0.00		
PSL-750	35.92	0.00		
PSL-750 (VMS)	31.84	0.00		
PSL-780	16.28	0.00		
PSL-DN300	31.74	0.00		
PSL-DN600	28.92	0.00		
PSL-DN160	29.51	0.00		
PSL-HP200	10.85	0.00		
PSL-HP-UX	12.48	0.00		
InterLispVax 780			110.28	
MV4000 CL			390.60	
MV8000 CL			310.00	
MV10000 CL			138.20	
3600 + FPA	11.04			0.04
750 NIL	497.85		498.02	
8600 CL	15.53	0.00		

Raw Time Puzzle				
Implementation	CPU	GC	Real	Paging
780 CL	47.48	0.00		
785 CL	29.60	0.00		
750 CL	231.79	0.00		
730 CL	512.56	0.00		
Perq			75.80	
750 Franz				
TrlOn & LclfYes				
TrlOn & LclfNo				
TrlOff & LclfYes				
TrlOff & LclfNo				
780 Franz				
TrlOn & LclfYes				
TrlOn & LclfNo				
TrlOff & LclfYes				
TrlOff & LclfNo				
Franz 68000				
TrlOn & LclfYes	52.12	32.60		
TrlOn & LclfNo	51.32	31.67		
TrlOff & LclfYes	52.08	25.18		
TrlOff & LclfNo	52.80	24.45		
InterLisp-10	121.02	7.92		
LM-2			42.93	

216

Presumably this is because 2-dimensional array reference
is losing its lunch.

— Glenn Burke *explaining why PUZZLE runs slowly.* (August 5, 1983.)

3.16 Triangle

3.16.1 *The Program*

```
;;; TRIANG -- Board game benchmark.
(eval-when (compile load eval)
  (defvar *board* (make-array 16. :initial-element 1))
  (defvar *sequence* (make-array 14. :initial-element 0))
  (defvar *a* (make-array 37. :initial-contents
                '(1 2 4 3 5 6 1 3 6 2 5 4 11 12
                  13 7 8 4 4 7 11 8 12 13 6 10
                  15 9 14 13 13 14 15 9 10
                  6 6)))
  (defvar *b* (make-array 37. :initial-contents
                '(2 4 7 5 8 9 3 6 10 5 9 8
                  12 13 14 8 9 5 2 4 7 5 8
                  9 3 6 10 5 9 8 12 13 14
                  8 9 5 5)))
  (defvar *c* (make-array 37. :initial-contents
                '(4 7 11 8 12 13 6 10 15 9 14 13
                  13 14 15 9 10 6 1 2 4 3 5 6 1
                  3 6 2 5 4 11 12 13 7 8 4 4)))
  (defvar *answer*)
  (defvar *final*)
  (setf (aref *board* 5) 0))
(defun last-position ()
  (do ((i 1 (1+ i)))
      ((= i 16.) 0)
    (if (= 1 (aref *board* i))
        (return i))))
```

```
(defun try (i depth)
  (cond ((= depth 14)
         (let ((lp (last-position)))
           (unless (member lp *final*)
             (push lp *final*)))
         (push
          (cdr (map 'list #'quote *sequence*))
          *answer*)
         t)
        ((and (= 1 (aref *board* (aref *a* i)))
              (= 1 (aref *board* (aref *b* i)))
              (= 0 (aref *board* (aref *c* i))))
         (setf (aref *board* (aref *a* i)) 0)
         (setf (aref *board* (aref *b* i)) 0)
         (setf (aref *board* (aref *c* i)) 1)
         (setf (aref *sequence* depth) i)
         (do ((j 0 (1+ j))
              (depth (1+ depth)))
             ((or (= j 36.)
                  (try j depth)) ()))
         (setf (aref *board* (aref *a* i)) 1)
         (setf (aref *board* (aref *b* i)) 1)
         (setf (aref *board* (aref *c* i)) 0) ())))
(defun gogogo (i)
  (let ((*answer* ())
        (*final* ()))
    (try i 1)))
;;; call: (gogogo 22.))
```

3.16.2 *Analysis*

This program is similar in many respects to the Puzzle benchmark, but it does not use any two-dimensional arrays. Therefore it provides a differentiator between one-dimensional and two-dimensional array references.

The puzzle that this benchmark solves is this: Given a board that looks like

```
            1
         2     3
      4     5     6
   7     8     9     10
11    12    13    14    15
```

which is taken to have holes at each of the numbered spots, suppose that initially every hole has a peg in it except for 5 and that pieces can be removed by 'jumping' as in checkers. Find all ways to remove all but one peg from the board.

There are 775 solutions to this puzzle, and they can easily be found by search.

There are five arrays in this program. *Board* is a one-dimensional array that represents a board, where the array indices correspond to the picture above. *Sequence* is a one-dimensional array that is used to keep track of the moves made to reach a solution. *A*, *b*, and *c* are one-dimensional arrays that store the possible moves. The elements of *board* are either 0 or 1: 0 means that there is no peg in that hole and 1 means there is. If *board*[*a*[i]] = 1, *board*[*b*[i]] = 1, and *board*[*c*[i]] = 0, then the peg at *a*[i] can jump the peg at *b*[i] and end up at *c*[i]. After this move has been made, *board*[*a*[i]] = 0, *board*[*b*[i]] = 0, and *board*[*c*[i]] = 1; *sequence* stores the indices i for each such move made.

After a solution is found, the elements of *sequence* are put into a list, and the list of solutions is the final result. As in Puzzle, the search proceeds by altering *board* and by undoing those alterations in case of backtracking. In addition, the first move to try is given (the peg in 12 jumps the peg in 8 and ends up in 5).

Meter for Last-Position	
='s	20150
References to (board x)	10075
1+'s	9300
LAST-POSITION	775
Total	40300

Meter for Try	
='s	19587224
References to (board x)	7820920
1+'s	5963732
TRY	5802572
Stores into (board x)	971616
Stores into (board (c x))	323872
Stores into (board (b x))	323872
Stores into (board (a x))	323872
Stores into (sequence x)	161936
Listarray's	1550
Cdr's	1550
Cons's	776
Member's	775
Total	41284267

3.16.3 *Translation Notes*

The INTERLISP version uses the Common Lisp array package. 8ASET and
8AREF manipulate 8-bit byte arrays.

```
(RPAQQ TRIANGCOMS
        ((LOCALVARS . T)
         (SPECVARS ANSWER FINAL DEEPCOUNTER)
         (GLOBALVARS BOARD SEQUENCE A B C)
         (FNS GOGOGO LAST-POSITION TRY TEST TRIANG-INIT)
         (FILES (SYSLOAD FROM <RPG>) CMLARRAY NONDADDARITH)
         (BLOCKS
          (TRIANGBLOCK
            GOGOGO LAST-POSITION TRY TEST TRIANG-INIT
            (ENTRIES GOGOGO TRIANG-INIT)))
         (P (TRIANG-INIT))))
(DECLARE: DOEVAL@COMPILE DONTCOPY
(LOCALVARS . T)
)
(DECLARE: DOEVAL@COMPILE DONTCOPY
(SPECVARS ANSWER FINAL DEEPCOUNTER)
)
(DECLARE: DOEVAL@COMPILE DONTCOPY
(ADDTOVAR GLOBALVARS BOARD SEQUENCE A B C)
)
(DEFINEQ
(GOGOGO
  (LAMBDA (I)
    (PROG ((ANSWER NIL)
           (FINAL NIL))
          (RETURN (TRY I 1))))))
```

```
(LAST-POSITION
  (LAMBDA NIL
    (OR (find I to 16 suchthat (EQ 1 (8AREF BOARD I)))
        0)))
(TRY
  (LAMBDA (I DEPTH)
    (DECLARE (SPECVARS ANSWER FINAL)
             (GLOBALVARS BOARD SEQUENCE A B C))
    (COND
      ((EQ DEPTH 14)
        (PROG ((LP (LAST-POSITION)))
              (COND
                ((MEMBER LP FINAL))
                (T (push FINAL LP))))
        (push ANSWER (CDR (LISTARRAY SEQUENCE)))
        T)
      ((AND (EQ 1 (8AREF BOARD (8AREF A I)))
            (EQ 1 (8AREF BOARD (8AREF B I)))
            (EQ 0 (8AREF BOARD (8AREF C I))))
        (8ASET 0 BOARD (8AREF A I))
        (8ASET 0 BOARD (8AREF B I))
        (8ASET 1 BOARD (8AREF C I))
        (8ASET I SEQUENCE DEPTH)
        (bind (DEPTH ,(ADD1 DEPTH)) for J from 0 to 36
         until (TRY J DEPTH) do NIL)
        (8ASET 1 BOARD (8AREF A I))
        (8ASET 1 BOARD (8AREF B I))
        (8ASET 0 BOARD (8AREF C I))
        NIL))))
(TEST
  (LAMBDA NIL
    (DECLARE (SPECVARS ANSWER FINAL)
             (GLOBALVARS BOARD SEQUENCE A B C))
    (TRIANG-INIT)
    (PROG ((ANSWER NIL)
           (FINAL NIL))
          (TRY 22 1)
          (RETURN (EQ 775 (LENGTH ANSWER))))))
```

```
(TRIANG-INIT
  (LAMBDA NIL
    (SETQ BOARD (MAKEARRAY 16 (QUOTE ELEMENTTYPE)
                             (QUOTE BYTE)
                             (QUOTE INITIALELEMENT)
                             1))
    (ASET 0 BOARD 5)
    (SETQ SEQUENCE (MAKEARRAY 14 (QUOTE ELEMENTTYPE)
                                (QUOTE BYTE)
                                (QUOTE INITIALELEMENT)
                                255))
    (SETQ A
      (MAKEARRAY 37 (QUOTE ELEMENTTYPE)
                    (QUOTE BYTE)
                    (QUOTE INITIALCONTENTS)
                    (QUOTE (1 2 4 3 5 6 1 3 6 2
                            5 4 11 12 13 7 8 4
                            4 7 11 8 12 13 6 10
                            15 9 14 13 13 14
                            15 9 10 6 0))))
    (SETQ B
      (MAKEARRAY 37 (QUOTE ELEMENTTYPE)
                    (QUOTE BYTE)
                    (QUOTE INITIALCONTENTS)
                    (QUOTE
                     (2 4 7 5 8 9 3 6 10 5 9 8
                      12 13 14 8 9 5 2 4 7 5 8 9 3
                      6 10 5 9 8 12 13 14 8
                      9 5 0))))
    (SETQ C
      (MAKEARRAY 37 (QUOTE ELEMENTTYPE)
                    (QUOTE BYTE)
                    (QUOTE INITIALCONTENTS)
                    (QUOTE (4 7 11 8 12 13 6 10 15
                            9 14 13 13 14 15 9 10
                            6 1 2 4 3 5 6 1 3 6 2 5
                            4 11 12 13 7 8 4 0)))))
)
(TRIANG-INIT)
```

3.16.4 *Raw Data*

Raw Time Triang				
Implementation	CPU	GC	Real	Paging
SAIL	86.03	6.35	144.90	
Lambda	510.20			0.30
Lambda (MC)	225.50			0.00
3600	151.70			0.06
3600 + IFU	116.99			0.04
Dandelion	856.00	0.46		
Dolphin	1510.00	0.70		
Dorado	252.20	0.21		
S-1			62.06	
PSL-SUN	353.44	0.00		
PSL-20	86.94	0.00		
PSL-3081	25.43	0.00		
PSL-Cray	14.44	0.00		
PSL-750	523.19	0.00		
PSL-750 (VMS)	439.51	0.00		
PSL-780	212.19	0.00		
PSL-DN300	439.90	0.00		
PSL-DN600	416.47	0.00		
PSL-DN160				
PSL-HP200	261.07	0.00		
PSL-HP-UX	250.07	0.00		
InterLispVax 780			1076.53	
MV4000 CL			456.37	
MV8000 CL			384.03	
MV10000 CL			151.20	
3600 + FPA	116.99			0.04
750 NIL	649.73		652.35	
8600 CL	99.73	0.00		

Raw Time Triang				
Implementation	CPU	GC	Real	Paging
780 CL	360.85	0.00		
785 CL	233.00	0.00		
750 CL	1021.35	0.00		
730 CL	2865.87	0.00		
Perq			1297.53	

750 Franz
  TrlOn & LclfYes
  TrlOn & LclfNo
  TrlOff & LclfYes
  TrlOff & LclfNo				

780 Franz
  TrlOn & LclfYes
  TrlOn & LclfNo
  TrlOff & LclfYes
  TrlOff & LclfNo				

Franz 68000
  TrlOn & LclfYes
  TrlOn & LclfNo
  TrlOff & LclfYes
  TrlOff & LclfNo				

InterLisp-10	2326.43	1.12		
LM-2			763.00	

I also tried TRIANG,
but gave up after 10 (?) CPU minutes.

— Walter van Roggen *explaining a need to*
tune his implementation. (January 26, 1984.)

3.17 File Print

3.17.1 *The Program*

```
;;; FPRINT -- Benchmark to print to a file.
(defvar
 *test-atoms*
 '(abcdef12 cdefgh23 efghij34 ghijkl45 ijklmn56 klmnop67
   mnopqr78 opqrst89 qrstuv90 stuvwx01 uvwxyz12
   wxyzab23 xyzabc34 123456ab 234567bc 345678cd
   456789de 567890ef 678901fg 789012gh 890123hi))
(defun init-aux (m n atoms)
  (cond ((= m 0) (pop atoms))
        (t (do ((i n (- i 2))
                (a ()))
               ((< i 1) a)
             (push (pop atoms) a)
             (push (init-aux (1- m) n atoms) a)))))
(defun init (m n atoms)
  (let ((atoms (subst () () atoms)))
    (do ((a atoms (cdr a)))
        ((null (cdr a)) (rplacd a atoms)))
    (init-aux m n atoms)))
(defvar test-pattern (init 6. 6. *test-atoms*))

(defun fprint ()
  (if (probe-file "fprint.tst")
      (delete-file "fprint.tst"))
  ;;; defaults to STRING-CHAR
  (let ((stream (open
                  "fprint.tst"
                  :direction :output)))
    (print test-pattern stream)
    (close stream)))
(eval-when (compile load eval)
  (if (probe-file "fprint.tst")
      (delete-file "fprint.tst")))
;;; call:  (fprint)
```

3.17.2 *Analysis*

This benchmark measures the performance of file output. The program checks to see whether there is a file with a certain name (there should not be). Then it creates and opens a new file with that name, prints a test pattern into that file, and then closes it. The EVAL-WHEN guarantees that the file is not present when the benchmark is run.

The test pattern is a tree that is 6-deep and that has a branching factor of 6. The atoms in the tree have 8 characters each and are a mixture of alphabetic and numeric characters. Printing the tree using PRINT requires 17,116 characters, including spaces, to be output.

Meter for Init	
Cons's	2184
<'s	1456
Cdr's	1133
='s	1093
INIT1	1093
1−'s	1092
Car's	1092
Null's	21
Rplacd's	1
Subst's	1
INIT	1
Total	9167

3.17.3 *Translation Notes*

The translation of this benchmark is trivial: The meat of the program is PRINT.

3.17.4 *Raw Data*

Raw Time Fprint				
Implementation	CPU	GC	Real	Paging
SAIL	0.78	0.40	1.32	
Lambda	16.58			11.20
Lambda (MC)				
3600	2.60			0.10
3600 + IFU				
Dandelion	13.70	0.40		
Dolphin	14.90	0.00		
Dorado	2.93	0.00		
S-1				
PSL-SUN	5.13	0.00		
PSL-20	4.77	0.00		
PSL-3081	0.34	0.00		
PSL-Cray	0.37	0.00		
PSL-750	5.33	0.00		
PSL-750 (VMS)	3.90	0.00		
PSL-780	2.19	0.00		
PSL-DN300	4.19	0.00		
PSL-DN600	4.43	0.00		
PSL-DN160	1.89	0.00		
PSL-HP200	9.37	0.00		
PSL-HP-UX	3.40	0.00		
InterLispVax 780			0.60	
MV4000 CL			5.07	
MV8000 CL			4.51	
MV10000 CL			2.35	
3600 + FPA	2.60			0.10
750 NIL	37.65		38.23	
8600 CL	1.08	0.00		

Raw Time Fprint				
Implementation	CPU	GC	Real	Paging
780 CL	3.94	0.00		
785 CL	2.19	0.00		
750 CL	6.08	0.00		
730 CL	18.30	0.00		
Perq			19.13	
750 Franz				
TrlOn & LclfYes	1.11	0.00		
TrlOn & LclfNo	1.23	0.00		
TrlOff & LclfYes	1.09	0.00		
TrlOff & LclfNo	1.06	0.00		
780 Franz				
TrlOn & LclfYes	0.63	0.00		
TrlOn & LclfNo	0.61	0.00		
TrlOff & LclfYes	0.64	0.00		
TrlOff & LclfNo	0.63	0.00		
Franz 68000				
TrlOn & LclfYes	1.93	0.00		
TrlOn & LclfNo	1.90	0.00		
TrlOff & LclfYes	1.92	0.00		
TrlOff & LclfNo	1.94	0.00		
InterLisp-10	4.45	0.00		
LM-2			12.09	

... without the vigilance of your benchmarking activity,
this bug might have gone unnoticed
for years.

— Jonl White *voicing praise.* (February 8, 1984.)

232

3.18 File Read

3.18.1 *The Program*

```
;;; FREAD -- Benchmark to read from a file.
;;; Requires the existence of FPRINT.TST which is created
;;; by FPRINT.
(defun fread ()
  (let ((stream (open "fprint.tst" :direction :input)))
    (read stream)
    (close stream)))
(eval-when (compile load eval)
  (if (not (probe-file "fprint.tst"))
      (format
        t
        "~%Define FPRINT.TST by running the FPRINT benchmark!")))
;;; call: (fread))
```

3.18.2 *Analysis*

This benchmark tests file input. It reads the file produced by FPRINT.

3.18.3 *Translation Notes*

The translation of this benchmark is trivial.

3.18.4 *Raw Data*

Raw Time Fread				
Implementation	CPU	GC	Real	Paging
SAIL	0.98	0.00	1.80	
Lambda	19.70			0.54
Lambda (MC)				
3600	4.60			0.00
3600 + IFU				
Dandelion	8.00	0.13		
Dolphin	6.41	0.00		
Dorado	1.57	0.00		
S-1				
PSL-SUN	7.70	0.00		
PSL-20	5.82	0.00		
PSL-3081	0.40	0.00		
PSL-Cray	0.63	0.00		
PSL-750	7.54	0.00		
PSL-750 (VMS)	6.20	0.00		
PSL-780	3.36	0.00		
PSL-DN300	6.47	0.00		
PSL-DN600	6.82	0.00		
PSL-DN160	3.09	0.00		
PSL-HP200	5.16	0.00		
PSL-HP-UX	5.02	0.00		
InterLispVax 780			0.12	
MV4000 CL			10.28	
MV8000 CL			8.91	
MV10000 CL			4.64	
3600 + FPA	4.60			0.00
750 NIL	27.78		28.02	
8600 CL	2.34	0.00		

Raw Time Fread				
Implementation	CPU	GC	Real	Paging
780 CL	7.24	0.00		
785 CL	2.56	0.00		
750 CL	11.21	0.00		
730 CL	29.83	0.00		
Perq			20.60	
750 Franz				
TrlOn & LclfYes	1.99	0.33		
TrlOn & LclfNo	2.02	0.32		
TrlOff & LclfYes	2.05	0.33		
TrlOff & LclfNo	2.04	0.35		
780 Franz				
TrlOn & LclfYes	1.18	0.19		
TrlOn & LclfNo	1.17	0.30		
TrlOff & LclfYes	1.18	0.19		
TrlOff & LclfNo	1.17	0.19		
Franz 68000				
TrlOn & LclfYes	2.37	0.89		
TrlOn & LclfNo	2.37	0.88		
TrlOff & LclfYes	2.35	0.56		
TrlOff & LclfNo	2.35	0.54		
InterLisp-10	4.47	0.00		
LM-2			20.67	

>   ...we re-ran the benchmarks in the current release of the software,
>   in which some things were made faster
>   (and one thing accidentally got slower).
>   — Daniel Weinreb*explaining results*. (September 12, 1984.)

3.19 Terminal Print

3.19.1 *The Program*

```
;;; TPRINT -- Benchmark to print and read to the terminal.
(defvar
 *test-atoms*
 '(abc1 cde2 efg3 ghi4 ijk5 klm6 mno7 opq8 qrs9
   stu0 uvw1 wxy2 xyz3 123a 234b 345c 456d
   567d 678e 789f 890g))
(defun init (m n atoms)
  (let ((atoms (subst () () atoms)))
    (do ((a atoms (cdr a)))
        ((null (cdr a)) (rplacd a atoms)))
    (init-aux m n atoms)))
(defun init-aux (m n atoms)
  (cond ((= m 0) (pop atoms))
        (t (do ((i n (- i 2))
                (a ()))
               ((< i 1) a)
             (push (pop atoms) a)
             (push (init-aux (1- m) n atoms) a)))))
(defvar test-pattern (init 6. 6. *test-atoms*))
;;; call:  (print test-pattern)
```

3.19.2 *Analysis*

This benchmark tests terminal output. On the Xerox D-machines, the output is to a 10"x10" window.

Meter for Init	
Cons's	2184
<'s	1456
Cdr's	1133
='s	1093
INIT1	1093
1-'s	1092
Car's	1092
Null's	21
Rplacd's	1
Subst's	1
INIT	1
Total	9167

3.19.3 *Translation Notes*

The translation of this benchmark is trivial.

3.19.4 *Raw Data*

Raw Time Tprint				
Implementation	CPU	GC	Real	Paging
SAIL	0.81	0.00	6.52	
Lambda	7.20			0.61
Lambda (MC)				
3600	4.89			0.00
3600 + IFU				
Dandelion	34.00	0.00		
Dolphin	29.20	0.00		
Dorado	5.55	0.00		
S-1				
PSL-SUN	3.58	0.00		
PSL-20	4.25	0.00		
PSL-3081	0.30	0.00		
PSL-Cray	0.20	0.00		
PSL-750	4.27	0.00		
PSL-750 (VMS)	2.63	0.00		
PSL-780	1.92	0.00		
PSL-DN300	2.72	0.00		
PSL-DN600	2.73	0.00		
PSL-DN160	1.84	0.00		
PSL-HP200	11.19	0.00		
PSL-HP-UX	7.82	0.00		
InterLispVax 780			11.47	
MV4000 CL			5.55	
MV8000 CL			4.94	
MV10000 CL			2.83	
3600 + FPA	4.89			0.00
750 NIL	47.55		58.31	
8600 CL	0.70	0.00		

Raw Time Tprint				
Implementation	CPU	GC	Real	Paging
780 CL	2.85	0.00		
785 CL	1.43	0.00		
750 CL	4.11	0.00		
730 CL	12.56	0.00		
Perq			15.55	
750 Franz				
TrlOn & LclfYes	0.88	0.00		
TrlOn & LclfNo	0.87	0.00		
TrlOff & LclfYes	0.87	0.00		
TrlOff & LclfNo	0.87	0.00		
780 Franz				
TrlOn & LclfYes	0.53	0.00		
TrlOn & LclfNo	0.52	0.00		
TrlOff & LclfYes	0.48	0.00		
TrlOff & LclfNo	0.52	0.00		
Franz 68000				
TrlOn & LclfYes	3.22	0.00		
TrlOn & LclfNo	2.12	0.00		
TrlOff & LclfYes	3.15	0.00		
TrlOff & LclfNo	2.55	0.00		
InterLisp-10	4.72	0.00		
LM-2			17.67	

I asked Moon, and he said it was complicated
and he didn't know the whole story.

— Daniel Weinreb*reflecting on the 3600's instruction cache.* (September 13, 1984.)

3.20 Polynomial Manipulation

3.20.1 *The Program*

```
;;; FRPOLY -- Benchmark from Berkeley based on polynomial
;;; arithmetic.  Originally writen in Franz Lisp by Richard
;;; Fateman.  PDIFFER1 appears in the code but is not defined;
;;; is not called for in this test, however.
(defvar ans)
(defvar coef)
(defvar f)
(defvar inc)
(defvar i)
(defvar qq)
(defvar ss)
(defvar v)
(defvar *x*)
(defvar *alpha*)
(defvar *a*)
(defvar *b*)
(defvar *chk)
(defvar *l)
(defvar *p)
(defvar q*)
(defvar u*)
(defvar *var)
(defvar *y*)
(defvar r)
(defvar r2)
(defvar r3)
(defvar start)
(defvar res1)
(defvar res2)
(defvar res3)
```

```
(defmacro pointergp (x y) '(> (get ,x 'order)
                              (get ,y 'order)))
(defmacro pcoefp (e) '(atom ,e))
(defmacro pzerop (x)
  '(if (numberp ,x)
       (zerop ,x)))
(defmacro pzero () 0)
(defmacro cplus (x y) '(+ ,x ,y))
(defmacro ctimes (x y) '(* ,x ,y))
(defun pcoefadd (e c x)
  (if (pzerop c)
      x
      (cons e (cons c x))))
(defun pcplus (c p)
  (if (pcoefp p)
      (cplus p c)
      (psimp (car p) (pcplus1 c (cdr p)))))
(defun pcplus1 (c x)
  (cond ((null x)
         (if (pzerop c)
             nil
             (cons 0 (cons c nil))))
        ((pzerop (car x))
         (pcoefadd 0 (pplus c (cadr x)) nil))
        (t
         (cons
          (car x)
          (cons
           (cadr x)
           (pcplus1 c (cddr x)))))))
(defun pctimes (c p)
  (if (pcoefp p)
      (ctimes c p)
      (psimp (car p) (pctimes1 c (cdr p)))))
(defun pctimes1 (c x)
  (if (null x)
      nil
      (pcoefadd (car x)
                (ptimes c (cadr x))
                (pctimes1 c (cddr x)))))
```

```
(defun pplus (x y)
  (cond ((pcoefp x)
         (pcplus x y))
        ((pcoefp y)
         (pcplus y x))
        ((eq (car x) (car y))
         (psimp (car x) (pplus1 (cdr y) (cdr x))))
        ((pointergp (car x) (car y))
         (psimp (car x) (pcplus1 y (cdr x))))
        (t
         (psimp (car y) (pcplus1 x (cdr y))))))
(defun pplus1 (x y)
  (cond ((null x) y)
        ((null y) x)
        ((= (car x) (car y))
         (pcoefadd (car x)
                   (pplus (cadr x) (cadr y))
                   (pplus1 (cddr x) (cddr y))))
        ((> (car x) (car y))
         (cons
          (car x)
          (cons (cadr x) (pplus1 (cddr x) y))))
        (t
         (cons
          (car y)
          (cons (cadr y) (pplus1 x (cddr y)))))))
(defun psimp (var x)
  (cond ((null x) 0)
        ((atom x) x)
        ((zerop (car x))
         (cadr x))
        (t
         (cons var x))))
```

```
(defun ptimes (x y)
  (cond ((or (pzerop x) (pzerop y))
         (pzero))
        ((pcoefp x)
         (pctimes x y))
        ((pcoefp y)
         (pctimes y x))
        ((eq (car x) (car y))
         (psimp (car x) (ptimes1 (cdr x) (cdr y))))
        ((pointergp (car x) (car y))
         (psimp (car x) (pctimes1 y (cdr x))))
        (t
         (psimp (car y) (pctimes1 x (cdr y))))))
(defun ptimes1 (*x* y)
  (prog (u* v)
        (setq v (setq u* (ptimes2 y)))
     a
        (setq *x* (cddr *x*))
        (if (null *x*)
            (return u*))
        (ptimes3 y)
        (go a)))
(defun ptimes2 (y)
  (if (null y)
      nil
      (pcoefadd (+ (car *x*) (car y))
                (ptimes (cadr *x*) (cadr y))
                (ptimes2 (cddr y)))))
```

```
(defun ptimes3 (y)
  (prog (e u c)
    a1 (if (null y)
           (return nil))
       (setq e (+ (car *x*) (car y))
             c (ptimes (cadr y) (cadr *x*) ))
       (cond ((pzerop c)
               (setq y (cddr y))
               (go a1))
             ((or (null v) (> e (car v)))
               (setq u* (setq v (pplus1 u* (list e c))))
               (setq y (cddr y))
               (go a1))
             ((= e (car v))
               (setq c (pplus c (cadr v)))
               (if (pzerop c) ; never true, evidently
                   (setq
                     u*
                     (setq
                       v
                       (pdiffer1
                         u*
                         (list (car v) (cadr v)))))
                   (rplaca (cdr v) c))
               (setq y (cddr y))
               (go a1)))
    a  (cond ((and (cddr v) (> (caddr v) e))
               (setq v (cddr v))
               (go a)))
       (setq u (cdr v))
    b  (if (or (null (cdr u)) (< (cadr u) e))
           (rplacd u (cons e (cons c (cdr u)))) (go e))
       (cond ((pzerop (setq c (pplus (caddr u) c)))
               (rplacd u (cdddr u))
               (go d))
             (t
               (rplaca (cddr u) c)))
    e  (setq u (cddr u))
    d  (setq y (cddr y))
       (if (null y)
           (return nil))
       (setq e (+ (car *x*) (car y))
             c (ptimes (cadr y) (cadr *x*)))
    c  (cond ((and (cdr u) (> (cadr u) e))
               (setq u (cddr u))
               (go c)))
       (go b)))
```

3.20.2 *Analysis*

This program, which was supplied by Richard Fateman of the University of California, Berkeley, computes powers of particular polynomials. There are fours sets of three tests: The first squares the polynomials $x + y + z + 1$, $100000x + 100000y + 100000z + 100000$, and $1.0x + 1.0y + 1.0z + 1.0$; the second takes the 5_{th} power of those three polynomials; the third takes the 10_{th} power of those three polynomials; and the fourth takes the 15_{th} power of those three polynomials.

The polynomial $100000(x+y+z+1)$ requires BIGNUMs for the higher powers, and $1.0(x + y + z + 1)$ requires floating-point numbers. Not all implementations can handle BIGNUMs, and so this benchmark is not performed on all of the implementations in this study.

This benchmark is a good one because it uses an interesting representation for polynomials in several variables and because it is programmed in an unusual and somewhat unpleasant programming style. Polynomials are represented as lists.

The variables in the polynomial are given an arbitrary, but fixed, total order. This identifies a main variable. If that variable is x, then the list

$$(x \quad e_1 \quad c_1 \ldots e_n \quad c_n)$$

represents the polynomial

$$c_1 x_{e_1} + \ldots + c_n x_{e_n}$$

The coefficients, c_i, are allowed to be polynomials in 'less main' variables. For example, the polynomial

$$x^2 + 2xy + y^2 + 7$$

is represented as

```
(x 2 1 1 (y 1 2) 0 (y 2 1 0 7))
```

Using the above formula to decode this we have

$$1x^2 + (2y)x^1 + (1y^2 + 7y^0)x^0 = x^2 + 2xy + y^2 + 7$$

With the total ordering on variables and with the assumption that $e_1 > \ldots > e_n$, it is possible to uniquely represent polynomials.

The total order is kept as entries on the property lists of the symbols that represent the variables, and the main variable is the one whose ORDER property is numerically the lowest.

Implementing addition, multiplication, and exponentiation of polynomials represented this way is theoretically simple but practically unpleasant. The main routine used in multiplying polynomials is written as a tangled web of GO's. This program side-effects a special variable to accomplish its task.

In another routine in the multiplication package, a special variable is bound in the argument list. Both fixnum and generic arithmetic are performed.

In order to manipulate the polynomial representation, destructive list operations are performed along with a fair amount of CONSing.

Meter for Setup	
Car's	98
Signp's	94
Atom's	72
Null's	66
Cons's	54
Cdr's	48
PCTIMES1	36
PTIMES	28
PCTIMES	28
PCOEFADD	26
Zerop's	18
PSIMP	18
*'s	16
Get's	12
PCPLUS	12
Putprop's	6
Eq's	6
PPLUS	6
Oddp's	0
/'s	0
PEXPTSQ	0
Rplacd's	0
<'s	0
Rplaca's	0
PTIMES3	0
PTIMES2	0
PTIMES1	0
>'s	0
='s	0
PPLUS1	0
+'s	0
Total	644

Meter for (Bench 2)		Meter for (Bench 5)	
Signp's	381	Car's	4413
Car's	369	Cdr's	4257
Cdr's	324	Signp's	3516
Null's	315	Null's	3501
Atom's	300	Atom's	3294
Cons's	180	Cons's	1656
PTIMES	123	PCOEFADD	1110
PCTIMES1	117	PTIMES	1038
PCOEFADD	117	PCTIMES	942
PCTIMES	114	*'s	768
*'s	78	+'s	714
Zerop's	60	PCTIMES1	624
PSIMP	54	PPLUS	609
+'s	36	PPLUS1	555
PTIMES2	27	='s	543
='s	27	PCPLUS	465
PPLUS1	27	Zerop's	423
PPLUS	27	PSIMP	414
>'s	18	>'s	366
Eq's	18	PTIMES2	345
PCPLUS	18	Eq's	240
Rplacds	9	<'s	198
<'s	9	Rplaca's	198
Rplaca's	9	Rplacd's	132
PTIMES3	9	PTIMES3	132
PTIMES1	9	PTIMES1	96
Oddp's	6	Oddp's	9
/'s	6	/'s	9
PEXPTSQ	3	PEXPTSQ	3
Putprop's	0	Putprop's	0
Get's	0	Get's	0
Total	2790	Total	30570

Meter for (Bench 10)	
Cdr's	50682
Car's	46686
Atom's	38700
Signp's	37161
Null's	36909
Cons's	15285
PCOEFADD	10968
PTIMES	10641
+'s	10239
PCTIMES	9864
*'s	9003
PPLUS	8709
PCPLUS	7485
='s	6708
PPLUS1	6477
>'s	5589
PCTIMES1	3822
PTIMES2	3531
<'s	3456
Rplaca's	3456
Zerop's	2874
PSIMP	2862
Eq's	2001
Rplacd's	1455
PTIMES3	1455
PTIMES1	777
Oddp's	12
/'s	12
PEXPTSQ	3
Putprop's	0
Get's	0
Total	336822

Meter for (Bench 15)	
Cdr's	384381
Car's	293511
Atom's	278784
Signp's	247089
Null's	242352
Cons's	79140
+'s	78024
PTIMES	71817
PCTIMES	67983
PPLUS	67575
*'s	65643
PCPLUS	62145
PCOEFADD	56466
>'s	54225
='s	42726
PPLUS1	37086
<'s	35919
Rplaca's	35919
PTIMES2	19713
Zerop's	11616
PSIMP	11604
PCTIMES1	11271
Rplacd's	11070
PTIMES3	11070
Eq's	9264
PTIMES1	3834
Oddp's	12
/'s	12
PEXPTSQ	3
Putprop's	0
Get's	0
Total	2290254

3.20.3 *Raw Data*

Raw Time				
Frpoly Power = 2 $r = x + y + z + 1$				
Implementation	CPU	GC	Real	Paging
SAIL	0.00	0.00	0.02	
Lambda	0.00			0.00
Lambda (MC)	0.00			0.00
3600	0.00			0.00
3600 + IFU	0.00			0.00
Dandelion				
Dolphin				
Dorado				
S-1			0.00	
PSL-SUN	0.03	0.00		
PSL-20	0.02	0.00		
PSL-3081	0.00	0.00		
PSL-Cray	0.00	0.00		
PSL-750	0.06	0.00		
PSL-750 (VMS)	0.07	0.00		
PSL-780	0.00	0.00		
PSL-DN300	0.40	0.00		
PSL-DN600	0.35	0.00		
PSL-DN160				
PSL-HP200	0.07	0.00		
PSL-HP-UX	0.06	0.00		
InterLispVax 780				
MV4000 CL			0.04	
MV8000 CL			0.04	
MV10000 CL			0.01	
3600 + FPA	0.00			0.00
750 NIL	0.04		0.00	
8600 CL	0.01	0.00		

Raw Time				
Frpoly Power $= 2 \; r = x + y + z + 1$				
Implementation	**CPU**	**GC**	**Real**	**Paging**
780 CL	0.03	0.00		
785 CL	0.02	0.00		
750 CL	0.06	0.00		
730 CL	0.17	0.00		
Perq				
750 Franz				
TrlOn & LclfYes	0.03	0.00		
TrlOn & LclfNo	0.05	0.00		
TrlOff & LclfYes	0.03	0.00		
TrlOff & LclfNo	0.08	0.00		
780 Franz				
TrlOn & LclfYes	0.02	0.00		
TrlOn & LclfNo	0.02	0.00		
TrlOff & LclfYes	0.02	0.00		
TrlOff & LclfNo	0.05	0.00		
Franz 68000				
TrlOn & LclfYes	0.02	0.00		
TrlOn & LclfNo	0.05	0.00		
TrlOff & LclfYes	0.03	0.00		
TrlOff & LclfNo	0.10	0.00		
InterLisp-10				
LM-2				

Raw Time				
Frpoly Power = 2 $r2 = 1000r$				
Implementation	CPU	GC	Real	Paging
SAIL	0.00	0.00	0.02	
Lambda	0.01			0.00
Lambda (MC)	0.00			0.00
3600	0.00			0.00
3600 + IFU	0.00			0.00
Dandelion				
Dolphin				
Dorado				
S-1			0.00	
PSL-SUN	0.20	0.00		
PSL-20	0.03	0.00		
PSL-3081	0.01	0.00		
PSL-Cray	0.00	0.00		
PSL-750	0.28	0.00		
PSL-750 (VMS)	0.16	0.00		
PSL-780	0.06	0.00		
PSL-DN300	0.13	0.00		
PSL-DN600	0.14	0.00		
PSL-DN160				
PSL-HP200	0.15	0.00		
PSL-HP-UX	0.15	0.00		
InterLispVax 780				
MV4000 CL			0.05	
MV8000 CL			0.05	
MV10000 CL			0.02	
3600 + FPA	0.00			0.00
750 NIL	0.15		0.15	
8600 CL	0.01	0.00		

Raw Time Frpoly Power $= 2$ $r2 = 1000r$				
Implementation	CPU	GC	Real	Paging
780 CL	0.04	0.00		
785 CL	0.02	0.00		
750 CL	0.06	0.00		
730 CL	0.17	0.00		
Perq				
750 Franz				
TrlOn & LclfYes	0.03	0.00		
TrlOn & LclfNo	0.03	0.00		
TrlOff & LclfYes	0.03	0.00		
TrlOff & LclfNo	0.12	0.00		
780 Franz				
TrlOn & LclfYes	0.02	0.00		
TrlOn & LclfNo	0.02	0.00		
TrlOff & LclfYes	0.02	0.00		
TrlOff & LclfNo	0.07	0.00		
Franz 68000				
TrlOn & LclfYes	0.03	0.00		
TrlOn & LclfNo	0.05	0.00		
TrlOff & LclfYes	0.05	0.00		
TrlOff & LclfNo	0.10	0.00		
InterLisp-10				
LM-2				

Raw Time				
Frpoly Power = 2 $r3 = r$ in flonums				
Implementation	CPU	GC	Real	Paging
SAIL	0.00	0.00	0.02	
Lambda	0.01			0.00
Lambda (MC)	0.00			0.00
3600	0.00			0.00
3600 + IFU	0.00			0.00
Dandelion				
Dolphin				
Dorado				
S-1			0.00	
PSL-SUN	0.08	0.00		
PSL-20	0.02	0.00		
PSL-3081	0.00	0.00		
PSL-Cray	0.00	0.00		
PSL-750	0.11	0.00		
PSL-750 (VMS)	0.07	0.00		
PSL-780	0.03	0.00		
PSL-DN300	0.43	0.00		
PSL-DN600	0.42	0.00		
PSL-DN160				
PSL-HP200	0.09	0.00		
PSL-HP-UX	0.14	0.00		
InterLispVax 780				
MV4000 CL			0.05	
MV8000 CL			0.04	
MV10000 CL			0.02	
3600 + FPA	0.00			0.00
750 NIL	0.05		0.05	
8600 CL	0.02	0.00		

Raw Time				
Frpoly Power = 2 $r3 = r$ in flonums				
Implementation	**CPU**	**GC**	**Real**	**Paging**
780 CL	0.04	0.00		
785 CL	0.02	0.00		
750 CL	0.06	0.00		
730 CL	0.16	0.00		
Perq				
750 Franz				
TrlOn & LclfYes	0.02	0.00		
TrlOn & LclfNo	0.03	0.00		
TrlOff & LclfYes	0.02	0.00		
TrlOff & LclfNo	0.08	0.00		
780 Franz				
TrlOn & LclfYes	0.02	0.00		
TrlOn & LclfNo	0.02	0.00		
TrlOff & LclfYes	0.03	0.00		
TrlOff & LclfNo	0.07	0.00		
Franz 68000				
TrlOn & LclfYes	0.05	0.00		
TrlOn & LclfNo	0.05	0.00		
TrlOff & LclfYes	0.05	0.00		
TrlOff & LclfNo	0.08	0.00		
InterLisp-10				
LM-2				

Raw Time				
Frpoly Power = 5 $r = x + y + z + 1$				
Implementation	CPU	GC	Real	Paging
SAIL	0.04	0.00	0.02	
Lambda	0.10			0.02
Lambda (MC)	0.04			0.00
3600	0.05			0.01
3600 + IFU	0.04			0.01
Dandelion				
Dolphin				
Dorado				
S-1			0.03	
PSL-SUN	0.23	0.00		
PSL-20	0.09	0.00		
PSL-3081	0.02	0.00		
PSL-Cray	0.01	0.00		
PSL-750	0.40	0.00		
PSL-750 (VMS)	0.33	0.00		
PSL-780	0.20	0.00		
PSL-DN300	0.29	0.00		
PSL-DN600	0.29	0.00		
PSL-DN160				
PSL-HP200	0.25	0.00		
PSL-HP-UX	0.24	0.00		
InterLispVax 780				
MV4000 CL			0.37	
MV8000 CL			0.30	
MV10000 CL			0.14	
3600 + FPA	0.04			0.01
750 NIL	0.36		0.36	
8600 CL	0.08	0.00		

Raw Time				
Frpoly Power $= 5\ r = x + y + z + 1$				
Implementation	CPU	GC	Real	Paging
780 CL	0.23	0.00		
785 CL	0.13	0.00		
750 CL	0.37	0.00		
730 CL	0.94	0.00		
Perq				
750 Franz				
TrlOn & LclfYes	0.27	0.00		
TrlOn & LclfNo	0.35	0.00		
TrlOff & LclfYes	0.27	0.00		
TrlOff & LclfNo	0.93	0.00		
780 Franz				
TrlOn & LclfYes	0.15	0.00		
TrlOn & LclfNo	0.15	0.00		
TrlOff & LclfYes	0.02	0.00		
TrlOff & LclfNo	0.60	0.00		
Franz 68000				
TrlOn & LclfYes	0.33	0.00		
TrlOn & LclfNo	0.45	0.00		
TrlOff & LclfYes	0.37	0.00		
TrlOff & LclfNo	0.90	0.00		
InterLisp-10				
LM-2				

Raw Time				
Frpoly Power $= 5$ $r2 = 1000r$				
Implementation	CPU	GC	Real	Paging
SAIL	0.06	0.00	1.06	
Lambda	0.16			0.05
Lambda (MC)	0.11			0.00
3600	0.19			0.02
3600 + IFU	0.14			0.01
Dandelion				
Dolphin				
Dorado				
S-1				
PSL-SUN	2.04	0.00		
PSL-20	0.37	0.00		
PSL-3081	0.09	0.00		
PSL-Cray				
PSL-750	1.58	0.00		
PSL-750 (VMS)	1.54	0.00		
PSL-780	0.90	0.00		
PSL-DN300	1.63	0.00		
PSL-DN600	1.77	0.00		
PSL-DN160				
PSL-HP200	1.34	0.00		
PSL-HP-UX	1.60	0.00		
InterLispVax 780				
MV4000 CL			0.64	
MV8000 CL			0.51	
MV10000 CL			0.25	
3600 + FPA	0.14			0.01
750 NIL	2.15		2.15	
8600 CL	0.12	0.00		

Raw Time				
Frpoly Power $= 5$ $r2 = 1000r$				
Implementation	**CPU**	**GC**	**Real**	**Paging**
780 CL	0.36	0.00		
785 CL	0.23	0.00		
750 CL	0.60	0.00		
730 CL	1.46	0.00		
Perq				
750 Franz				
TrlOn & LclfYes	0.48	0.37		
TrlOn & LclfNo	1.18	0.57		
TrlOff & LclfYes	0.48	0.37		
TrlOff & LclfNo	1.80	0.57		
780 Franz				
TrlOn & LclfYes	0.67	0.37		
TrlOn & LclfNo	0.67	0.37		
TrlOff & LclfYes	0.38	0.00		
TrlOff & LclfNo	1.18	0.42		
Franz 68000				
TrlOn & LclfYes	0.73	0.00		
TrlOn & LclfNo	0.85	0.00		
TrlOff & LclfYes	0.80	0.00		
TrlOff & LclfNo	1.32	0.00		
InterLisp-10				
LM-2				

Raw Time				
Frpoly Power = 5 $r3 = r$ in flonums				
Implementation	CPU	GC	Real	Paging
SAIL	0.04	0.00	0.08	
Lambda	0.15			0.04
Lambda (MC)	0.08			0.00
3600	0.05			0.01
3600 + IFU	0.04			0.01
Dandelion				
Dolphin				
Dorado				
S-1			0.03	
PSL-SUN	0.40	0.00		
PSL-20	0.13	0.00		
PSL-3081	0.03	0.00		
PSL-Cray	0.02	0.00		
PSL-750	0.49	0.00		
PSL-750 (VMS)	0.49	0.00		
PSL-780	0.28	0.00		
PSL-DN300	0.44	0.00		
PSL-DN600	0.44	0.00		
PSL-DN160				
PSL-HP200	0.41	0.00		
PSL-HP-UX	0.41	0.00		
InterLispVax 780				
MV4000 CL			0.40	
MV8000 CL			0.33	
MV10000 CL			0.16	
3600 + FPA	0.04			0.01
750 NIL	0.42		0.43	
8600 CL	0.10	0.00		

Raw Time				
Frpoly Power = 5 $r3 = r$ in flonums				
Implementation	CPU	GC	Real	Paging
780 CL	0.30	0.00		
785 CL	0.18	0.00		
750 CL	0.48	0.00		
730 CL	1.29	0.00		
Perq				
750 Franz				
TrlOn & LclfYes	0.30	1.83		
TrlOn & LclfNo	1.02	0.67		
TrlOff & LclfYes	0.30	1.83		
TrlOff & LclfNo	1.62	0.63		
780 Franz				
TrlOn & LclfYes	0.22	0.00		
TrlOn & LclfNo	3.85	1.83		
TrlOff & LclfYes	0.98	0.40		
TrlOff & LclfNo	3.85	1.83		
Franz 68000				
TrlOn & LclfYes	0.43	0.00		
TrlOn & LclfNo	0.53	0.00		
TrlOff & LclfYes	0.48	0.00		
TrlOff & LclfNo	0.98	0.00		
InterLisp-10				
LM-2				

Raw Time				
Frpoly Power $= 10$ $r = x + y + z + 1$				
Implementation	CPU	GC	Real	Paging
SAIL	0.46	0.79	1.90	
Lambda	1.20			0.22
Lambda (MC)	0.54			0.05
3600	0.49			0.08
3600 + IFU	0.39			0.06
Dandelion				
Dolphin				
Dorado				
S-1			0.42	
PSL-SUN	2.75	0.00		
PSL-20	0.92	0.00		
PSL-3081	0.25	0.00		
PSL-Cray	0.14	0.00		
PSL-750	4.52	0.00		
PSL-750 (VMS)	3.54	0.00		
PSL-780	2.00	0.00		
PSL-DN300	3.45	0.00		
PSL-DN600	3.60	0.00		
PSL-DN160				
PSL-HP200	2.24	0.00		
PSL-HP-UX	2.44	0.00		
InterLispVax 780				
MV4000 CL			3.77	
MV8000 CL			3.01	
MV10000 CL			1.45	
3600 + FPA	0.39			0.06
750 NIL	3.85		3.88	
8600 CL	0.64	0.00		

Raw Time				
Frpoly Power $= 10$ $r = x + y + z + 1$				
Implementation	**CPU**	**GC**	**Real**	**Paging**
780 CL	2.13	0.00		
785 CL	1.19	0.00		
750 CL	3.38	0.00		
730 CL	8.91	0.00		
Perq				
750 Franz				
TrlOn & LclfYes	3.15	0.00		
TrlOn & LclfNo	5.37	1.38		
TrlOff & LclfYes	3.15	0.00		
TrlOff & LclfNo	12.07	1.37		
780 Franz				
TrlOn & LclfYes	2.60	0.83		
TrlOn & LclfNo	2.60	0.83		
TrlOff & LclfYes	2.33	0.00		
TrlOff & LclfNo	7.67	0.88		
Franz 68000				
TrlOn & LclfYes	4.17	0.00		
TrlOn & LclfNo	5.63	0.00		
TrlOff & LclfYes	4.72	0.00		
TrlOff & LclfNo	10.43	0.00		
InterLisp-10				
LM-2				

Raw Time				
Frpoly Power = 10 $r2 = 1000r$				
Implementation	CPU	GC	Real	Paging
SAIL	0.92	5.94	12.48	
Lambda	2.30			0.68
Lambda (MC)	1.56			0.03
3600	2.89			0.26
3600 + IFU	2.10			0.18
Dandelion				
Dolphin				
Dorado				
S-1				
PSL-SUN	37.60	0.00		
PSL-20	6.46	0.00		
PSL-3081	0.35	0.00		
PSL-Cray				
PSL-750	27.77	0.00		
PSL-750 (VMS)	23.38	0.00		
PSL-780	13.02	0.00		
PSL-DN300	32.67	0.00		
PSL-DN600	33.33	0.00		
PSL-DN160				
PSL-HP200	26.06	0.00		
PSL-HP-UX	30.51	0.00		
InterLispVax 780				
MV4000 CL			10.05	
MV8000 CL			13.84	
MV10000 CL			3.74	
3600 + FPA	2.10			0.18
750 NIL	38.71		38.98	
8600 CL	1.40	0.00		

Raw Time				
Frpoly Power $= 10$ $r2 = 1000r$				
Implementation	**CPU**	**GC**	**Real**	**Paging**
780 CL	4.45	0.00		
785 CL	2.64	0.00		
750 CL	7.25	0.00		
730 CL	17.30	0.00		
Perq				
750 Franz				
TrlOn & LclfYes	11.82	3.52		
TrlOn & LclfNo	11.82	3.52		
TrlOff & LclfYes	14.95	5.82		
TrlOff & LclfNo	22.27	5.93		
780 Franz				
TrlOn & LclfYes	8.87	3.70		
TrlOn & LclfNo	8.87	3.70		
TrlOff & LclfYes	8.00	2.27		
TrlOff & LclfNo	14.87	3.83		
Franz 68000				
TrlOn & LclfYes	15.07	2.08		
TrlOn & LclfNo	16.53	0.00		
TrlOff & LclfYes	15.71	2.16		
TrlOff & LclfNo	21.35	0.00		
InterLisp-10				
LM-2				

Raw Time				
Frpoly Power = 10 $r3 = r$ in flonums				
Implementation	CPU	GC	Real	Paging
SAIL	0.47	2.98	5.89	
Lambda	1.60			0.45
Lambda (MC)	1.08			0.01
3600	0.54			0.08
3600 + IFU	0.43			0.06
Dandelion				
Dolphin				
Dorado				
S-1			0.43	
PSL-SUN	4.43	0.00		
PSL-20	1.50	0.00		
PSL-3081	0.22	0.00		
PSL-Cray	0.23	0.00		
PSL-750	7.19	0.00		
PSL-750 (VMS)	5.59	0.00		
PSL-780	3.06	0.00		
PSL-DN300	5.61	0.00		
PSL-DN600	5.69	0.00		
PSL-DN160				
PSL-HP200	4.27	0.00		
PSL-HP-UX	4.72	0.00		
InterLispVax 780				
MV4000 CL			4.08	
MV8000 CL			3.49	
MV10000 CL			1.64	
3600 + FPA	0.43			0.06
750 NIL	4.64		4.66	
8600 CL	0.97	0.00		

Raw Time				
Frpoly Power = 10 $r3 = r$ in flonums				
Implementation	**CPU**	**GC**	**Real**	**Paging**
780 CL	2.89	0.00		
785 CL	1.67	0.00		
750 CL	4.69	0.00		
730 CL	12.80	0.00		
Perq				
750 Franz				
TrlOn & LclfYes	3.47	0.00		
TrlOn & LclfNo	7.27	2.95		
TrlOff & LclfYes	3.47	0.00		
TrlOff & LclfNo	13.87	2.88		
780 Franz				
TrlOn & LclfYes	3.85	1.83		
TrlOn & LclfNo	3.85	1.83		
TrlOff & LclfYes	2.60	0.00		
TrlOff & LclfNo	8.62	1.43		
Franz 68000				
TrlOn & LclfYes	5.17	4.20		
TrlOn & LclfNo	6.65	0.00		
TrlOff & LclfYes	5.70	4.25		
TrlOff & LclfNo	11.43	0.00		
InterLisp-10				
LM-2				

Raw Time				
Frpoly Power $= 15$ $r = x + y + z + 1$				
Implementation	**CPU**	**GC**	**Real**	**Paging**
SAIL	3.15	4.82	12.57	
Lambda	7.80			1.28
Lambda (MC)	3.86			0.13
3600	3.45			0.41
3600 + IFU	2.65			0.29
Dandelion				
Dolphin				
Dorado				
S-1			2.87	
PSL-SUN	86.10	6.10		
PSL-20	12.68	0.00		
PSL-3081	4.04	0.00		
PSL-Cray	0.95	0.00		
PSL-750	81.66	3.16		
PSL-750 (VMS)	63.76	0.00		
PSL-780	35.46	1.39		
PSL-DN300	70.27	3.27		
PSL-DN600	75.10	3.21		
PSL-DN160				
PSL-HP200	39.98	0.00		
PSL-HP-UX	47.19	0.00		
InterLispVax 780				
MV4000 CL			25.93	
MV8000 CL			21.27	
MV10000 CL			10.15	
3600 + FPA	2.65			0.29
750 NIL	24.93		25.81	
8600 CL	4.13	0.00		

| Raw Time | | | | |
| Frpoly Power $= 15$ $r = x + y + z + 1$ | | | | |
Implementation	CPU	GC	Real	Paging
780 CL	13.21	0.00		
785 CL	7.60	0.00		
750 CL	21.51	0.00		
730 CL	55.45	0.00		
Perq				
750 Franz				
TrlOn & LclfYes	29.47	6.65		
TrlOn & LclfNo	37.23	9.12		
TrlOff & LclfYes	29.47	6.65		
TrlOff & LclfNo	82.57	9.38		
780 Franz				
TrlOn & LclfYes	18.48	5.63		
TrlOn & LclfNo	18.48	5.63		
TrlOff & LclfYes	20.60	4.02		
TrlOff & LclfNo	52.52	5.32		
Franz 68000				
TrlOn & LclfYes	31.12	4.39		
TrlOn & LclfNo	42.70	6.77		
TrlOff & LclfYes	34.67	4.48		
TrlOff & LclfNo	73.02	6.80		
InterLisp-10				
LM-2				

Raw Time Frpoly Power $= 15$ $r2 = 1000r$				
Implementation	CPU	GC	Real	Paging
SAIL	9.41	50.48	94.77	
Lambda	18.90			5.50
Lambda (MC)	14.35			0.54
3600	22.35			2.78
3600 + IFU	15.63			1.89
Dandelion				
Dolphin				
Dorado				
S-1				
PSL-SUN				
PSL-20	68.18	0.00		
PSL-3081	20.13	1.34		
PSL-Cray				
PSL-750	394.17	22.27		
PSL-750 (VMS)	293.68	8.04		
PSL-780	161.61	8.66		
PSL-DN300				
PSL-DN600	485.28	23.65		
PSL-DN160				
PSL-HP200	410.20	2.52		
PSL-HP-UX	476.42	4.30		
InterLispVax 780				
MV4000 CL			143.03	
MV8000 CL			107.98	
MV10000 CL			40.48	
3600 + FPA	15.63			1.89
750 NIL	479.48		482.87	
8600 CL	10.45	9.37		

Raw Time				
Frpoly Power = 15 $r2 = 1000r$				
Implementation	CPU	GC	Real	Paging
780 CL	34.48	26.99		
785 CL	22.20	7.30		
750 CL	57.00	51.82		
730 CL	139.49	122.14		
Perq				
750 Franz				
TrlOn & LclfYes	129.57	48.22		
TrlOn & LclfNo	155.45	67.14		
TrlOff & LclfYes	129.57	48.22		
TrlOff & LclfNo	202.68	67.47		
780 Franz				
TrlOn & LclfYes	93.87	41.75		
TrlOn & LclfNo	93.87	41.75		
TrlOff & LclfYes	86.50	30.38		
TrlOff & LclfNo	132.79	43.00		
Franz 68000				
TrlOn & LclfYes	176.77	30.73		
TrlOn & LclfNo	188.30	21.68		
TrlOff & LclfYes	180.50	30.83		
TrlOff & LclfNo	218.67	21.65		
InterLisp-10				
LM-2				

Raw Time				
Frpoly Power $= 15$ $r3 = r$ in flonums				
Implementation	CPU	GC	Real	Paging
SAIL	3.16	48.86	81.33	
Lambda	11.00			2.47
Lambda (MC)	7.66			0.23
3600	3.84			0.40
3600 + IFU	3.04			0.30
Dandelion				
Dolphin				
Dorado				
S-1			3.09	
PSL-SUN				
PSL-20	11.13	0.00		
PSL-3081	2.54	0.00		
PSL-Cray	1.66	0.00		
PSL-750	61.11	3.63		
PSL-750 (VMS)	40.79	0.00		
PSL-780	21.84	1.56		
PSL-DN300				
PSL-DN600	44.20	4.88		
PSL-DN160				
PSL-HP200	30.66	0.00		
PSL-HP-UX	33.71	0.00		
InterLispVax 780				
MV4000 CL			27.23	
MV8000 CL			23.95	
MV10000 CL			11.02	
3600 + FPA	3.04			0.30
750 NIL	30.70		31.18	
8600 CL	5.84	0.00		

Raw Time				
Frpoly Power = 15 $r3 = r$ in flonums				
Implementation	CPU	GC	Real	Paging
780 CL	17.83	13.78		
785 CL	10.40	0.00		
750 CL	31.05	26.80		
730 CL	85.16	61.52		
Perq				
750 Franz				
TrlOn & LclfYes	36.69	11.20		
TrlOn & LclfNo	41.47	11.00		
TrlOff & LclfYes	36.69	11.20		
TrlOff & LclfNo	86.83	11.22		
780 Franz				
TrlOn & LclfYes	21.70	6.97		
TrlOn & LclfNo	21.70	6.97		
TrlOff & LclfYes	25.08	6.77		
TrlOff & LclfNo	54.27	6.95		
Franz 68000				
TrlOn & LclfYes	37.60	20.53		
TrlOn & LclfNo	49.18	17.18		
TrlOff & LclfYes	40.88	20.55		
TrlOff & LclfNo	79.72	17.23		
InterLisp-10				
LM-2				

*Well, it certainly is hard to explain
because there are several
different cases. There is a prefetcher....*

— Bruce Edwards *explaining the 3600's instruction cache.* (September 18, 1984.)

*This article couldn't do nearly as much damage
as the Gabriel and Brooks "critique"
or the upcoming publication
of last year's Lisp benchmarks by MIT Press.*

— Anonymous *commenting on the author of this book.* (April 1985)

Would you like to volunteer?

— Peter Deutsch—*the question I should have said 'no' to.* (February 27, 1981)

3.21 Conclusions

Benchmarks are useful when the associated timings are accompanied by an analysis of the facets of Lisp and the underlying machine that are being measured. To claim that a simple benchmark is a uniform indicator of worth for a particular machine in relation to others is not a proper use of benchmarking. This is why this book goes to great lengths to explain as many of the trade-offs as possible so that the potential benchmarker and the benchmarker's audience are aware of the pitfalls of this exercise.

Benchmarks are useful for comparing performance of Lisp implementations. They help programmers tailor their programming styles and make programming decisions where performance is a consideration, although it is not recommended that programming style take a back seat to performance. Benchmarks help identify weak points in an implementation, so that efforts to improve the Lisp can focus on the points of highest leverage.

Computer architectures have become so complex that it is often difficult to analyze program behavior in the absence of a set of benchmarks to guide that analysis. It is often difficult to perform an accurate analysis without doing some experimental work to guide the analysis and keep it accurate; without analysis it is difficult to know how to benchmark correctly.

There were two major tangible benefits of the work reported in this book: an increasingly educated audience and improved implementations.

While the studies reported here were going on, many debates arose. These debates were focussed on two questions: Is this computer faster than that computer? and Can one benchmark show that a particular Lisp implementation is faster than another, while another benchmark shows the opposite? As the benchmarking work progressed, the level of discussion improved, and now the debates are about whether a particular Lisp implementation is best suited to a certain application. Rather than using one, often anonymous, benchmark, people started using a suite of benchmarks and started talking about the specific merits of an implementation.

The other benefit was that running these benchmarks turned up two sorts of bugs in implementations; one caused incorrectness and the other caused inefficiency. The ultimate benefactor of the removal of these bugs is the user of sophisticated Lisp implementations—a user who relies on the implementors for a correct and efficient Lisp system.

The final arbiter of the usefulness of a Lisp implementation is the ease that the user and programmer have with that implementation. Performance is an issue, but it is not the only issue.

References

[**Baker 1978a**] Baker, H. B. *List Processing in Real Time on a Serial Computer*, Communications of the ACM, Vol. 21, no. 4, April 1978.

[**Baker 1978b**] Baker, H. B. *Shallow Binding in Lisp 1.5*, Communications of the ACM, Vol. 21, no. 7, July 1978.

[**Bates 1982**] Bates, R., Dyer, D., Koomen, H. *Implementation of InterLisp on a Vax*, Proceedings of the 1982 ACM Symposium on Lisp and Functional Programming, August 1982.

[**Bobrow 1973**] Bobrow, D., Wegbreit, B., *A Model and Stack Implementation of Multiple Environments* in **Communications of the ACM**, Vol. 16, No. 10, Oct. 1973.

[**Bobrow 1979**] Bobrow, D., Clark, D., *Compact Encodings of List Structure"* in **ACM Trans. on Prog. lang. and Systems**, Vol 1 No 2 p.266 October 1979.

[**Brooks 1982a**] Brooks, R. A., Gabriel, R. P., Steele, G. L. *An Optimizing Compiler For Lexically Scoped Lisp*, Proceedings of the 1982 ACM Compiler Construction Conference, June, 1982.

[**Brooks 1982b**] Brooks, R. A., Gabriel, R. P., Steele, G. L. *S-1 Common Lisp Implementation*, Proceedings of the 1982 ACM Symposium on Lisp and Functional Programming, August 1982.

[**Burton 1981**] Burton, R. R, et. al. *InterLisp-D Overview* in **Papers on InterLisp-D**, Xerox Palo Alto Research Center, CIS-5 (SSL-80-4), 1981.

[**Clark 1981**] Clark, D., Lampson B., and Pier, K. *The Memory System of a High-Performance Personal Computer* in **IEEE Transactions on Computers**, vol C-30, No 10, October 1981.

[**Cohen 1981**] Cohen, J. *Garbage Collection of Linked Data Structures*, ACM Computing Surveys, Vol. 13, no. 3, September 1981.

[**Correll 1979**] Correll, Steven. *S-1 Uniprocessor Architecture (SMA-4)* in **The S-1 Project 1979 Annual Report**, Chapter 4. Lawrence Livermore National Laboratory, Livermore, California, 1979.

[**Deutsch 1976**] Deutsch, L. P., Bobrow, D., *An Efficient, Incremental, Automatic Garbage Collector* in **The Communications of the ACM**, July 1976.

[**Fateman 1973**] Fateman, R. J. *Reply to an Editorial*, ACM SIGSAM Bulletin 25, March 1973.

[Foderaro 1982] Foderaro, J. K., Sklower, K. L. **The FRANZ Lisp Manual**, University of California, Berkeley, Berkeley, California, April 1982.

[Griss 1982] Griss, Martin L, Benson, E. *PSL: A Portable LISP System*, Proceedings of the 1982 ACM Symposium on Lisp and Functional Programming, August 1982.

[Lampson 1982] Lampson, Butler W. *Fast Procedure Call*, Proceedings of the 1982 ACM Symposium on Architectural Support for Programming Languages and Operating Systems, SIGARCH Computer Architecture News, Vol. 10 no.2, March 1982.

[Masinter 1981a] Masinter, L. **InterLisp-VAX: A Report**, Department of Computer Science, Stanford University, STAN-CS-81-879, August 1981.

[Marti 1979] Marti, J,. Hearn, A. C., Griss, M. L. *Standard Lisp Report* in **SIGPLAN Notices 14, 10** October 1979.

[Masinter 1981b] Masinter, L. M., Deutsch, L. P. *Local Optimization For a Compiler for Stack-based Lisp Machines* in **Papers on InterLisp-D**, Xerox Palo Alto Research Center, CIS-5 (SSL-80-4), 1981.

[Moon 1974] Moon, David. **MacLisp Reference Manual, Revision 0**, M.I.T. Project MAC, Cambridge, Massachusetts, April 1974.

[Moon 1984] Moon, David. *Garbage Collection in a Large Lisp System*, in the Proceedings of the 1984 ACM Symposium on Lisp and Functional Programming, August 1984.

[Steele 1977a] Steele, Guy Lewis Jr. *Data Representations in PDP-10 MacLisp*, Proceedings of the 1977 MACSYMA Users' Conference. NASA Scientific and Technical Information Office, Washington, D.C., July 1977.

[Steele 1977b] Steele, Guy Lewis Jr. *Fast Arithmetic in MacLisp*, Proceedings of the 1977 MACSYMA Users' Conference. NASA Scientific and Technical Information Office, Washington, D.C., July 1977.

[Steele 1979] Steele, Guy Lewis Jr., Sussman, G. J. *The Dream of a Lifetime: A Lazy Scoping Mechanism*, Massachusetts Institute of Technology AI Memo 527, November 1979.

[Steele 1982] Steele, Guy Lewis Jr. et. al. *An Overview of Common Lisp*, Proceedings of the 1982 ACM Symposium on Lisp and Functional Programming, August 1982.

[Teitelman 1978] Teitelman, Warren, et. al. **InterLisp Reference Manual**, Xerox Palo Alto Research Center, Palo Alto, California, 1978.

[**Weinreb 1981**] Weinreb, Daniel, and Moon, David. **LISP Machine Manual**, Fourth Edition. Massachusetts Institute of Technology Artificial Intelligence Laboratory, Cambridge, Massachusetts, July 1981.

[**Weyhrauch 1981**] Weyhrauch, R. W., Talcott, C. T., Scherlis, W. L., Gabriel, R. P.; personal communication and involvement.

[**White 1979**] White, J. L., *NIL: A Perspective*, Proceedings of the 1979 MAC-SYMA Users Conference, July 1979.

Index

2005 (Puzzle Benchmark), 208.
=, 21.
'RSET (MacLisp), 11.
8AREF (InterLisp), 221.
8ASET (Interlisp), 221.
16AREF (InterLisp), 209.
16ASET (InterLisp), 209.

A register (MacLisp), 32.
A-list lambda-binding, 6.
abstract data structure, 156.
Accent (SPICE Operating System), 61.
address space, 1.
analysis, 1.
AOS/VS (Data General Operating
    System), 76.
Apollo, 66.
Apollo Dn160, 70.
Apollo DN300, 70.
Apollo DN600, 70.
APPEND, 18.
APPLY, 12, 177.
AR1 register (MacLisp), 32.
AR2A register (MacLisp), 32.
areas, 36.
arguments in registers, 8.
arithmetic, 16, 57.
arrays, 12, 13, 31, 48, 52, 59, 64, 71,
    74, 78, 195, 206, 218.
array headers, 31.
array references, 195, 206, 218.
assembly language, 31.
ASSOC, 18.
atoms, 5.

backtracking, 207.
Baskett, 206.
benchmarking, 1, 2, 81, 23.
benchmarks, 1, 2, 81.
Berkeley, 51.
BIBOP, 15, 31, 51, 64, 77.
Big Bag Of Pages, 15, 31, 51, 64, 77.
bigfloat, 17.
bignums, 17, 36, 43, 52, 55, 57, 64, 245.

binding, 5, 6, 38, 93.
binding stack, 38.
black art (Benchmarking), 23.
block compilation, 9, 11.
block-packing puzzle, 206.
Bob Boyer, 116.
bottleneck registers (RTA, RTB, S-1), 46.
boxed numbers, 9, 16, 23, 33.
Boyer (Benchmark), 45, 139.
Boyer (Human), 116.
Browse (Benchmark), 136.
buckets, 22.
buddy-block system, 31.
bus size, 4.

cache memory, 2, 3, 4, 6, 25, 40, 43,
    47, 61, 75, 110, 140.
CADR (Lisp Machine), 36, 40, 42.
CALLS instruction (Vax), 10.
CAR, 12, 13.
Carnegie-Mellon University, 58.
CATCH (Lisp primitive), 9, 44, 60, 79, 99.
CDR, 12.
CDR-coding, 14, 37, 39, 43, 73.
CHAOSNET, 22.
circular lists, 156.
circular queue, 3.
clock rate, 3.
closed-coding, 17.
closed-compiling, 17.
closing a file, 227.
closures, 7, 79.
CMACROs (PSL), 67.
Common Lisp, 8, 19, 54, 58.
common-subexpression elimination, 23.
compilation, 44.
compiler, 8, 20, 22.
complex numbers, 49.
computer algebra, 66.
CONS, 12.
constant-folding, 23.
constants, 5.
Conway, 206.
contagion code, 57.

context-switching, 7.
Cray-1, 42, 66, 69.
Cray-XMP, 69.
cross optimizations, 23.
Ctak (Benchmark), 99.
CTSS (Cray Operating System), 69.

D-LAST (CADR Microcode), 35.
DandeLion (Xerox), 75.
DandeTiger (Xerox), 75.
data base, 139.
data-driven derivative, 175, 181.
Data General Common Lisp, 76.
Data General MV Architecture
    Computers, 76.
data paths, 3.
data stack, 39.
data structures, 12.
DATATYPE (InterLisp), 12, 160.
data types, 47, 51, 52, 54, 71, 73, 77.
Dderiv (Benchmark), 91, 175.
debuggabilly, 11.
debugging, 1.
DEC-20, 13, 31, 66, 69.
deep binding, 5, 6, 20, 93.
DEFSTRUCT, 12, 158.
DEFSUBST, 40.
DEFVST, 12.
deleting a file, 227.
depth-first search, 207.
Deriv (Benchmark), 170.
derivative, 170.
Destructive (Benchmark), 146.
destructive list operations, 246.
DG-UX (Data General Operating
    System), 76.
directed graph, 156.
disk service, 2.
Div2 (Benchmark), 186.
division by 2, 186.
Dolphin (Xerox), 74.
Dorado (Xerox), 75.
DRECONC, 18.
dynamic, 5.
dynamic binding, 93.
dynamic variables, 6.

EBOX, 25, 111.
ECL logic, 65.
ELISP, 66.
EQ, 21.
EQUAL, 21.
error correction, 4, 37.
Ethernet, 22.

expert system, 139.
EXTEND, 12.

FASL (File Format), 67.
fast fourier transform, 193.
fast links, 11.
Fateman, 51, 245.
Fdderiv (Benchmark), 181.
FFT (Benchmark), 40, 193.
file input, 232.
file management, 20, 21.
file output, 227.
file print, 227.
file read, 232.
file system, 20, 21.
firmware, 18.
fixed-point arrays, 13.
fixnums, 35, 55, 58, 64, 78, 148.
FIXSW, 148.
FLAVORS, 12, 38.
FLENGTH, 149.
flexibility, 1.
floating point arrays 13.
floating point numbers, 40, 57, 58, 64,
    71, 78, 195, 245.
flonums (see Floating Point Numbers), 35.
FLOOR, 148.
FLPDL (MacLisp), 33.
fluid, 5.
Forest Baskett, 206.
FORTRAN-like programming style, 195.
forwarding pointer, 14.
Fprint (Benchmark), 227.
frames, 139.
Franz Lisp, 2, 11, 51.
Fread (Benchmark), 232.
free, 5.
free/special lookup, 7.
free variables, 6.
FRPLACA, 13, 149.
Frpoly (Benchmark), 40, 240.
FUNCALL, 12, 176.
function calls, 6, 8, 35, 39, 43, 50, 51,
    55, 59, 63, 72, 78, 82.
funny quotes, 92, 98, 104, 109, 115, 135,
    145, 152, 169, 174, 180, 185, 192, 202,
    216, 226, 231, 235, 239, 274.
FXPDL, 33.

G-vectors (SPICE), 59.
garbage collection, 6, 13, 20, 28, 30,
    57, 63, 67, 74, 78.
generic arithmetic, 15, 17.
GENSYM, 140.
GET, 176.
global, 5.
global variables, 20.
Griss, 66.

hardware, 2.
hardware considerations, 3.
hardware tagging, 36.
hash table, 21.
hayseed hackers, 11.
heap, 10.
Hewlitt-Packard, 66.
history of the address space, 29.
HP9000, Series 200, 69.
HP-9836, 66, 69.
HRRZ, 13.
hunks (MacLisp), 12, 31.

I-vector (SPICE), 59.
IBM 370, 66, 40, 70.
IBM 3081, 42, 70.
IEEE proposed standard floating-point, 46.
IEEE single precision specifications, 40.
IFU (Symbolics), 40.
Ikuo Takeuchi, 81.
implementation strategies, 5.
implementation tactics, 5.
inner loops, 28, 30.
instruction-counting methodology, 3.
instruction fetch, 3.
instruction pre-fetch unit (Symbolics), 40.
InterLisp, 2, 9, 11, 12, 13, 15, 17, 19,
    73, 160, 196, 221.
InterLisp-10, 2, 11, 13, 17.
InterLisp-D, 2, 15, 73.
InterLisp-Vax, 2.
interpreter, 7, 11, 20.
iteration versus recursion, 186.

J Moore, 116.
John Conway, 206.
John McCarthy, 81.
JonL White, 31.
JSB, 51.
jumping (Triang Benchmark), 218.

KA-10 (DEC), 6, 9.
KL-10 (DEC), 6, 9.

lambda binding (see Binding), 5, 20.
lambda-list, 56.
Lambda machine (LMI), 42.
LAP (Lisp Assembly Program), 67.
least recently used (LRU), 36.
levels of Lisp system architecture, 2.
lexical, 5, 6, 7.
lexical binding, 6.
lexical contour, 7.
lexical variables, 6.
Lisp-in-Lisp, 46, 58, 66.
Lisp compiler, 8, 20, 22.
Lisp instruction level, 5.
Lisp machines, 10, 12 ,15, 34, 35, 36.
Lisp machine hardware, 35, 36.
Lisp Machine Inc, 34, 42.
Lisp operation level, 18.
list utilities, 147.
LM-2 (Lisp machine), 36.
LMI, 34, 42.
load average, 2, 30.
loading compiled Lisp code, 32.
local function call, 51.
local variable, 5.
locality, 3, 25.
locative, 37.
loop-unwinding, 23.
LRU (Least Recently Used), 36.

MacLisp, 10, 11, 12, 15, 16, 19, 31,
    50, 148, 181.
MACRO32 (Assembly language), 57.
MACSYMA, 28, 51.
MACSYMA-like system, 28.
MAPCAR, 18.
Martin Griss, 66.
MBOX, 111.
MC68000, 25, 66, 69.
McCarthy, 81.
MDL (Language), 15.
memory bandwidth, 4.
methodology, 2.
microcode, 3, 15, 18, 20, 58, 73.
microcoded machines, 18.
microcompiler (LMI), 44.
micro-micro function call, 44.
mircostack (LMI), 44.
MIT Artificial Intelligence Laboratory, 34.
MIT CADR, 34.
monitor calls, 32.
Moore, 116.
Multics-like ring protection, 46.
multiple values, 9, 45, 60.

multi-processing Lisp, 7.
MV4000 (Data General), 80.
MV8000 (Data General), 80.
MV10000 (Data General), 80.
MV memory structure (Data General), 76.
MV-UX (Data General Operating System), 76.

natural benchmarks, 2.
NCONC, 18.
New Implementation of Lisp, 54.
NIL, 15, 54.
NOUUO (MacLisp), 11.
NuBus, 42.
NULL, 15.
number-CONSing, 16, 23, 33, 49, 52, 55.
number-format sizes, 17.
obarray, 21.
object oriented programming, 12.
oblist, 21.
one-dimensional arrays, 218.
open-coding, 17, 22.
open-compiling 17, 22.
opening a file, 227, 232.
operand fetch and decode, 6.
&optional, 56, 63.
order of evaluation, 23.

P0 space (Vax), 55.
P1 space (Vax), 55.
page boundaries, 30.
paging, 2, 14, 30, 34, 36, 38, 42, 61, 70, 73, 140.
PASCAL, 5.
pattern matching, 139.
PDL buffer, 3.
PDL numbers, 10, 16, 27, 33, 50.
PDP-6, 31.
PDP-10 MacLisp, 2.
PDP-10, 9, 16, 31.
peephole optimization, 23.
performance, 1.
performance evaluation defined, 1.
performance profile, 23.
PERQ Systems Corporation, 58.
PERQ T2, 62.
personal machines, 29.
pipeline, 4, 44, 47, 50, 65.
polynomial manipulation, 240.
Portable Standard Lisp (PSL), 8, 16, 63, 66, 67, 68, 69.
position-independent code, 56.
powers of polynomials, 245.
pre-fetch units, 4.

Prettyprint, 21.
PRINT, 21, 227, 236.
programming style, 23, 245.
property lists, 139, 246.
PSL (Portable Standard Lisp), 8, 16, 63, 66, 67, 68, 69.
PSL compiler, 67.
PSL versions, 68.
PSL-HP200, 68.
PSL-HP-UX (Hewlit-Packard Operating System), 69.
Puzzle (Benchmark), 59, 203, 218.

QUOTIENT, 148.

random graph, 156.
random numbers, 140.
random number generator, 140, 156.
range checking of arrays, 13.
raw-data tables, 81.
READ, 21, 232.
real-benchmark methodology, 3.
recursion versus iteration, 186.
reference count (Garbage Collection), 14, 74.
register A (MacLisp), 32.
register allocation, 6, 9, 23, 39.
register AR1 (MacLisp), 32.
register AR2A (MacLisp), 32.
register B (MacLisp), 32.
register C (MacLisp), 32.
register optimization, 23.
registers, 6.
&rest, 44, 55, 56.
&rest arguments, 39, 44, 55, 56.
RETFROM (InterLisp), 9, 100.
REVERSE, 18.
Richard Fateman, 51, 245.
rings, 76.
Rlisp (PSL), 68.
roots of Common Lisp, 33.
RPLACA, 12, 13, 147.
RPLACD, 12, 140.
RTA (S-1), 46.
RTB (S-1), 46.
runtime typing, 14, 17.
runtime type checking, 14, 17.

S-1 Lisp, 2, 11, 15, 16, 46, 93.
S-1 Mark IIA, 46.
SAIL (Operating System), 25, 29, 33, 110.
search problem, 206.
segmented memory, 76
SEUS (Language), 10.

shallow binding, 5, 20, 93.
small-benchmark methodology, 3.
small-number-CONS, 27.
small-number scheme, 16.
Smalltalk (Language), 12, 15.
spaghetti stack (InterLisp), 74, 99, 101.
special, 5, 6, 10, 12, 20, 93.
special variables, 6, 20.
special binding, 10, 12, 83.
SPICE Lisp byte codes, 63.
SPICE Lisp (CMU), 58, 63, 76.
stack-allocated number, 16.
stack architecture, 59.
stack buffer (Symbolics), 3, 38, 43.
stack cache, 3, 38, 43.
stack group (ZetaLisp), 38.
stacks, 38.
stack vectors, 55.
Stak (Benchmark), 93.
Stanford Artificial Intelligence Laboratory
     (SAIL), 33.
Standard Lisp, 66.
stock hardware, 15.
stop-and-copy (Garbage Collection), 57, 78.
strings, 12, 64, 74.
SUBRCALL, (MacLisp), 182.
SUN II, 70.
symbolic derivative, 171.
Symbolics 3600, 3, 36, 39, 40, 44.
Symbolics 3600 compiler, 39.
Symbolics 3600 data formats, 40.
Symbolics Inc, 3, 34, 36, 39, 40, 44.
Symbolics LM-2, 34.
symbols, 5, 6.
Syslisp (PSL), 66.
systemic quantities vector, 50.

tagged architecture, 14, 58.
tagging, 54, 58, 64.
tags, 14.
tail recursion, 9, 26, 72, 111, 186.
tail recursion removal, 186.
Tak (Benchmark), 12, 24, 30, 42, 61,
     81, 93, 99, 105.
Takeuchi, 81.
Takl (Benchmark), 105.
Takr (Benchmark), 61, 110.
TENEX (Operating System), 29.
terminal output, 236.
terminal print, 236.
theorem-proving benchmark, 129.
three operand instructions, 46.
THROW (Lisp primitive), 9, 44, 60, 79, 99.

time-shared machine, 29.
top-of-stack register, 38.
Tprint (Benchmark), 62, 236.
trampolines, 11.
TRANSLINK (Franz), 11, 32, 33, 51.
Traverse (Bennchmark), 153.
Triang (benchmark), 217.
two-dimensional arrays, 218.
type checking facility, 15.
types, 31, 35, 37.

unboxing, 16.
units, 139.
University of California at Berkeley, 51.
University of Utah, 66.
unpleasant programming style, 245.
unsnapping links, 33.
unwinding, 9.
user-controlled paging, 36.
Utah, 66.
UUO, 32.
UUO links, 11.
UUOlinks, 33, 51.

value cell, 6.
value predication, 50.
variable lookup, 20.
variables, 5, 6.
Vax 11/750, 69.
Vax 11/750 Common Lisp, 94.
Vax 11/780, 25, 69.
Vax 8600, 65.
Vax Common Lisp (DEC), 63.
Vax (DEC), 10, 25, 51, 54, 63, 65,
     69, 79, 94.
Vax NIL, 2, 11, 15, 94.
Vax Portable Standard Lisp (PSL), 16.
vectors, 12, 48, 52, 59, 64, 71, 74, 78.
Venus (Dec Vax 8600), 65.
VMS operating system (DEC), 63.

WAITS (Operating System), 33.
White, 31.
wholine time, 25.
windows, 236.
word alignment, 4.
working-set, 2, 14, 30.
write-through, 4.

XCT instruction, 32.
Xerox, 73.

ZEROP, 21.
ZetaLisp, 34.

www.ingramcontent.com/pod-product-compliance
Lightning Source LLC
Chambersburg PA
CBHW080355060326
40689CB00019B/4017